PUTTING THE EYFS CURRICULUM INTO PRACTICE

PUTTING THE EYFS CURRICULUM INTO PRACTICE

2E

Caroline Vollans & Julian Grenier

1 Oliver's Yard
55 City Road
London EC1Y 1SP

2455 Teller Road
Thousand Oaks
California 91320

10th Floor, Emaar Capital Tower 2
MG Road, Sikanderpur, Sector 26
Gurugram, Haryana – 122002
India

8 Marina View Suite 43-053
Asia Square Tower 1
Singapore 018960

Editor: James Clark
Assistant editor: Harry Dixon
Production editor: Martin Fox
Copyeditor: Jane Fricker
Proofreader: David Hemsley
Indexer: Elske Janssen
Marketing manager: Lorna Patkai
Cover design: Bhairvi Vyas
Typeset by: C&M Digitals (P) Ltd, Chennai, India
Printed in Great Britain by Bell and Bain Ltd,
BB0362727

Library of Congress Control Number is available

British Library Cataloguing in Publication data

A catalogue record for this book is available from the
British Library

ISBN 978-1-03-620693-2
ISBN 978-1-03-620692-5 (pbk)

Contents

About the Contributors

Rohan Allen is the Headteacher of Rebecca Cheetham Nursery School and Children's Centre. Originally from Australia, he began his teaching career in secondary education, specialising in English, PE and ICT, before expanding his expertise to primary and EYFS education in London. Rohan has served as Headteacher at Rebecca Cheetham for 8 of his 12 years at the school, where he has championed his passion for student and staff wellbeing and mindfulness. His efforts have helped cultivate a calm and nurturing learning environment, incorporating mindful breathing techniques to support emotional regulation. Rohan is also committed to fostering an understanding of diversity, ensuring that children are not only exposed to but also embrace the rich diversity within their community.

Aaron Bradbury is an Early Childhood academic, paying close attention to all aspects of Early Years and Child Centred Practice, Workforce Development, Child Development and Early Help. Aaron's current role is Principal Lecturer for Early Years and Childhood at Nottingham Trent University. He is also the Chair of the LGBTQ+ Early Years working group and manages his own website and community called Early Years Review. Aaron has published texts on apprenticeships and Early Years research.

Matilda Browne is the co-headteacher at Reach Academy Feltham and Reach Academy Hanworth Park. As a Primary Head, she passionately believes that a carefully laid out EYFS curriculum and highly trained staff are vital to a child's success throughout their education and that, therefore, the Early Years should be a priority in all primary schools. Alongside this, Matilda regularly leads training in instructional coaching and was the Primary Curriculum Lead for Humanities, English, Science and RSE for Oak National Academy during the pandemic.

Cassie Buchanan OBE is the CEO of Charter Schools Educational Trust, a cross-phase trust in South London. She serves on the Department for Education's (DfE) Curriculum and Assessment Review Panel (2024) and is a Non-Executive Director at Oak National Academy, the DfE's online curriculum provider. Under her leadership, the Trust has become a DfE Early Years Stronger Practice Hub. Cassie was Headteacher at Charles Dickens Primary School until 2020, leading its designation as a Teaching School, Education Endowment Foundation Research School and Behaviour Hub. Trained initially as an Early Years specialist, she remains passionate about early childhood education. Cassie was awarded an OBE for services to education in January 2021.

Siobhan Campbell is Assistant Director of East London Research School. She works with teachers and school leaders to effectively put evidence into practice. Siobhan was formerly the headteacher of an outstanding primary school and has been a teacher in a number of London boroughs.

Tania Choudhury is an accredited SENCO, Early Years teacher and SEN leader. She has completed a Master's in Special and Inclusive Education with a particular focus on Autism Studies and parental engagement of the BAME community. Tania has contributed towards writings and content for the Chartered College of Teaching, the Education Endowment Foundation, Oak National Academy and other institutes on a range of issues related to Early Years and SEND. Previously, Tania worked with the University of Oxford to learn more about how Bangladeshi children talk and play at home. Currently, she works as a SEND Manager for an Alternative Provision, working with 3- to 25-year-olds with a range of needs across the UK.

Felicity Dewsbery is the Deputy of the Pen Green Centre for Children and their Families leading the Research, Training and Development Base. She has been working in the field of Early Years for over 30 years in various roles. She passionately believes that outcomes for children and their families can be improved through robust professional development opportunities. Fliss has two Masters from two different disciplines, both of which have deepened her theoretical underpinning to support her to work and lead within Early Years. Her first MA is in Integrated Practice from Leicester University and her second in Psychoanalytical Observational Studies from the Tavistock and Portman Centre. She is currently writing a research doctorate to case study Early Years practitioners' lived experiences of supervision.

Jan Dubiel is an Independent Consultant and project director for hey! at Coram Hempsall's and is a nationally and internationally recognised specialist in Early Childhood Education. He was recently identified by the *Times Educational Supplement* as one of the 10 most influential people in British education and was previously Head of National and International Development at Early Excellence and Director of Early Years at AISL Harrow International Schools and Bilingual Kindergartens. He has worked as a YN, YR and Y1 teacher, senior leader, consultant and advisor and national lead on the management of the (Early Years) Foundation Stage Profile with QCA. Jan has written widely on different aspects of Early Years policy, pedagogy and practice.

Lindsey Foster is the Headteacher of Sheringham Nursery School and Children's Centre in the London Borough of Newham. During her 16 years at Sheringham, Lindsey has been SENCO, Forest School leader, mentor and tutor for school-based initial teacher training. She is passionate about inclusive education and working in partnership with parents. Lindsey has written for the East London Stronger Practice Hub and supported other colleagues with their writing. Lindsey has a particular interest in play-based learning and Forest School for young children.

Dr Julian Grenier is the Senior Content and Engagement Manager for Early Years at the Education Endowment Foundation (EEF). Before joining the EEF, he was the Head-teacher of Sheringham Nursery School and Children's Centre in Newham, East London. During that time, he was a National Leader of Education and was also the Director of East London Research School. He led Sure Start Children's Centres for over two decades and also served as one of His Majesty's Inspectors and Ofsted's Curriculum Lead for Early Education. He is a regular columnist for *TES* and has written and co-written several best-selling books about early childhood education. Julian was awarded a CBE for services to Early Years Education in 2022.

Lauren Grocott is a Content and Engagement Specialist for Early Years at the Education Endowment Foundation. Her focus is on supporting and promoting evidence use as a tool for developing practice and improving outcomes for socioeconomically disadvantaged children. Over the course of her career in education, Lauren has held a variety of roles across the sector in nurseries, schools, Sure Start Centres and as a local authority advisor. She holds an MSc in Psychology and has a particular interest in children's cognitive development, PSED and neurodiversity.

Dr Sinéad Harmey is an Associate Professor in Literacy Education based at the International Literacy Centre at the Institute of Education, UCL's Faculty of Education and Society. Sinéad's research and teaching focus on three interdependent and complementary fields: literacy development and instruction, review methodologies to ensure the successful translation of research to practice, and early literacy intervention. She is particularly interested in emergent writing.

Fliss James is the Director of the East London Research School and Assistant Head-teacher at Sheringham Nursery School and Children's Centre in Newham, London. She has worked in education for over 20 years and has had varied experiences across the breadth of the Early Years sector as a teacher, deputy head, ITE educator and Early Years Content Specialist for the Education Endowment Foundation. Fliss is passionate about the impact of high-quality evidence-informed Early Years education and care; what happens in the early years matters and can make a real difference to all children's life chances.

Honey Kaur is committed to Early Years care and education and has been working as a Childcare Provider for 16 years. Honey privileges building strong, trusting relationships with families and the local community. Her overall focus is on providing a nurturing, safe and challenging environment for each child and their family. To ensure that she is offering the best possible support, Honey prioritises training and professional development, keeping her skills up to date and striving to make a positive difference. She leads weekly sessions for childminders, providing a platform for colleagues to share their practices and help each another. Honey is currently working on developing ways of extending support for childminders, so that they feel connected to a community and have a useful network. Honey writes regularly about her practice for the East London Stronger Practice Hub and works alongside other childminders to do so.

Shaghaygh Khademian is an experienced Early Years teacher and Deputy Head-teacher. She is based at Mowlem and Marion Richardson Primary Schools in Tower Hamlets, East London. She is a qualified yoga teacher for children and has taught at an international school in the Middle East. Shaghaygh has a Master's degree from the University of Exeter in Teaching English to Speakers of Other Languages. During her years at Mowlem, Shaghaygh has had various experiences and roles as a Reception and Year One teacher, leading on Early Reading, safeguarding, Modern Foreign Languages and Personal, Social and Health Education. She is a mentor and tutor for school-based initial teacher training. She is an Evidence Lead in Education for the East London Research School and an Early Years Lead Practitioner for Tower Hamlets Education Partnership. Shaghaygh is bilingual and has a particular interest in second language acquisition.

Eunice Lumsden is the Professor of Child Advocacy and the Head of Childhood Youth and Families at the University of Northampton and a registered social worker. She has advised on Early Childhood policy, workforce qualifications and is a member of the Institute of Apprenticeships and Technical Qualifications, Education and Early Years Route Panel. She has also received awards for her 'Changemaking' work and research in the early years and child welfare. Nationally, she has been a member of several external expert groups advising the government on Early Years qualifications and inequalities in the early years and was an academic advisor for the Early Years Healthy Development Review, which led to the *Best Start for Life* policy. Eunice led the development of the Early Childhood Graduate Competencies for the Early Childhood Studies Network.

Dr Lala Manners has enjoyed a long and varied career in the field of Early Years Physical Development and Movement studies as a writer, researcher, mentor, practitioner, broadcaster, presenter and consultant. She is currently absorbed in a range of post-pandemic initiatives to support children's overall health and wellbeing. Lala continues to advocate for all things physical in children's lives.

Dr Sandra Mathers is a Senior Research Fellow at the Department of Education, University of Oxford. She began her career as a primary school teacher and her work remains strongly practice- and policy-relevant. Sandra's research focuses on adult–child interactions in the early years including: large-scale longitudinal studies (Children of the 2020s, Millennium Cohort Study); developing and evaluating early language and professional development programmes (Talking Time, URLEY); exploring how to encourage positive adult–child interactions with digital media (LIFT); evaluating the impact of government Early Years initiatives (Graduate Leader Fund, Early Education Pilot for Two-Year-Olds); and studying quality and inequality in early education provision.

Gemma Maclachlan is a childminder based in Kent. She is a level 3 Early Years Educator and a level 3 Forest School practitioner. Her setting is accredited by Natural Thinkers, reflecting her passion for outdoor learning. She is committed to bringing the outside into her indoor setting to create a curriculum which focuses on the two environments working in harmony, enabling every child to thrive, achieve and succeed. Gemma is a Practice Partner for Kent Early Years Stronger Practice Hub, raising the profile of childminders so that they are seen as the professionals that they are. She works on developing webinars and training sessions for a range of Early Years educators. She has worked with the Education Endowment Foundation (EEF) to create videos, blogs and case studies to show evidence-informed practice in action, in both Physical Development and Personal Social and Emotional Development.

Anni McTavish worked as a practitioner and manager of an under-fives pre-school in Camden, North London. During her 30 years in education, she has facilitated training and workshops, and written articles and books with a creative focus. She is currently artist in residence for a maintained Nursery School in London and a mentor for the Early Years Conversation Project (EYCP). She has also advised the Young V&A on the creative arts. Underlying all her work is an emphasis on children's emotional health and wellbeing.

Adam Mohamed is a teacher at Sheringham Nursery School and Children's Centre in the London Borough of Newham. He has been working in the sector for over 13 years. Adam has a strong interest in children's communication and language development. He is also an avid proponent of Forest School. Adam writes about his practice for the East London Stronger Practice Hub. In addition to his work, Adam loves climbing, cycling and music.

Dr June O'Sullivan OBE is an accomplished leader with a proven record of driving social impact in Early Years education. As the creator of the London Early Years Foundation's (LEYF) sustainable business model and the LEYF Pedagogy for Social Justice, she has championed the belief that every child, regardless of background, deserves the opportunity to thrive. Known as an inspiring speaker, author and media commentator, June's expertise spans social business, child poverty and sustainability. Awarded an MBE in 2013 and an OBE in 2023 for her services to education, she continues to advise international governments and organisations on Early Years Education and Care (EYEC) to foster long-term social change.

Dame Alison Peacock is Chief Executive of the Chartered College of Teaching, a charitable professional body that seeks to raise our status through empowering a knowledgeable and respected profession through membership and accreditation. Prior to joining the Chartered College, Dame Alison was Executive Headteacher of the Wroxham School in Hertfordshire. Her career to date has spanned primary, secondary and advisory roles.

She is an Honorary Fellow of Queens College and Hughes Hall, Cambridge, and UCL. She is a Visiting Professor of Glyndŵr University and a trustee for The Edge Foundation, Star Academies and Big Change. Her research is published in a series of books about Learning without Limits, offering an alternative approach to inclusive school improvement.

Liz Pemberton (she/her) is the Director of The Black Nursery Manager Ltd, a training and consultancy company specialising in anti-racist practice in Early Years education. With over 20 years in the sector, she has worked as a secondary school teacher, public speaker and nursery manager. She holds an MA in Early Childhood Studies and has delivered training across the UK, including Scotland and Wales, as well as internationally in Geneva, Hong Kong and the USA. In 2024 Serendipity Institute for Black Arts and Heritage recognised her as 1 of 100 Black Women Who Have Made a Mark, the Black Cultural Archives acknowledged her as one of their 2022 40×40 Future Leaders and she was nominated as a finalist for trainer of the year for the 2022 Nursery World Awards.

Sarah Porter is the Headteacher at Kay Rowe Nursery School and Children's Centre in East London. She grew up in the countryside but has worked in Early Years for many years in urban areas of London, Bristol and Dorset. Learning outdoors has been a passion for Sarah since the start of her teaching career. She has built wildlife ponds in almost every school she has worked in and really enjoyed seeing the delight and excitement experienced by young children watching tadpoles develop into frogs. Sarah has recently worked with the Froebel Trust to launch a Saturday Forest School. Sarah is also interested in young children's place in the community they live in and how they are seen and see themselves.

Melissa Prendergast is the Deputy Headteacher at Sheringham Nursery School and Children's Centre in Newham, London. With 20 years' experience in Early Years education, she is passionate about the vital role this phase plays in shaping a child's development and future opportunities. She strategically leads East London Research School and A Brighter Start Stronger Practice Hub, ensuring educators have access to evidence-informed practice. Together with the research school team, she has developed pedagogical strategies and professional development programmes to enhance the quality of interactions in Early Years settings. Melissa is collaborating with Peeple to explore effective ways to support the home learning environment, with a focus on integrating STEM learning into everyday experiences.

Iram Siraj OBE is Professor of Child Development and Education, Department of Education at the University of Oxford. She has directed a number of influential longitudinal studies on the impact of pre-school and primary education. Her current studies focus on process quality and key domains of learning, including interventions on the impact of evidence-based professional development promoting physical, language and mathematics learning. She has over 250 publications, including three widely-used rating scales which measure the quality of pedagogy in Early Childhood Education and Care (ECEC) that promotes child outcomes in the cognitive (ECERS-E 4th edn, 2010), social-emotional (SSTEW, 2015) and physical (MOVERS, 2017) domains. She was awarded an OBE for her services to ECEC in the Queen's honours in 2015.

Ed Vainker is the Managing Director of the Reach Foundation. He was the co-founder and Principal of Reach Academy Feltham and has developed a Cradle to Career model in Feltham. He works with groups of schools and leaders around the country to promote a coherent, all-through approach.

Caroline Vollans was a primary school teacher for 15 years, specialising in language and literacy development. Caroline then did an MA in Psychoanalysis followed by a clinical training. She practised as a psychotherapist in a hospital and secondary school. Caroline now works as a freelance writer and editor. She leads on the online output for the East London Stronger Practice Hub and writes for several Early Years publications. Caroline is particularly interested in the overlaps between Early Years education and psychoanalysis. In all her work, Caroline aims to give voice to the unspoken and unheard.

Foreword

Iram Siraj

Two big questions have shaped my thinking and enquiry since I became an early years teacher back in 1983. Why do some children succeed socially, physically and/or academically while others fail? And, how can we help more children fulfil their potential regardless of their background?

I am delighted to welcome the second edition of *Putting the EYFS Curriculum into Practice*, which begins to address these questions with leading professionals describing the best early-education, evidence-informed, practice. It has been completely revised and rewritten to ensure it is up to date, with many added case studies which bring the book to life.

My first years of teaching helped me to appreciate the role of those proximal factors which influence children's lives through their early experiences with significant others: parents, carers, siblings, health practitioners, pre-school staff and their immediate community. Similarly, background characteristics and contextual factors (such as poverty, class, developmental issues, ethnicity and gender) also shape children's experiences.

I learned later that these early experiences, from birth to 5, lay the foundations for all future development. My research shows that the life-course trajectories of all future learning are set early and rarely change during primary and secondary education. It is much easier to change trajectories in the early years.

Every child's life is part lottery, as none can determine their sex, ethnicity, parents or place of birth. These random, and often cruel, factors are the strongest determinants of life prospects, which is precisely why early education is so important. It is during the early years of rapid physical growth and brain development that children benefit the most from high-quality education and schooling – which then becomes a protective factor, ameliorating the risks from the birth lottery.

Despite this, it is only in the last two decades that Early Childhood Education and Care (ECEC) has been offered to all 3- and 4-year-olds (and to most 2-year-olds from families living with disadvantage, and now for children from 9 months upwards for working families). Although society has welcomed this provision, it has not been matched with an equal investment in the quality and coherence of the ECEC system, which remains fragmented and with some poorly qualified staff. There have been attempts to strengthen the sector because of the clear research evidence; but there is still a long way to go, and this is recognised by the number of All-Party Parliamentary

Groups (APPGs) and House of Commons select committees which have taken evidence over the last three decades.

In the absence of rapid progress in legislation and policy, it is gratifying to see how some leadership in the sector now supports staff in a variety of settings, and this book, edited by Caroline Vollans and Dr Julian Grenier, is an excellent example of this. It is also refreshing to see the ECEC sector starting to think seriously about context, curriculum, pedagogy and assessment in early education. In the heated debates between early years specialists, it is encouraging to find a book which is both broad and balanced, and which supports ECEC educators to improve their understanding of knowledge domains, pedagogical skills, curriculum design and how young children learn.

The book resonates well and extends the Early Years Foundation Stage (EYFS) and *Development Matters*. The authors of the chapters respect educators' ability to understand and appreciate the importance of solid research on important topics like inclusion, early communication and language, literacy and maths development.

The extensive collection of case studies of practice brings the book to life, and include babies, toddlers, pre-schoolers and Reception-class children. They also draw on a variety of providers, including childminders and pre- and primary school provision. The 15 chapters provide a comprehensive guide to an early education curriculum for ECEC educators and leaders, helping them to design and implement a strong curriculum supported by appropriate pedagogy and effective assessment.

In particular this book helps every early educator to dampen the effects of the birth lottery and provides them with tools and knowledge to give children from the most disadvantaged backgrounds the start they deserve to fulfil their potential.

Iram Siraj OBE
Professor of Child Development and Education at the University of Oxford

Introduction

The Importance of Curriculum in the Early Years

Julian Grenier and Cassie Buchanan

Caring for and teaching young children in the early years is undoubtedly a challenge. But it is also the best and most rewarding job either of us has ever done, and the most important. For that reason, it is a privilege for us both to introduce this second edition of *Putting the EYFS Curriculum into Practice* and celebrate the success of a book which sits on many desks and bookshelves in schools and early years settings across England.

A child's early years are a period of rapid growth and learning. For example, a newborn's brain is about 25% of its adult size, reaching around 50% by age 1, 80% by age 2 and 90% by age 5. In the first years of life, a child's brain forms more than 1 million new neural connections every second.

This extraordinary growth in brain capacity can leave us facing some dilemmas. Does this mean that development will surge ahead of its own accord, as long as conditions are favourable enough? Does this imply that a child's future is already determined by the first 1,000 days of their life?

Young children are, as Alison Gopnik famously said, 'the best learning machines in the universe' (Gopnik, 2009). Yet, whilst acknowledging that they are rich in potential, we also need to face up to an unpleasant reality: England does not yet ensure that each one of those children gets off to a fair start.

At the time of writing this, approximately 30% of children in England are growing up in poverty (House of Lords Library, 2024). As the leading health researcher Sir Michael Marmot argues, this has a toxic effect: the 'stress associated with poverty will damage children's brains, it will damage child development'. Indeed, by the end of the Early Years Foundation Stage (EYFS), we see one aspect of this damage with children from low-income families already 4.6 months behind their peers in their learning (Education Policy Institute, 2024). On average, that learning gap widens as children grow up, roughly doubling by the end of primary school and doubling again by the end of secondary. As a result, young people eligible for free school meals are only half as likely as their more advantaged classmates to gain GCSEs in English and Maths at grade 5 or above (National Audit Office, 2024).

Similar gaps affect many children from ethnic minority backgrounds, most notably children of Gypsy/Roma, Black Caribbean and Pakistani heritage. Boys achieve considerably worse outcomes than girls. Children with special educational needs and disabilities (SEND) are at risk of making less progress than their peers in the early years.

We think that this is unacceptable.

As educators and leaders, we both have a track record of working towards narrowing or eliminating these sorts of gaps. We want to share our thinking about curriculum to encourage readers working in diverse contexts and facing unique challenges to redouble their efforts to ensure that a child's background is not a barrier to learning – both in the early years and beyond.

We start from the conviction that development and learning are not simply child-led. From the earliest days, babies thrive on 'serve and return' interactions with parents, other caregivers and educators. As sociocultural theory explains (Rogoff, 2003; Vygotsky, 1978), those serve and return interactions between the child and a more skilled partner are the essential force behind the child's learning and development. If children have experienced fewer of those sustained and supportive interactions by the time they start in an early years setting, they will need additional support, nurture and teaching.

If we focus on communication and language as an instructive example, every child needs regular 'serve and return', language-rich interactions with educators, memorably called 'language nutrition' by Zauche et al. (2016). Some children may benefit from plenty of language nutrition in their early years classrooms and settings, spending time talking and playing with educators. Others may hardly speak at all and mostly play away from educators. In the same way that we would always think about a child's nutrition in the day, and seek to ensure that they ate well and kept hydrated, we should also bear in mind that every child needs daily 'language nutrition'. Approaches like interactive reading, explained in Chapter 3 by Sandra Mathers, offer children nourishing, language-rich interactions. Educators need to ensure that children with less-developed language get more of this nutrition to make sure they develop well. To turn these aims into daily reality for every child, educators need to take part in sustained, high-quality professional development programmes (Siraj et al., 2024); Siobhan Campbell and Melissa Prendergast explain how to make this happen in Chapter 15. As a safety net, we might also use an evidence-informed programme like Nuffield Early Language Intervention (NELI) in the Reception year, which gives children eligible for free school meals an average 7-month boost to their progress in language and communication, preventing gaps from widening (Smith et al., 2023).

Intervening early to support language development improves children's learning and wellbeing in the early years, enabling them to use communication to make friends, play with others, solve disputes and talk about how they are feeling. Furthermore, as the Education Endowment Foundation's guidance report, *Preparing for Literacy* (EEF, 2018) explains, 'language provides the foundation of thinking and learning and should be prioritised'. Without well-developed language and communication, children will struggle to access the curriculum in Key Stage 1 and beyond. Indeed, longitudinal studies like the British Cohort Study (reported in Shuey and Kankaraš, 2018) clearly show us the benefits of well-developed language and communication. Children who are better communicators at age 5 will go on to:

- become better readers at age 11
- get better exam results at age 16
- gain higher-paid employment as adults
- be more likely to complete a degree by age 30
- feel healthier at age 42

Research into early language development is instructive in another way, too. It is the quality of early interactions which makes the biggest difference, not the quantity (Hirsh-Pasek et al., 2015). We can apply this lesson to all our thinking about the early years curriculum. It may be tempting to map out complex and comprehensive long-term plans to provide the foundations for learning each subject in the National Curriculum, but an early years curriculum like this will almost certainly be overloaded with content. It will be impossible to check whether each child has securely grasped all the skills and knowledge that we intended them to learn. It is preferable to focus instead on secure, deep-level learning, as Fliss James argues in Chapter 7 on Mathematics. Additionally, as the section on early science in Chapter 8 argues, to prepare children well for their future learning it is important to have a balanced approach which focuses on quality early years practice as well as specific knowledge and skills. When it comes to curriculum design in the early years, we need to be parsimonious.

A range of needs

In any group of young children, we expect to see a wide range of development. Child development is not much like a stepladder, with children progressing steadily upwards through the ages and stages. Instead, it is more like a series of overlapping waves. Children make progress in some areas whilst they might seem to stand still in others. One 2-year-old is chatty and loves to share books and sing songs, but is timid outdoors. Another only says a couple of words at a time, but charges outdoors and up to the top of the climbing frame given half a chance. We expect to see both types of development in a group of 2-year-olds. Neither is problematic, but we will need to keep a watchful eye on both children and give them the experiences, equipment and teaching they need to foster their all-round development. We will also expect any group of young children to include some who are neurodiverse and some who have other additional needs, like delayed communication or developmental coordination disorder (dyspraxia). An effective curriculum will be suitable for every child.

Meeting that range of needs is never going to be easy. Every day is different in the early years, and we have both enjoyed the diversity of the children we have worked with and the unexpected joys as well as the challenges they have brought. It is especially positive to note that in the last decade we have been able to draw increasingly on research evidence about a set of approaches which will support the large majority of the children we work with. These are approaches which most early years educators already know about, or can readily bring into daily practice. Taken together, these are the core of an effective curriculum in the early years.

The six priorities are:

- All-round quality: warm and loving care, appropriate routines and sensible boundaries – all of these help children to learn about managing life in a social group beyond their family
- Extended back-and-forth conversation
- Building a larger and richer vocabulary, using more complex forms of language to talk about things which are 'beyond the here and now'
- Developing the skills to focus attention, screen out distractions and work towards a goal
- Gaining a deep understanding of numbers and patterns
- Having the physical skills and coordination for active play and for the use of tools

In tandem with their increasing knowledge of the world, it is important for children to develop their all-round intellectual skills. These skills will enable them to solve problems, think and act creatively, and work with others. They will help children to enjoy their time in the early years, make friends and manage conflicts, and develop their artistic and musical creativity. In turn, all this learning lays the foundations for their future success in school and life. If those early foundations are not laid well, we run the risk of gaps opening and widening as children progress through school.

Effective pedagogy – teaching and caring for the children – consists of a toolbox of approaches which we can draw on at the appropriate time. That toolbox includes:

- creating and managing spaces where children can play independently
- sensitively interacting with children as they play
- guiding children's play towards learning specific skills or knowledge
- scaffolding children's learning by providing temporary support during a task, to adjust the level of challenge
- directly teaching children, across a broad spectrum of skills and knowledge, from handwashing, to using scissors, to learning phonics

Intentional teaching

When we think of children's learning, we need to be careful and thoughtful about balancing time for independent play, guided play and direct teaching. Epstein (2007) describes this as 'intentional teaching': drawing on a range of pedagogical strategies and holding specific outcomes or goals in mind for the child's learning. To be intentional teachers, we need:

- a detailed knowledge of each child
- a broad understanding of child development
- curriculum knowledge about what children need to learn
- pedagogical knowledge and the skills to use the right strategy at the right time, ensuring the child achieves that learning

We turn our thinking into action by playing with children, developing conversations with them, teaching them new skills and knowledge, and preparing the learning environment. These acts of intentional teaching are the key drivers of children's early learning in settings and schools. The impact of the planned curriculum depends on this intentional teaching, together with high-quality responsive care and interactions. As a result, effective professional development for educators in the early years is a crucial dimension of quality. We might think of educator development in three broad stages:

- Instinctive practice: the educator describes their response to children in terms of instinct ('I just knew that was a good time to get involved with their play')
- Reflective practice: the educator reflects on their practice, or the practice of others ('I was so glad I remembered not to talk too much when I joined in with her play')
- Intentional practice: the educator knows the range of strategies they can draw on, and can explain why they chose a specific strategy in response to the child ('I know that children learning English as an additional language need time for processing, so I waited 10 seconds for Jamil to reply, rather than asking another question')

As Mathers (2020, p. 3) argues, 'in order to most effectively support young children's language development, practitioners need to explicitly understand which pedagogical strategies they are using and why they are using them'.

Scripted programmes, like Nuffield Early Language Intervention (NELI), have an important role to play for targeted groups of children who need extra help. However, to be effective minute-by-minute in dynamic early years settings and schools, educators need:

- secure understanding of research evidence about learning and child development
- knowledge of the pedagogical strategies they can draw on

Educators also need to be able to link these two sources of knowledge: we need to understand what effect our strategies might have and then be able to deploy them intentionally. To put it simply, we need to know why we are doing what we are doing. We need to be able to link our knowledge of child development and pedagogy to be intentional.

There is no shortcut to implementing the curriculum effectively.

Child development and play

Sometimes, it is argued that children and child development have not changed, so we should stick to practices which served children perfectly well in the past. We would argue otherwise. Child development is an interactive process. It involves the child and their biology, and it also involves important people and the wider culture. For example, children now are 'digital natives'. They switch smoothly between the online world and the real world. They watch a Spider-Man cartoon on YouTube, fashion a cape from a bit of material and set about saving the world. The impact of ICT on child development may be cause for concern, or something to welcome. Either way it has changed childhood and child development. We could make the same argument about the loss of street-play. Fifty years ago, the streets around the London schools where we have taught for decades would have been teeming with children at play. Now they are lined with parked cars and clogged by traffic.

We have seen a great many changes to childhood. Children now spend much more time away from their families, in early years settings. They have many more social connections. This means that early education and care now provide a space for the experiences children would once have had in the home and on the street. Child development has changed. Early education and care must change with it.

One important implication of changing childhoods is that play is, if anything, even more important in the early years than it used to be.

There is no serious debate about the importance of play in the EYFS. It is a requirement of the Statutory Framework (Department for Education [DfE], 2024a). There is also research evidence to support the importance of play to young children's wellbeing, learning and progress. For example, the EEF Early Years Toolkit (EEF, 2025) estimates that play-based learning has a 'positive impact (+ four months) on learning outcomes'.

However, the EEF add a note of caution to their findings in the Toolkit: 'the evidence base is very limited' (EEF, 2025). Likewise, a recent research synthesis and meta-analysis by Skene et al. into learning through guided play concludes that 'the existing evidence is not of a quantity, quality, or consistency within any one outcome area to allow very confident conclusions to be drawn' (Skene et al., 2022, p. 1178). It is also important to note that despite these cautions, the review has several positive findings. For example, the review finds that guided play is an effective approach to maths, having 'a greater positive effect than direct instruction on early maths skills, shape knowledge, and task switching, and a greater positive effect than free play on spatial vocabulary' (Skene et al., 2022, p. 1173).

In schools, an additional challenge is that play is not always appreciated. As Julie Fisher says, 'play is a word that chills the hearts of some headteachers, and senior leaders, particularly those who have never taught young children in their careers' (Fisher, 2020, p. 62). Like any other aspect of early years provision, play-based learning can be done poorly. In their classic paper, 'Crisis in the kindergarten: Why children need to play in school', Miller and Almon describe the scenario of 'ample play but without active adult support, often resulting in chaos' (Miller and Almon, 2009, p. 5).

Play and the curriculum

We think it is important to consider both how play can support the curriculum, and also how it has an intrinsic value to children's development and wellbeing.

At Charles Dickens Primary School, Head of Mathematics Themistocles Bakas comments on the fundamental value of play alongside direct teaching, as part of a carefully planned, consistent approach:

> Each lesson in reception is a small step, recalling and then building on the previous day's learning. Throughout, there is a strong focus on mastery, on the learning and practising of core mathematical principles through play. These core principles are then built upon in Year 1 seamlessly. Our use of language, concrete resources and visual representations is consistent across EYFS to the end of Key Stage 2.

Crucially, although there is a strong focus on the direct teaching of numeracy skills, this does not detract from the importance of play-based learning, ensuring that children develop positive attitudes and an interest in maths.

The team at Charles Dickens have also thought long and hard about how to harness the power of play-based learning to develop self-regulation and communication skills. Careful thought goes into the curation of activities, zones and resources that will engage children, deepen and extend their learning, and foster their imaginations.

In this rich context, often the best thing the educator can do is to take a step back. This gives children the freedom to learn from each other, negotiate their play and problem solve. Older children can lead the play, scaffolding the language and social interactions with deftness. They cannot do this if we are hovering.

As children play, educators observe carefully so they can:

- Step in to support children with resources or resolving conflict
- Evaluate the impact of the taught curriculum. Is it being practised and secured by the children? Are adaptations to the curriculum or the environment needed?
- Identify children who need further support

Educators will also focus on those children who need further support by:

- sharing stories and modelling play
- sitting alongside children, sharing attention with them and developing conversations
- picking an activity linked to a child's interests such as a jigsaw – this will help them to develop their learning as well as 'stick' at the task

This focus on teaching children to persist with difficult tasks, make decisions independently and work things out for themselves is based on research that shows self-regulation is important for both academic attainment and wellbeing in later life (Schoon et al., 2015).

Vertical integration

An effective early years curriculum is right for children today whilst also setting them up for success tomorrow.

For example, when evaluating the curriculum at Sheringham Nursery School, the team acted on the insight from health practitioners and early years educators across the neighbourhood that children needed more support with their early language development. Sheringham worked with local settings and local schools on a joint project called Newham Communication Project (NCP) to address this priority. As Grenier (2025) explains, this collaborative model was important not only for its impact on developing quality practice, but also for promoting collaboration across the system:

> This partnership between early years settings and schools was important for another reason: interventions that work in the early years can fade as children grow older. By engaging Reception teachers and school leaders, the approaches in NCP could be continued into the first years of school. This follow-through is important. The American researchers Jenkins et al. (2018) investigated why the benefits of a high-quality early childhood maths curriculum appeared to fade as children went through school. They found that additional professional development for kindergarten and first grade teachers (equivalent to Reception and Year 1 in England) 'all but eliminated the fadeout of effects on math achievement observed between kindergarten and first grade' (Jenkins et al., 2018, p. 369).
>
> (Grenier, 2025, p. 15)

As well as training alongside each other, educators developed a single reporting format to support transition. This enabled Reception teachers in local schools to value and build on children's prior learning in their early years settings, improving the coherence of the EYFS across different settings.

Similarly, an evaluation of the whole school's curriculum at Charles Dickens Primary School highlighted a lack of coherence between Early Years and Key Stage 1. Though the school's outcomes were in line with, or above, national averages, some children were struggling with the Year 1 curriculum. A lack of coherence meant that children did not experience a seamless transition into Key Stage 1.

A coherent curriculum is 'vertically integrated' – it keeps working as children move up into older age groups. In *Principled Curriculum Design*, Dylan Wiliam identifies vertical integration as one of the seven key principles. He explains: 'it needs to be clear how material taught at one point in time builds on materials taught earlier and feeds into what is to be taught later' (Wiliam, 2013, p. 28).

Using a different analogy, Christine Counsell considers the curriculum as a racecourse or running track (from the Latin *currere*, meaning to run or proceed). Like Dylan Wiliam, she emphasises continuity in children's learning: 'Curriculum is content structured over time ... it points to the curriculum as continuous. Not just a sequence or a chronology, it's much more like a narrative. Curriculum is content structured as narrative over time' (Counsell, 2018).

For this narrative to make sense, it needs to be carefully sequenced so that the foundations are securely laid for the next stage of learning. However, we must not be so busy thinking about the next that we neglect the now. Each element of the curriculum must have both a short-term and a long-term function (Counsell, 2018) so that we can answer these two questions:

- Why is this particular piece of learning important now?
- How will it contribute to future learning?

At Charles Dickens, the curriculum in Reception and Year 1 must be fully understood by both groups of practitioners. They need a shared understanding of the 'now' and 'next' of each element of the curriculum. Without this, teams may operate in isolation, resulting in a lack of coherency.

Sheringham Nursery School is a standalone early years setting, so it needs to link closely to the primary schools children will be joining. Joint evaluation with primary school headteachers concluded that Sheringham children achieved well as they went through the primary years, but some children left nursery without the secure learning they needed in Reception. For example, whilst the team at Sheringham had been putting a lot of focus on counting and encouraging children to develop their understanding of pattern, there was an insufficient focus on making sure that every child was secure in all the different components of understanding number:

- knowing the count sequence
- knowing that you say one number name for each object
- knowing that the last number you say tells you how many objects are in a set
- understanding the composition of number (numbers are made up of other numbers and you can 'see the numbers inside' other numbers)

Without 'vertical integration' between early years settings and primary schools, or between EYFS and Key Stage 1 within a school, children may not secure the important knowledge they need for a successful transition and smooth continuation of their learning journey.

Achieving a balanced approach

We have argued above that we need a balanced approach to early education and care. By thinking like this, we can avoid false polarities, like 'the child's right to play in the early years' versus 'preparing children for their future learning'. Play which is sensitively supported and guided by practitioners who are 'intentional teachers' is essential to ensuring that children are ready for the curriculum in Key Stage 1 and beyond. High-quality direct teaching is needed so that children secure important knowledge in key areas like phonics and number by the end of the EYFS. Thoughtful Key Stage 1 teachers will be mindful that the EYFS is called the 'foundation stage' for a reason. They will take care to ensure that every child consolidates foundational learning and skills through direct teaching and through play, by applying the programmes of study flexibly in Year 1.

Achieving this balance also means that we need robust approaches to assessment. Where a child does not yet have all the skills, concepts and vocabulary they need to start writing sentences, we will do them a disservice if we just expect them to write because that is on our curriculum plan. Few things are more depressing than watching a young child toiling to write a few words, with a well-intentioned educator next to them suggesting the words they might want to use, and how to spell them. It is enough to put children off writing for life. You cannot write a sentence if you cannot say a sentence. Similarly, we also do children a disservice if we merely 'wait for them to be ready' to write. We could wait a very long time, and during that time a child could fall further and further behind their classmates. Instead, effective curriculum thinking means that we identify the prior skills and concepts the child needs in order to be ready to learn handwriting, and design appropriate and motiving activities, including:

- outdoor play with a focus on large muscle development (arms and shoulders)
- games which involve starting and stopping, going up and going back down
- activities to develop small muscle skills; for example: picking up bits of gravel and putting them in a pot (finger strength, coordination and pincer grip)

In Chapter 6, Sinéad Harmey explores some practical approaches to help children develop strong hands for writing as well as the oral language skills they need to compose a sentence before they write it down.

Taking a balanced, carefully considered approach to the EYFS curriculum ensures that children are provided with the knowledge, vocabulary and skills they need for a successful future in school and beyond. This is important for all children. But we wish to stress that this is especially important for children from lower-income backgrounds or facing other types of disadvantage. As Iram Siraj and her colleagues point out:

> Although the importance of high quality ECEC [Early Childhood Education and Care] for fostering children's development and learning extends across the gradient of social disadvantage, it is particularly significant for children from highly disadvantaged backgrounds.
>
> (Siraj et al., 2016, p. 4)

Conclusion

Ever since the poet Wordsworth invented the concept of 'early childhood', we have been aware of what a special and sensitive time this is. As the nursery school pioneer Margaret McMillan wrote, 'to move, to run, to find things out by new movement, to feel one's life in every limb, that is the life of early childhood' (McMillan, 1930, p. 23). It is important that we do not over-programme early education and dampen that joy. It is important that we value every child and recognise their special talents and unique character.

However, that does not mean taking up a romanticised view. Every child's development will not flow as naturally as the caterpillar's development into a butterfly. As the Center on the Developing Child (2011) at Harvard University argues, 'brains are built, not born'. To play our part in building brains, we need to think through our approach to pedagogy, curriculum and assessment with care and precision.

That is exactly what the authors of the following chapters have done so eloquently. As Alison Peacock reminds us at the book's Afterword, this is a rich conversation which we need to carry on. There is much to celebrate in the early years. Yet there is still so much we need to learn and do.

A note on the text

Throughout this book, 'parent' refers to parents, carers, adoptive and foster parents, and guardians.

'Educator' refers to teachers, early years educators, teaching assistants, childminders and all other professionals working in the early years.

2

A Curriculum That Promotes Equality and Challenges Racism and Sexism

Eunice Lumsden

Introduction

I began my career in higher education in 2002 and some of my earliest memories include visiting Early Childhood Education and Care (ECEC) settings that had sections labelled 'Multi-Cultural Area'. In my previous role as a social worker, valuing difference and diversity and addressing how they impact people's lives were embedded in practice. Consequently, I was rather taken aback that for some in ECEC inclusion was an 'add on'. They were unable to see that all children, regardless of the demographics of the setting, needed experiences that reflected the fact that England is a multi-cultural society.

Practice has evolved and the Early Years Foundation Stage Statutory Framework (DfE, 2025, p.7) 'seeks to provide ... equality of opportunity and anti-discriminatory practice, ensuring that every child is included and supported'. In other words, differences should be 'seen as assets to be appreciated, rather than problems to be solved' (Thompson, 2021, p. 6). Early years practice must recognise these 'assets' and value 'differences' in gender, sexual identity, heritage, religion, family background, class, disability and country of origin.

This chapter will demonstrate why equality in our work is not optional: it is the right of every child and enshrined in law. The discussion will illustrate how different areas of inequality are connected and that a holistic approach in practice is important. The language of equality will be discussed, and you will be supported to examine and reflect on your own beliefs, including how unconscious bias can impact on your work with children and how you respond to others. You will be introduced to the MANDELA Model (Lumsden, 2024), a strengths approach framework that supports those working in the early years to have different conversations between each other, with children, families and their local community. Conversations that will lead to real and sustainable change in practice.

Exploring these areas, regardless of your background, gender, sexuality, disability, religion and culture, will be challenging. However, embracing anti-oppressive and anti-discriminatory practice is an essential, not a desirable, outcome in our work with children and families. Through addressing your values, beliefs and attitudes, you will begin to understand the role you play in providing a curriculum focused on inclusivity that does not shy away from the challenges of addressing the inequality, oppression and discrimination experienced by staff and the children and families you work with.

The legal and policy context

The importance of equality is firmly embedded in legislation and the policies that govern our work in the early years. The United Nations Convention on the Rights of the Child (United Nations Children's Fund [UNICEF], 2019) is ratified by the United Kingdom and should underpin all our work in the early years. Article 2 is pertinent to the focus of this chapter:

> The Convention applies to every child without discrimination, whatever their ethnicity, gender, religion, language, abilities or any other status, whatever they think or say, whatever their family background.

(UNICEF, 2019)

This right not to be discriminated against is also embedded in the Children Act (1989) and the Equality Act (2010). The Equality Act replaced and consolidated former legislation to simplify the law. It identifies all unlawful areas of discrimination and includes the legal duty for all institutions to ensure equality of opportunity and protection of rights for all. It is against the law to discriminate against someone because of:

- age
- disability
- gender reassignment
- marriage and civil partnership

- pregnancy and maternity
- race
- religion or belief
- sex
- sexual orientation

These are called protected characteristics. They can offer us a useful framework to reflect on our own values, beliefs and attitudes. The MANDELA Model presented at the end of this chapter will enable you to reflect further on yourself and the inclusivity of your practice.

Despite legislation, we live in a society that is not equal, nor is the aspiration for an inclusive society held by all. Research by the Equality and Human Rights Commission (Abrams et al., 2018) found that at least 42% of people indicated they had faced prejudice. Some people also expressed negative responses to some of the protective factors, including sexual orientation, gender identity and specific ethnic groups.

More recent research by the Youth Futures Foundation (2024) reinforces the challenges, especially for young people from diverse backgrounds joining the workforce. A survey of 3,250 ethnically minoritised young people aged between 18 and 25 in England found that:

- Nearly half of the young people (48%) said they had experienced some level of prejudice or discrimination when seeking to enter the workplace
- 41% of the young people who had experienced discrimination agreed that it had a negative emotional impact in their everyday lives, with 38% saying it had resulted in a loss of confidence
- Despite a high proportion of young people experiencing workplace discrimination, many do not report it formally
- Almost seven in ten (69%) of those who did not report their experience of discrimination said it was because they did not believe it would make a difference

The Young Foundation conducted an online survey involving 12 professional groups to find out about over 7,000 members' perceptions and experiences of equality, diversity and inclusion (EDI) in their professions and organisations (Bell, 2024). More than half (53%) of the professionals surveyed said that they had considered leaving their profession and/or organisation because of issues related to EDI. They reported that they felt 'overlooked or undervalued, with further concerns around progression, management, workload, pay and culture' (Bell, 2024, p. 5).

Recently, the debates on intersectionality (Bernard, 2022) have provided a theoretical framework for understanding the multiple and multifaceted oppression and discrimination faced by people. For example, the Youth Futures survey (2024) shows how young Black and Asian women report facing discrimination that is not just based on their race or their gender alone, but on a combination of both.

Everyone who works in the EYFS needs to understand this interlayered area and the wider context that early years practice is nested in. Legal requirements, policies and procedures, including those set out in the EYFS, should be explicit and known by all, including the importance of:

- equal opportunity
- principles of uniqueness, difference and inclusion
- partnership working with parents and carers

However, it is not just about knowing – it is about actions. What is the ethos of your place of work and how do you continually focus on your development in this area? Those working with infants, children and families must be committed to learning, discussing, reflecting and developing their practice, as well as challenging others. It is this continual cycle that will enable settings to embed high-quality practice that meets the overarching principles of the EYFS.

The language of equality

Understanding the terms that are used in legislation, policy documents and practice to promote equality is an important starting point. One of the challenges is ensuring a shared understanding of the same terms. There also needs to be an understanding that practice in this area is about social justice. To promote social justice, you need to understand diversity and the challenges, inequalities, oppression and discrimination experienced by children and families.

Participating in these debates will enhance our work and make us address our value base and reflect on the judgements we make and the language we use. As Betteridge (2024, p. 24) states:

All educators have a moral and ethical pedagogical responsibility to support every child in thriving, to help them build a positive self-identity, and to shape their understanding of the world.

As you engage with the discussion that follows, reflect on the words of Betteridge and hold in mind this quotation from the *Nurturing Care Framework* (World Health Organization [WHO], 2018, p. 2): 'if we change the beginning of the story, we change the whole story'.

Social justice

This broad term and its principles are captured effectively by Tedam (2020), who states:

Social justice is the fair, just and respectful treatment of all people, while recognising that unfairness, corruption and inequalities are the leading causes of war, conflict, inhumane treatment, suffering, pain, exploitation and many other ills that confront our world today.

(Tedam, 2020, p. 60)

Embedded in this definition is the idea that social justice is broader than fairness for the individual. It is a *sociopolitical* term that embraces what is happening in society as well as at a political level. In short, social justice is about how the systems we operate in can perpetuate injustice. For those working in the EYFS, this is important as you will work with infants, children and families who have been discriminated against.

Anti-oppressive and anti-discriminatory practice

These two terms are closely aligned and often used together. For some, reading this chapter may be the first time you have explored the terms in greater detail. Anti-discriminatory practice is embedded in the EYFS and practitioner and professional standards. These terms are complex and need to be understood holistically, drawing on the sociological, economic and political contexts as well as the legal frameworks that govern our work.

Arguably, the language of oppression does not sit well with the language of the early years. However, to provide young children with the best start, we must understand the unique child and their story. In ECEC, we are ideally placed to work with children and their families. We can provide new ways to eliminate the barriers they may face now and in the future.

This can be done by embedding anti-oppressive practices which proactively address the oppression faced by individuals, groups and communities in our work. This involves understanding that some are oppressed, some are the oppressors, and that those who have been oppressed can become the oppressors. Also, being oppressed can lead people to fight for their rights and freedom (Tedam, 2020).

If we consider child poverty, the number of children in this category is increasing year on year, even when at least one of their parents is working (Child Poverty Action Group [CPAG], 2025). The impact of child poverty is well documented, yet the research by Simpson, Lumsden, McDowall Clark and others (Simpson et al., 2015, 2017, 2018) highlights how the effects of poverty on child development are not always understood by practitioners. Understanding the causes and impact of poverty is important to meet the requirements of the EYFS. Staff need training that addresses this. It will enable practitioners to understand how their views about families living in poverty have developed, challenge myths and allow them to safely explore how practice can be enhanced. However, the challenges of this cannot be underestimated. Poor pay and working conditions permeate the sector (Bonetti, 2019), which means that members of the ECEC workforce are themselves part of the 'in work' poverty statistics.

Through developing our knowledge, understanding and appreciation of the experiences of others, we begin to develop our empathy and skills in anti-discriminatory practice: practice that acknowledges our *power* in situations to make a difference. Understanding that in ECEC we all have the power to act in ways that can make a difference, is key to creating change. You can explore this further through the reflective questions at the end of this chapter.

When we exert power over someone, or someone uses it over us, we need to consider two things:

1   the occurrence itself
2   the feelings evoked in us

Our experiences, whether positive or negative, have an impact on our feelings. Those of us who choose to work with infants, children and their families have a responsibility to understand the *power* we have in our interactions with others. Through this understanding, we can begin to advocate more effectively and address specific areas of discrimination, including racism, sexism and unconscious bias.

Unconscious bias

It may be hard to comprehend that our actions towards others are influenced by factors that are not in our immediate consciousness. These factors are deep-rooted and have been formed from previous experiences and exposure, or lack of them, to certain groups in society. Even if we *think* we are being fair, unconscious bias may lead us to think about different groups in society in certain ways as well as influencing our choices and actions. It can influence the decisions we make about friends and the groups we join or avoid. It can influence how we think about certain issues, like men working in ECEC or the impact of the Travelling Community staying near an early years setting. It can influence our choices, like buying boys dolls. For those we interact with, our actions can have wider implications. For instance, gender, sexual orientation, age, ethnicity and disability are some of the protected factors under the Equality Act (2010), yet while interviewing someone for a job, our (unconscious) beliefs and prejudices may influence who is successful.

I appreciate the complexity of this area, but educators have an important role to play in creating enabling environments that are representative, inclusive and empowering for every child. Importantly, they need to understand that inclusion means that those being included need to feel they belong. If you think about the example at the start of this chapter – a separate 'multi-cultural' area – the message is one of exclusion, not inclusion. This shows that the environments we are in can leave messages in our unconscious that last a lifetime.

I want to share an example from my journey to reinforce this point. My special doll from childhood was something rarely seen in the 1960s as it was a 'Black Doll' and that is what I called her. I remember people asking me why she didn't have a name, but to me, she did. You can read many things into my actions as a child but, looking back as an adult, I think it reflected what I was experiencing. My mother was from Sri Lanka and my father was White British. I was often referred to by many names other than the name my parents gave me.

Can you think of examples when you have referred to others in a discriminatory way or challenged others who have? The language we use is powerful and can lead to discrimination.

To change this, we need to be open to learning, reflecting on our practice and to personal and professional challenge. We also need to see the world through the experiences of others. This cannot happen unless we recognise that unconscious bias exists and, while we cannot change what has happened to us, we can explore where our views come from and undertake training. Through these processes, we can minimise the impact of unconscious bias on our work.

Anti-racist practice

We live in a society where racism is prevalent. The murder in May 2020 of George Floyd in the USA by Derek Chauvin, a 44-year-old white police officer, led to a considerable public outcry. The 'Black Lives Matter' movement has led to a renewed focus on the role of the early years in addressing racism. The issues are not new in early years practice, but it is a multifaceted and challenging area. Research indicates that children as young as 3 can be negatively influenced by their experiences of racism (Seltzer and O'Brien, 2024). As Tedam (2015, p. 93) states, 'early years practitioners will need to be aware of racism and its long-term effects on children's self-esteem and identity'. She highlights that if incidents of racism are not addressed, the message received by others is that 'the practitioners in early years provisions condone racist and discriminatory behaviours and attitudes'. Rather, the victims and perpetrators of racist behaviour need to know it is wrong.

Lane (2008) points out that we must not get into a 'blame' culture or feel guilty when mistakes are made; nor should practitioners think they are better than others if they understand issues and see racist actions that others cannot. The important point is that racism is a complex area where unconscious bias plays a significant role in how we view the world. However, we must address it in our work and make it visible to others when we see it in action. As Thomas (2025, p. 20) suggests, 'to be truly transformative, anti-racist approaches in the early years must be activated in a sustained and tolerant manner that is forward thinking'.

Understanding racism and the impact it has is an area of ongoing development for us all. Discussions and training need to be addressed sensitively and in non-threatening environments where people feel able to explore the issues, as well as seeing them through the eyes of others. This is not always easy to achieve. As the discussion in this chapter highlights, you cannot fulfil your duties unless you open yourself up to the ongoing learning journey that is required. To be an anti-racist practitioner, you first need to understand the many different forms racism can take and that it is deeply embedded in the history of our society.

Jane Lane (2008, p. 32) argues that myths and misunderstandings about racism can be removed if the different types of racism are understood. She identifies these as:

- racial prejudice
- racial discrimination
- racial harassment
- racial hatred
- racial violence
- racial assumptions
- racial stereotyping
- cultural racism
- sectarianism and anti-religious racism
- xenoracism
- institutional racism
- structural racism
- state racism

The list shows that racism is not just about how we may act, or how it impacts the individual. Racism can be embedded throughout the workplace (institutional racism) and in the society we live in (structural racism). You will also see how intersectionality as a framework can support your learning and understanding of different people's experiences. Understanding racism through these different lenses is an important step in the journey to create inclusive early years environments and develop an anti-racist pedagogy.

For Thomas (2025), embracing an anti-racist approach to early years pedagogy is an important next step on the journey for early years educators. This approach recognises structural and institutional racism and the setting's role as a change agent that can address racism rather than perpetuate it. The approach has four core areas that need to shape actions (Thomas, 2025, p. 24):

- celebrate diverse races and cultures
- enact anti-racist teaching for learning
- cultivate critical skills
- maintain inclusivity and belonging

For educators, it is important to think about the 'how' – how do we go beyond the Early Learning Goals and explore in depth how anti-racist practice is embedded in the methods, practices and theories of learning?

Anti-sexist practice

To understand why anti-sexist practice is important in the early years, practitioners need to understand:

1   what sexist behaviour is
2   the impact of sexual discrimination, and
3   how to address sexual discrimination

Sex is a protected characteristic in the Equality Act 2010. Sex discrimination can be experienced personally as well as being embedded in the structures and organisations we interact with. While it can impact all, women are particularly affected because of the historical context of the relationship between men and women and gender assumptions. The terms 'patriarchy' and 'male privilege' are much used. These are complex areas concerned with understanding the dominance of men over women in all structures of society.

Anti-sexist practice is about addressing these gender assumptions and taking action to eradicate or minimise inequality because of your sex. In the UK, there is an ongoing focus addressing sexual discrimination, including action to proactively address the gender pay gap between men and women. This is gradually reducing (Office for National Statistics, 2024), though we have a long way to go. We now have women on active duty in the armed forces and more women in leadership roles, but equality of opportunity for all women is still an aspiration requiring considerable work.

The early years sector provides a mirror to the many challenges faced by women in the workplace. Despite the increasing requirements on the workforce to prepare children for school and their future as citizens, the early years is a low-pay, low-status occupation. The challenges of this were captured effectively by Cooke and Lawton (2008, p. 6), who highlighted the importance of early years services in 'delivering both economic prosperity and social justice' for young children yet offering no financial reward for the workforce to upskill themselves. Furthermore, debates still exist about whether pre-school provision is about early learning or providing 'childcare' while parents work. Traditionally, childcare is viewed as women's work and closely connected to motherhood. This has negatively impacted pay scales in the sector and how it is valued by others (Bonetti, 2019; Osgood, 2011).

Inclusivity: The MANDELA model

This final section introduces you to the MANDELA Model of Inclusivity in Early Childhood (see Table 2.1). Drawing on the reflective model developed by Tedam (2011), it provides a framework to facilitate the critical discussions that need to take place in early years settings, drive change and create new ways of thinking and working (Lumsden, 2024).

The need to develop the work of Tedam (2011) for the early years sector was reinforced when I was working on the version of this chapter for the first edition of the book. I was writing about core areas of social change that are embedded in legislation and the EYFS, but putting these approaches into action is complicated because of individual perspectives and institutional and structural inequalities. However, as this chapter has evidenced, it is not sufficient to say 'I am not racist' or sexist, etc. We must take action, individually and collectively, to address these areas.

Think back to the earlier discussion that highlighted that whilst people may experience prejudice for a range of reasons, most feel unable to raise this with their employers (Bell, 2024). I know I am one of those people that have struggled to raise issues that relate to me – what about you? What are the barriers that prevent us raising issues?

The word MANDELA was originally chosen by Professor Tedam as it represented the hope that Nelson Mandela gave communities facing oppression. The early years model is not prescriptive, rather it is a framework in which each letter has several suggested questions (see Table 2.1). You could adapt the questions to make them bespoke to your group or home-based setting. They are there to support ongoing, sustainable change through shaping discussions that critically explore all aspects of the practice, knowledge and understanding of those working in the setting about inclusivity and their role as drivers of change. As the MANDELA Model workbook states:

It provides the opportunity to explore how the organisation can embrace inclusivity in all aspects of their work to address the structural inequalities embedded in our society. It also allows the organisation to understand these issues in the context of individual settings. It is an ongoing whole team approach that includes policies, day to day practice, recruitment and how we engage and work with families, infants and young children.

(Lumsden, 2024, p. 1)

Table 2.1 The MANDELA Model of Inclusivity in Early Childhood Framework of Change

MANDELA model	Action	Questions to promote inclusivity
Make Time	Make time to really understand the community that uses the setting – staff, children, families. Use this information to shape different conversations, develop relationships, co-construct action plans and ensure they are enacted.	Do you audit the diversity of staff, families, children regularly?
		How do you use this information to value all and guide practice? Areas to consider:
		1 Anti-oppressive and Anti-discriminatory practice*
		2 Anti-racist practice*
		3 Inclusivity*
		4 Appreciation of religious and spiritual beliefs*
		5 Value the individuals in the staff team
		6 Whole setting training
		7 Individual training
		8 Supervision
		9 Mentoring
		10 Pedagogy
		11 How do families know about the ethos and values of the setting?
		Do you thoroughly understand these terms?

MANDELA model	Action	Questions to promote inclusivity
Acknowledge	This is about striving for inclusivity in all we do through acknowledging our **Needs**, **Differences**, **Educational experiences**, **Life experiences** and **Age**.	How does the organisation acknowledge and value the diversity of those working in the setting and the children and families that use it? How do those working in the organisation know they are acknowledged and valued?
		How do children and families know they are acknowledged and valued?
Needs	What are the different needs of those using the setting, remembering people have the right not to share? How can you ensure the setting is inclusive of all needs? How do staff know and feel their needs are being addressed? How do parents and carers know their child's needs will be met?	How does the setting address the individual needs of staff members, children, parents and families in relation to:
		1 Language differences 2 Language proficiency 3 Verbal and non-verbal communication 4 Relationship building 5 Writing skills 6 Training needs 7 Neurodiverse needs of staff members, children and parents?
		How does the organisation support the needs of the local community?
Differences	This is about recognising we are all different. How do I know I am safe in your setting? Do you see me? To you value who I am?	What are the differences and similarities of staff members?
		These could include:
		1 Culture 2 Ethnicity 3 Religious beliefs 4 Age
		How does the organisation use these characteristics to support and enhance their work?
		How does the organisation embrace the cultural heritage, religion and ethnicity of their local community and the infants, young children and families using the setting?
		How does the organisation use these characteristics to support and enhance their work?
Educational Experiences	Acknowledging previous educational experiences, providing training and further development of staff. Supporting parents and carers develop their knowledge about child development.	How does the organisation recognise and value previous and different educational experiences?
		How does this understanding inform training and development opportunities?
		How does the organisation ensure high-quality early learning experiences for the children?
		How does the organisation support families to know about and understand the importance of child development and early learning?

(Continued)

Table 2.1 (Continued)

MANDELA model	Action	Questions to promote inclusivity
Life Experiences	Our journeys are all different – how do we value these and how do we create safe environments for people to use and work? How do we ensure our staff are safe practitioners? How does the setting value family diversity and the different experiences of the children using the setting?	We know that those choosing to work in the early years are often motivated by their childhood experiences. How do you: 1 Support staff who share their previous experiences? 2 Maintain confidentiality? 3 Ensure all staff are 'seen', heard' and 'safe'? 4 Provide opportunities for individual staff to develop?
Age	How does the setting value people of different ages? What is its approach to intergenerational sharing? Does it know how age is viewed in different cultures?	1 Do you know how age is viewed in different cultures? 2 How do you value people of different ages in your organisation? 3 What is the age range of staff in your organisation? 4 Do children meet and interact with people of different ages? 5 How do you organise the children in relation to their ages in your setting? (e.g. mixed age groups).

(Adapted from Lumsden, 2024)

Conclusion

This chapter has provided an overview of the complexities of embedding the EYFS requirement of providing 'equality of opportunity and anti-discriminatory practice, ensuring that every child is included and supported' (DfE, 2025, p. 7). The key message is that to meet these requirements and those of the Equality Act (2010), practitioners must understand how inequality and discrimination manifest and take action to promote inclusive practice and drive social change. Not only do those working in the early years need the knowledge, but they also need empathy and insight into the lived experiences of others and the skills to promote anti-discriminatory practice for all. Consequently, we are all on a challenging learning journey that will always be ongoing. The MANDELA Model provides a framework to facilitate this learning journey and support a sustainable, ongoing agenda for change. This is based on the firm belief that we make a difference.

In conclusion, I would like to draw on the words of Martin Luther King. In 1964 he stated, 'The time is always right to do what is right.' Yes, the meaning of his words is so true, but real change will only come when, one by one, we can say, 'I've noticed this...', 'I have challenged others to...', 'We need to...' and 'I am open to...' (Lumsden, 2021).

Reflective questions

1   It is against the law to discriminate against someone because of:

- age
- disability
- gender reassignment
- marriage and civil partnership
- pregnancy and maternity
- race
- religion or belief
- sex
- sexual orientation

How do you think the MANDELA Model could help your setting tackle prejudice and promote understanding between people from different groups? Are there areas of practice that you could improve?

2   Research shows that many young people from diverse groups face significant challenges in gaining employment and also face discrimination in the workplace. Think about your workplace. How diverse is it? How are all staff supported in their work? How easy is it to share any difficulties you are experiencing?

3   When was the last time you exerted power over someone? When was the last time someone used their power over you? How did it make you feel? How do you think it made them feel?

3

Communication and Language

Sandra Mathers

EYFS Statutory Educational Programme

The development of children's spoken language underpins all seven areas of learning and development. Children's back-and-forth interactions from an early age form the foundations for language and cognitive development. The number and quality of the conversations they have with adults and peers throughout the day in a language-rich environment are crucial. By commenting on what children are interested in or doing, and echoing back what they say with new vocabulary added, practitioners will build children's language effectively. Reading frequently to children, and engaging them actively in stories, non-fiction, rhymes and poems, and then providing them with extensive opportunities to use and embed new words in a range of contexts, will give children the opportunity to thrive. Through conversation, story-telling and role play, where children share their ideas with support and modelling from their teacher, and sensitive questioning that invites them to elaborate, children become comfortable in using a rich range of vocabulary and language structures.

(DfE, 2025, p. 9)

Introduction

It is hard to overstate the importance of early language. Children need strong oral language skills to underpin their social communication, relationships, literacy and learning in all areas of development.

The aspects of oral language are outlined in Table 3.1. They include both receptive language (understanding) and expressive language (speaking). Understanding and speaking are related but can develop at different rates. For example, a child learning English as an additional language may have good understanding, but not yet be ready or able to communicate verbally in English. Most children follow the same pattern in their language development. But the different phases overlap greatly. This means that children reach milestones at very different times within the 'typical' range.

Table 3.1 Communication throughout the Early Years Foundation Stage (EYFS)

Aspect of language development	Birth to 3 years old	3-, 4- and 5-year-olds
Vocabulary knowledge underpins children's understanding and use of language and sets the foundation for later literacy and learning.	**From 6 months**, children begin to understand words. **Between 9 and 14 months** they typically produce their first words. Given the right conditions, vocabulary increases dramatically during the early years (an estimated 7–10 words per day) but the developmental range is great. **By 18 months**, word production can range from 10 to 200 words.	**Around age 3**, children will have more words to describe categories (*birds* or *fruit*), emotions (*happy*, *sad*, *angry*) and time and space. **Between ages 4 and 5** children will have more words for emotions (*upset*, *unsure*, *thrilled*). They will use words to explain position (*between*, *above, below*) and use more adjectives (*rough, huge, funny*).
Social communication involves learning how to use language in social contexts and mastering the 'rules' of conversation. This forms the foundation for building relationships, engaging in social interaction and later literacy and learning.	**At 4–7 months**, social communication begins with vocalisations (e.g. growls, squeaks). **From 7 months** babbling begins. **Between 7 and 15 months**, children begin to use gestures, eye-gaze and pointing. Through the **toddler years** to the end of the EYFS, children continue to master social conversation, including initiation, turn-taking and using language in a wider range of contexts.	
Grammar includes knowledge about the structure of words and how words and phrases are combined into sentences.	**At 16–26 months** children begin to understand short sentences and create two-word sentences of their own (e.g. *Daddy shirt*). **Between ages 2 and 3**, children typically begin to understand and produce more complex sentences (e.g. *Daddy putting shirt on*) including function words (*a, the, I, we*), word beginnings (*mis-, un-*) and word endings (*-ing, -ed*). Errors such as 'me runned' are common as children over-generalise the rules they are beginning to grasp.	**Around age 3**, children's language becomes more adult-like. **By age 5**, children can typically express ideas and feelings using quite complex sentences, including connectives (*and, but, when, because*) and different tenses.

Aspect of language development	Birth to 3 years old	3-, 4- and 5-year-olds
Higher-order language Narrative skills include the ability to link ideas together to retell events and tell stories coherently using all the important details (e.g. who, where, when). Children also need to develop the skills which bring narratives to life such as description and inference. Narrative skills underpin later reading comprehension and writing.		**Between ages 3 and 5,** children use these skills to increasingly talk about a wide range of topics (e.g. past events, causes and consequences, predictions and explanations).

The Role of the adult

Children's language is most mouldable in their first 5 years, and whilst the home environment has the strongest influence, early education is also very important. As early years educators, we play a vital role in supporting young children's oral language development. To do this effectively, we need to consider:

1   planning
2   opportunities in your daily routine
3   environment and resourcing
4   language-supporting interactions
5   how to support language at home

We will consider each aspect in turn. Many of the practices described are appropriate for children with language delays as well as children within the typical range. This chapter does *not* provide detailed guidance on how to support children with specific speech, language and communication needs (SLCN). Noticing and taking prompt action if a child might have SLCN is vital. You can learn more about this through a free online course from Speech and Language UK, *An introduction to speech, language and communication* (https://speechandlanguage.org.uk/educators-and-professionals/training-courses/an-introduction-to-speech-language-communication/).

Planning

Every context, experience and interaction provides opportunities to support oral language. Careful planning helps us make the most of these opportunities. Think about:

- Planning for language **within all activities and contexts**. Include contexts which may not be obviously language focused. Identify key vocabulary and oral language goals for all planned activities. For example, during nappy changes we might plan to focus on commentary. We might talk aloud to interpret babies' feelings and intentions (e.g. *I'm going to put your nappy on now. I know, you don't like that very much, we'll be done soon…*).
- Planning for language across the **week, term and year**. Use **observations and assessments** to inform language planning. Knowing where children are in their language development helps us to provide the right experiences for them. We need to plan experiences which are just above their current level. There is a range of tools which can support us. This includes simple free screeners like the TROLL (Dickinson et al., 2003) and comprehensive toolkits such as the Wellcomm, which have costs attached.

Planning to Support Word Learning

Word learning should form part of a broad approach to developing oral language. Word learning is best supported when we:

- plan interesting and meaningful experiences to talk about
- build on these experiences to support word learning *in context* and *through conversation*
- identify the *key words* which the children need
- explicitly teach and support the children to learn those key words
- reinforce children's learning by linking new words to broader topics and continuous provision, and planning engaging follow-up activities. Children will need to hear and practise their new words in lots of different contexts.

When selecting key words, choose words which:

- the children do not already know, understand or use
- will be useful to help them interact with others, understand emotions, manage daily routines or learn new ideas and concepts
- the children will be exposed to in other contexts, for example from the books you are using, or which relate to other planned activities and experiences
- go beyond nouns: make sure to include *verbs* (action words), key grammatical items such as pronouns (*I, me, he, she*) and adjectives (describing words)

Opportunities in your daily routine

Think carefully about how to create time and space for communication. Research suggests that the 'ingredients' of a language-supporting day include the approaches outlined below.

Daily shared reading

In a language-rich setting, children of all ages share books with adults daily. Books are a powerful tool for supporting language development. They contain richer language than everyday conversation. They also offer great opportunities for conversation in a context which is meaningful and engaging for children.

Shared reading is most powerful when it is *interactive*. Children will gain most from reading individually or in a small group because they can be actively involved. We should not rule out whole-group reading but must think carefully about what the children will gain from this.

Remember to read books more than once. Children love to re-read stories. Research shows they learn words introduced in a new book faster when that book is read three or four times in a short period (e.g. a week) than from a single reading.

Songs, rhymes and poems

Songs and rhymes provide a great opportunity to develop communication and language in a way that babies and children (and adults!) enjoy. *Development Matters* (DfE, 2023) offers useful guidance. It suggests we should sing songs with babies and toddlers often, play a wide range of music types, move with babies to music, use action rhymes, and encourage babies and children to join in with and anticipate the words and actions in songs and rhymes. Older children should learn a wide range of songs and rhymes and perhaps create their own. By Reception, we should be focusing on the sound and structure of songs/rhymes. We should draw attention to rhyme, pausing for children to predict the next rhyming word and encouraging them to create their own rhymes or clap out the beats in words.

Small-group opportunities for talk

Once children become old enough to take part in short group activities, we should plan regular opportunities for structured conversations with adults. In a small-group context, children have more opportunities to engage in the back-and-forth conversation which will support their language development. Structured does not mean formal or adult led. It means we have a planned focus on oral language, and we are actively scaffolding children's communication, language and conversation. Including children with mixed language levels in groups will enable children with lower language levels to benefit from the language of their peers. We also need to think about how to scaffold children's conversations with each other.

Case Study 3.1

Talking Time, by Melissa Prendergast

At Sheringham Nursery School, children take part in weekly small-group conversation activities as part of 'Talking Time' (Dockrell et al., 2023), a universal intervention for 3- and 4-year-olds. Educators and children love this special time together. While all children benefit, it is particularly valuable for those facing learning barriers.

Adam, who loves technology, often brings electrical items to nursery. He has difficulties with attention, social communication and interaction. He understands Bengali and English and communicates in English using short phrases and some jargon (strings of sounds or babble that mimic adult speech patterns and intonation, without clear words).

His key person, Sara, plans sessions around his needs, centring him in the conversation and ensuring he is engaged. She gives him a copy of *Peace at Last* (Murphy, 1990). In Talking Time, the focus is on using the pictures in story books to spark child-led conversation.

Sara: Adam, this is your book.
Adam: Yeah.
Sara: Leo, Maria, and I are going to share. Ready, Adam?

Adam looks at the cover and smiles.

Sara: It's about Mr Bear and Mrs Bear.
Adam: Mr Bear!
Sara: Yes, Mr Bear. He is the biggest bear, the baba.

Sara encourages Adam to turn the pages with her. The children notice the cat and discuss their pets. Adam flips through the pages as they talk. Sara brings him back into the conversation.

Sara: I have also noticed something else.

She traces the moon with her finger and moves the book towards him, knowing he recognises the word.

Adam: Look, it's moon!
Sara: It's the moon, Adam, and the stars! Is it daytime or night-time?
Children
chorus: Night-time!

They discuss sometimes seeing the moon in the morning. When Adam loses focus, Sara brings him back in.

Sara: Turn the page, Adam. One more.
Adam: Yeah. Page. Yeah.

Excited by the picture, Adam turns to his friend.

Adam: Woah!!

Sara: I wonder what we can see in this picture?

Adam's friend describes shadows and reflections. Sara explains these concepts and includes Adam in the discussion.

Sara: Adam, Maria said the window is lit up, someone must be inside, and she can see the window's reflection on the grass.

Adam studies the picture and speaks, though some words are unclear. Sara listens attentively, smiling and nodding to show she is interested.

Adam: I... (jargon) ... is house.

Sara: Yes! It is a house. It is the bear's house.

Leo and Maria discuss the houses in the background. Adam continues studying the image and speaks as they do.

Adam: Shadow. It closed on the window.

Sara encourages everyone to listen. She interprets what he said.

Sara: Did you hear Adam? He said he could see the shadow. I see it too! It's the tree's shadow, made by the bright moon shining down.

By using the pictures in the book as prompts, Sara engages Adam in conversation at his developmental level. Through this interaction, Adam develops his oral language and gains confidence in communication, all while enjoying this special time with Sara and his friends.

Play and exploration

Play, exploration and investigation offer particularly engaging and meaningful contexts for language learning. They build on children's interests and allow them to practise language, social and self-regulation skills with peers. While babies are playing with toys and resources, we can name objects and talk about what they (and we) are doing. This provides language in context. For toddlers and pre-schoolers, pretend, dramatic and role play offer rich early language and literacy experiences.

Using every opportunity

We need to make use of every opportunity for language learning, both planned and unplanned. This includes routines such as tidying up, mealtimes and getting ready to go outside. Routines provide rich opportunities for giving children the language they need to negotiate what they are expected to do, and for relaxed conversations in an informal context. Create regular one-to-one opportunities to talk with children whenever you can.

Connecting it all together

We need to think about how to link language and experiences across different activities and contexts. This will give children repeated opportunities to hear and rehearse new language. For example, we can:

- provide activities which follow on from books, stories or songs
- choose books which relate to other experiences and activities
- plan for language learning across activities and areas

Environment and resourcing

When planning a communication-rich environment, we need to consider:

- Which areas are hotspots for communication, and which are not.
- Whether our resources and activities are meaningful and engaging for children, thinking about *each* child's experiences and interests.
- How to group resources together, in the way we naturally do in the early years. For example, grouping different foods and kitchen tools in the home corner. This helps children to learn the words related to these resources more quickly because they are meaningful.
- Whether our books reflect a wide range of types (fiction, non-fiction, rhymes), levels of challenge, topics and people. Choose books for the vocabulary and concepts they will introduce to children. Consider offering some wordless books, even for older children.

Using props, pictures and real experiences during activities and when reading books also supports language learning. This is particularly important for children with less-developed language or those learning English.

Language-supporting interactions

We move on now to consider adult–child interactions and the strategies we can use to nurture children's language skills. Ten evidence-based strategies are set out below.

Be a magnet for communication

The first step is to engage babies and children and motivate them to communicate with you. You can do this by:

- *Making children feel noticed and valued.* Encourage children to initiate communication by showing you are relaxed and have time to talk. Show interest using eye contact, body language and children's names. Know and enjoy your children as individuals and let this show. Give each baby and child individual attention. Use specific praise and encouragement.

- *Putting children in charge.* Children are most confident and motivated to talk about things they have experienced, and which are meaningful to them. Talk about what babies, toddlers and children are doing, know about and are interested in. Let them lead in interactions and conversation.
- *Using non-verbal and verbal invitations.* Use eye contact, body language and facial expressions to engage children. Then use a mix of open comments and questions to get the conversation going. A comment (e.g. *I wonder what will happen next...*) can sometimes be more natural than a question, allowing children to respond in their own way.
- *Engaging with all children*, including reluctant communicators, children with language delay and children in the early stages of learning English. These children may not 'ask' for our attention directly but will benefit greatly from interacting with us.

Support children to engage and reply

Help children communicate successfully by being a responsive language partner:

- *Give space and time* for children to think and respond.
- *Listen and respond.* Tune in to what babies, toddlers and children are trying to communicate verbally and non-verbally. Let them know they have been understood and encourage more communication by:
  - ○ confirming (e.g. nodding, repeating the child's words)
  - ○ verbalising babies' gestures (*Oh, you want to give me the toy – thank you!*)
  - ○ responding with interest.
- *Support turn-taking* using facial expressions and gestures to cue a baby or child to take their turn, verbally or non-verbally.
- *Give extra support where needed.* For example, a child might find it hard to respond to the question *Do you want an apple or a banana?* We might repeat the question, pointing to the fruit to make the words more concrete. If an older child struggles with *How does he feel?*, we might give a forced alternative like *Do you think he looks happy or sad?* Or we might verbalise what the child is trying to communicate (e.g. *Are you telling me that Teddy is tired?*) – but be sure not to jump in too soon. Support children with limited language by using concrete gestures, props and pictures.
- *Use lots of different techniques to keep the conversation going*: questions, comments, adding information, non-verbal cues, making links to children's knowledge, experiences, interests and lives. Match and adapt your language in response to the child.

Converse with children

Conversations with a more experienced language partner are one of the best ways for children to develop their communication, language and thinking. They can be verbal or non-verbal. Conversations allow children to:

- hear new language in context
- practise using language to express their ideas, feelings and wishes
- get responses from adults that support their understanding and talking

Make your room or class a place for conversation. Talk about a wide range of subjects with babies and children in many different contexts, including during routines. Aim for genuine conversations about things that interest the children and you. Use the techniques outlined above to support children in having meaningful conversations with multiple turns.

Case Study 3.2

ShREC at Snack Time, by Fliss James

Maya involves the children in preparing a snack. She knows the value of this daily routine and has thought carefully about which children she wants to benefit from this experience. She intentionally focuses on Aiden and Farah and uses the four ShREC strategies (James, 2022) to encourage responsive back-and-forth conversation.

She shares attention with the children and responds by purposefully giving them the words they need. She uses comments to talk about what they are doing and experiencing, and expands on what they communicate by repeating and adding more words.

Maya: It's time for snack. We have crackers, cream cheese and grapes. I need some help to get the snacks ready.

Aiden smiles and nods, joining Maya at the snack table. She gives him some plates to carry.

Maya: We need plates, you can carry the plates to the table.

Aiden points at the crackers.

Maya: You can put the crackers on the plate.

Once finished, Aiden reaches for a cracker.

Maya: You'd like a cracker, Aiden. A crunchy cracker!
Maya: Farah, Aiden is helping me prepare snack, you can help too.

Farah: Me cracker, me cracker!

Maya: One cracker for you too Farah. Here is a knife so you can spread some cream cheese onto your cracker.

Farah: Oooh it cheese butter. I do it.

Maya: Soft cream cheese, it's a bit like butter. We had butter on our rice cakes yesterday.

Aiden eats his plain cracker. Then he signals to Maya that he does not want any cream cheese by shaking his head, frowning and putting up his hand. Maya notices Aiden's non-verbal communication and responds sensitively by narrating his experience.

Maya: You don't want any cheese. You prefer a plain cracker without cream cheese.

Farah: Maya, I need grapes.

Maya: Yes Farah, you can have some grapes. First, we need to cut the grapes in half. You can both help me. Here is the chopping board and a knife.

Farah points at the chopping board.

Farah: I got this... in my home. My mum got a red one.

Maya: This is a chopping board. We use it to chop up fruit and vegetables. You have got a white chopping board and Aiden has a green chopping board.

Aiden: Green.

Maya: Yes, you've got a green chopping board, and it is the same colour as your green cup!

Aiden picks up his cup and notices it is empty. He pauses and frowns. He lifts his cup and points to the milk jug.

Maya: Oh, you'd like some milk Aiden. Here is the jug, you can pour some milk into your cup.

Aiden tentatively pours some milk into the cup and smiles. He takes a sip.

Aiden: Milk is yummy.

Challenge each child at their level

Children learn most when we match and adapt our language to their level. Pitch new language just above their current level and adapt it based on their response – stepping up or stepping down as needed. Use a range of prompts to give each child 'just enough' challenge.

- *Low-challenge (high-support) language* focuses on what children are doing, experiencing or can see in front of them. For example:

- o labelling (*That's your cup*)
- o commenting (*Mr Bear is going upstairs to bed*)
- o closed questions (*What is the mouse holding?*)
- o simple 'wh' questions (*What is the man doing?*)

- *Mid-range prompts* extend language and thinking. For example:
  - o use more open 'wh' prompts (*What's happening here?*)
  - o encourage children to recall (*Which animals did we see on the farm?*)
  - o encourage children to make links between a story and their life (*Have you ever felt scared like Ali?*)
  - o talk about preferences or opinions (*What's your favourite fruit?*)

- *High-challenge prompts* extend children even further. For example:
  - o encourage children to infer or predict (*How do you think he feels? What do you think will happen next?*)
  - o encourage children to explain (*Why is Mr Bear carrying a torch?*)
  - o ask open questions with no right answer (*Why do you like that one best?*)
  - o talk about abstract topics like feelings

Introduce new words and language

Educators play an important role in modelling new language for children. You can support word learning by:

- introducing new language through concrete, engaging, playful experiences
- modelling a rich and varied vocabulary just above children's current level
- providing the words for objects, actions and feelings
- describing and narrating what children and adults do, experience and think (e.g. *You're standing up! I'm cutting the peel off the orange because we don't eat that part.*)
- speaking slowly, clearly and matching your language to the child
- repeating words
- demonstrating: using gestures, actions, pictures or simple activities to support understanding

Build understanding of word meanings

When learning new words, children need information about word meanings as well as the word labels. This information is best provided in context and by building on what children already know. For example, we might say '*knitting* is a bit like sewing but you use wool and a really big needle'. We might give information or examples about the wider concept: 'Your mum or dad might *knit* a jumper for you to wear in the winter.' Again, having physical objects available can help children's understanding.

Extend children's language

We can extend and deepen children's word learning by expanding their own language. This gives children a more complex model which is just above their current level. We might:

- Add more information or ideas. For example, if the child says, *'that a lion'*, we might say *'yes, that lion* is <u>eating a juicy bone</u>'.
- Add grammatical details. For example, if the child says, *'climb out'*, we might say *'yes, <u>he</u> is climb<u>ing</u> out'*.
- Add new words to bring richer meaning. For example, if the child says, *'mouse got banana'*, we might say *'oh yes, the mouse* is <u>pulling</u> that <u>heavy</u> banana'.

Support children to use new words and language

To build confidence and depth of understanding, children need to practise using new language in a range of concrete contexts. Prompt children to use new words and language using comments and questions, and by having conversations which allow them to practice their new language. Plan lots of practical activities for children to use and act out new words/concepts in different concrete contexts. For example, to reinforce the word *behind*, we might demonstrate it. We might ask the children to line up and take turns to stand behind each other. We might hide behind something in hide and seek or treasure hunting games. We might use small-world play to show which objects are *'behind'*.

Support peer communication and conversation

Supporting peer communication and conversation will enhance children's social skills and relationships, as well as their language development. Hold and place babies where they can communicate with each other. Encourage children to talk with and listen to each other. Techniques such as descriptive commenting can help children to notice each other, drawing them into peer conversation. For older children, plan for small-group discussions supported by an adult. We might consider talk-partner techniques (Think, Pair, Share) during whole-group times.

Support children to understand and build narratives

As children become older, they need support to understand and create narratives. These might be fictional (e.g. stories) or personal (e.g. talking about events in their own lives). Children need practice at:

- *Scene-setting* (who, where, when) – talking about the characters and where/when the event or story happened

- *Talking about events in order.* Help children tell or retell events and stories, linking ideas together (e.g. *After Sami threw the ball, what happened...?*) and summarise the 'story so far'. Support children to talk about their own experiences clearly (e.g. *And what did you choose when you went into the shop?*)
- *Ending a narrative* (e.g. *They all went home for tea...*)

How to support language at home

Parents and the home environment have the greatest influence on children's language development. Let parents know how important their role is and how they can help children to develop their language. Support them in playing and talking with children at home, for example by sharing books and resources. We can discuss our themes or activities with parents and share ideas for talking about them with their children. We might ask parents to help us to understand their child's interests and experiences. What will they be keen to talk about? We might share our assessments and understandings about children's language development with parents. Then, we can ask them to help *us* in gaining an accurate picture of their child's language abilities and progress.

Early Learning Goal: Listening, Attention and Understanding

Children at the expected level of development will:

- Listen attentively and respond to what they hear with relevant questions, comments and actions when being read to and during whole class discussions and small group interactions.
- Make comments about what they have heard and ask questions to clarify their understanding.
- Hold conversation when engaged in back-and-forth exchanges with their teacher and peers.

(DfE, 2025, p. 12)

Early Learning Goal: Speaking

Children at the expected level of development will:

- Participate in small group, class and one-to-one discussions, offering their own ideas, using recently introduced vocabulary.

- Offer explanations for why things might happen, making use of recently introduced vocabulary from stories, non-fiction, rhymes and poems when appropriate.
- Express their ideas and feelings about their experiences using full sentences, including the use of past, present and future tenses and making use of conjunctions, with modelling and support from their teacher.

(DfE, 2025, p. 12)

Conclusion

Early language ability is one of the strongest predictors of later development through school and in life. Children who struggle with oral language at school entry are unlikely to catch up without extra support. They are at risk of poorer outcomes throughout their lives. Language is essential for thinking, expressing our feelings, making friends and finding solutions to conflicts. For these reasons, it should be a priority in curriculum planning. Use the insights and ideas in this chapter – and the questions below – to create a communication-supporting class or room.

Reflective questions

1   As a team, consider how you could **plan** more effectively for supporting communication and language across activities and contexts.

2   Make a map of your outdoor and indoor **environment**. Mark areas which are communication 'hot spots' and where communication and talk happen less often. What can you learn from this?

3   Consider **the 'ingredients' of a language-supporting day** set out in this chapter (shared reading, small-group opportunities, etc.). Identify one aspect to focus on over the next term to improve language opportunities for your children.

4   Reflect on the **language-supporting interactions** set out in this chapter. Which are part of your regular practice and which might you need to work on? Choose one strategy to focus on for a week. Be intentional about *rehearsing* and *reflecting* on your use of this strategy during the week to refine your practice.

5   As a team, reflect on how you could work with parents more closely to support **children's language at home**.

Acknowledgements

The author would like to acknowledge Clare Williams, Janice Woodcock and Iram Siraj (URLEY), and Wendy Lee, Clare Williams and Julie Dockrell (Talking Time).

4

Personal, Social and Emotional Development

Julian Grenier and Fliss Dewsbery

—EYFS Statutory Educational Programme—

Children's personal, social and emotional development (PSED) is crucial for children to lead healthy and happy lives, and is fundamental to their cognitive development. Underpinning their personal development are the important attachments that shape their social world. Strong, warm and supportive relationships with adults enable children to learn how to understand their own feelings and those of others. Children should be supported to manage emotions, develop a positive sense of self, set themselves simple goals, have confidence in their own abilities, to persist and wait for what they want and direct attention as necessary. Through adult modelling and guidance, they will learn how to look after their bodies, including healthy eating, and manage personal needs independently. Through supported interaction with other children, they learn how to make good friendships, co-operate and resolve conflicts peaceably. These attributes will provide a secure platform from which children can achieve at school and in later life.

(DfE, 2025, p. 9)

Introduction

It has never been more important to prioritise children's personal, social and emotional development (PSED) in the early years. Since the COVID-19 pandemic, lockdowns and cost of living crisis, educators have reported increasing numbers of children struggling with their emotions and finding it difficult to manage the social demands of being in a group with other children. Educators also report concerns about the role of passive screentime in children's lives, and its negative impact on children's play and social interaction. It is notable that one in five children has their own device (mobile phone or tablet) by the age of 3 (Ofcom, 2023, p. 7).

On a more positive note, we have much more research evidence to draw on when considering how to support children's social and emotional development, and their mental health. Most notably, the Education Endowment Foundation (EEF) has summarised evidence-informed approaches to PSED as well as publishing an online guide to promoting children's mental health and wellbeing. Both the PSED theme and the mental health and wellbeing guide are available on the EEF's Early Years Evidence Store (www.educationendowmentfoundation.org.uk/early-years).

Sensitive, thoughtful approaches to caring for children are at the foundations of an effective approach to PSED, supplemented with an intentional pedagogy to help children become more aware of their emotions, which can help them to benefit 'in terms of recognising, expressing and regulating emotions as well developing their ability to collaborate, negotiate and solve problems with others' (EEF, 2024a).

Alongside this sensitive teaching, high-quality care provides an enabling context for children's PSED. When we think about education and childcare in an integrated way, we can achieve the greatest impact. As the Effective Pre-School, Primary and Secondary Education project (EPPSE) researchers comment, 'our evidence suggests that those settings which see cognitive and social development as complementary achieve the best profile in terms of child outcomes' (Siraj-Blatchford et al., 2002, p. 10). Interestingly, the more recent Study of Early Education and Development (SEED) report found that 'the overall quality of childcare which children experience prior to starting school [aged 2–4 years old] may be more significant for their later academic development than the specifically educational element of the childcare' (Melhuish and Gardiner, 2021, p. 18).

Attachment and the key person role

The key person approach is an important aspect of high-quality care, as well as a legal requirement in the EYFS. The theory and practice behind the key person approach were developed by Elinor Goldschmied and Sonia Jackson in the 1990s (Goldschmied and Jackson, 1993), building on decades of research about attachment (Bowlby, 1969) and children's need for personalised, warm and responsive care in nursery settings (Bain and Barnett, 1980). In a busy group setting, the adults and children will be engaged in lots of activity. Within that busy-ness, it is important that the child is aware that there is a special person in the team of adults who knows them intimately and can anticipate their needs or respond quickly to them.

As part of the key person approach, it is important to have a clear protocol for settling-in, which allows the process to be gradual and humane. This is especially important when we consider the difficulties many young children currently experience when adjusting to life in a larger group. Children will benefit greatly from the support of their parents in the early days, as they get to know us and the setting.

Children's confidence develops from feeling safe and secure. This is especially important for babies and toddlers. Children need to know that their key person is a reliable 'safe base', someone they can return to when they need a little extra care or sympathy. In addition to this warm and responsive care, it is also important for the educator to transmit a positive sense of 'you can do this' to the child. This can help children to develop resilience in the face of difficulties. In the following case study, Lauren Grocott explains how a well-managed approach to settling-in helps a young child to make a positive start to life in nursery and also learn about recognising and managing their emotions.

Case Study 4.1

Helping Zariah to Settle In, by Lauren Grocott

Key person Ashley is helping Zariah settle in at nursery. Zariah was confident during her settling-in sessions when accompanied by her dad but has arrived on her first day looking quite apprehensive.

Ashley smiles warmly and welcomes Zariah in, 'It's so good to see you at nursery this morning. Say goodbye to your dad, then we will hang your things up.'

After waving goodbye, Ashley shows Zariah to her new peg. Zariah stands still with her coat fastened, watching the other children. When Ashley asks if she needs any help to take her coat off, Zariah says 'I don't want to.'

Ashley says 'Ok. You can keep it on for now, if you'd like?' Zariah nods, sniffs and then quietly says 'I want Daddy.'

Ashley smiles and replies, 'It can be really hard to be away from your daddy. It looks like you are feeling sad.' Zariah nods and then begins to cry. Ashley gets Zariah's teddy out of her backpack and offers her a hug. Zariah accepts, sitting down on Ashley's knee.

Here, Ashley sensitively acknowledges Zariah's emotions without judgement. She verbally labels what Zariah might be feeling. Evidence suggests this can build children's awareness of their emotions and develop the vocabulary to express them (EEF, 2024a). She uses what she knows about Zariah to comfort her, including the offer of a hug.

When she has calmed a little, Zariah asks, 'When is Daddy coming back?' Ashley shows Zariah their daily routine, which is displayed as a picture timetable. She explains each step of the routine, ending at the 'lunchtime' picture, adding 'This is when your daddy will come to get you.'

Ashley introduces the timetable to help Zariah begin to predict the routine of the nursery day. Research evidence suggests that having a consistent, predictable daily routine can support children's emotional wellbeing (EEF, 2024a).

(Continued)

The next day, Zariah is upset again after her dad drops her off, though she does choose to remove her coat. Ashley suggests they could go to the book corner and read some stories. Zariah nods and they settle themselves on the beanbags.

Ashley points to a character with a smiling face and says 'I feel happy this morning – I've got a big smile, just like him. I am happy because I like being at nursery. How are you feeling?' Zariah finds a picture of a crying character, 'Sad. I was crying like her.' Ashley nods, 'You have been feeling sad, because it is hard to be away from your dad. You did cry a little bit this morning, but that's ok. I'll look after you – although you're feeling a bit sad, I know you'll be alright.'

Ashley draws some other children into the discussion to think about what they do to help themselves when they feel sad. They suggest having a hug with their key person or a friend or cuddling a teddy in the calm tent. Zariah says, 'I have my teddy from my house in my bag.' Ashley nods, 'That's right. If you are feeling very sad, you can cuddle him.'

Ashley continues to label emotions and draw Zariah's attention to what they might look or feel like. She also scaffolds Zariah's reflections on why she has been feeling sad, and what she can do when she is feeling that way. Evidence suggests that proactively teaching children strategies for managing their emotions can improve their self-regulation and personal, social and emotional development (EEF, 2024a). Discussions about how to use the strategies, like the one above between Ashley and Zariah, help children learn how to apply strategies successfully. In addition, nurturing, warm and responsive relationships between adults and children are key for children's overall, healthy development (National Scientific Council on the Developing Child, 2004).

Research suggests that this way of working with children and their families, acknowledging and thinking about feelings, supports children's PSED, self-regulation and mental health and wellbeing. It can also be emotionally demanding on the educators. In the following section, Fliss Dewsbery considers how leaders can help educators to manage this.

Supervision and work discussion, by Fliss Dewsbury

Supervision is a statutory requirement in the Early Years Foundation Stage (EYFS) (DfE, 2025), which applies to everyone who works in the sector. In her 2011 review of the EYFS, Clare Tickell recommended that it should be 'clear what supervision means in practice, including some good practice examples, and that settings should agree their own procedures for supervision. Childminders should also have access to the challenge and professional support that supervision can provide' (Tickell, 2011, p. 47).

One of the most influential versions of supervision is 'Work Discussion', developed by Peter Elfer. Elfer (2018, p. 4) describes the aim of Work Discussion as being to enable 'practitioners to be more attuned to the child holistically, in the context of that child's family culture and wider culture, in order to support their practice and strengthen outcomes for children'.

Michael Rustin describes the purpose of a Work Discussion group as providing an 'understanding [of] what is going on, and the emotions and anxieties that are in play in a situation, but also of actively trying to help a participant observer to cope better with a situation and, through this, to enable practice to become more thoughtful' (Rustin, 2008, p. 269).

Peter Elfer argues that supervision must not be understood as a 'tick-box approach'. It is not a system for setting and monitoring staff targets, for example. Instead, he proposes that 'supervision should be part of a setting's culture, recognising that there are many dilemmas in early years work. Thoughtful reflection, including attention to emotion, may not produce simple solutions but it is an integral part of a respectful, whole-setting approach to the complexities of the work' (Elfer, 2015).

However, others have argued for a broader understanding of supervision. We can understand supervision as offering an individual or a group a reflective and containing space to discuss a variety of different work-related issues. John (2012) suggests that supervision should:

- offer a developmental or formative aspect … providing an opportunity to discuss skills and understanding
- provide a management/organisational aspect to discuss aims, principles, policies and standards
- be supportive or restorative, offering an opportunity to discuss how the work is affecting supervisees

Supervision has been of particular importance since 2020. The COVID-19 pandemic has had a negative effect on children and the early years workforce. Many educators have reported facing difficult circumstances in their work with young children with social or emotional difficulties, or mental health problems (Nelinger et al., 2021). Supervision is a mechanism to explore some of these difficulties.

Case Study 4.2

Supervision through the Stronger Practice Hubs programme

The East Midlands Stronger Practice Hub has been offering supervision sessions to leaders and managers of early years settings who rarely receive supervision for themselves, although they provide it to their practitioners. To start the session, an experienced early years supervisor starts by asking the supervisee what is the most 'pressing' or 'top issue' for them in the hope that together they can explore

(Continued)

some of the demand they are facing in their work. It is explained that each session lasts for approximately an hour and is a confidential space unless any safeguarding concerns are disclosed. Participants can be offered additional sessions, if they so wish.

Nicky, an experienced early years teacher, told me how she felt she was approaching a crossroad in her career. She said that she felt frozen to make a decision because of low self-confidence. We discussed some of the aspects surrounding her low self-esteem, and she shared how in a previous role she had experienced bullying and the impact this still had on her. I listened intently as Nicky recalled the series of events and how these experiences had impacted on her. Together we explored some of the ways she had managed this experience and the journey she had been on to cope with such adversity. During the supervision, I tried to enable her to see the early years teacher in front of her, to recognise her strength and focus on her achievements since these experiences.

After each session the supervisee is asked to provide a short overview on how the supervision has helped them. Nicky responded by stating 'It helped me reflect and provided a way forward in a supportive way. The session was enlightening, and I felt like an emotional weight had been lifted from my shoulders. It instantly gave me greater confidence to make professional and personal choices.'

Self-regulation and executive function skills

Self-regulation is the ability of children to manage their emotions, thoughts and behaviours in different situations. It helps them work towards goals, whether set by themselves or guided by adults. As the EEF's guide to self-regulation and executive function explains, 'very young children begin to develop their self-regulation, in part, through close support and co-regulation from the adults around them' (EEF, 2024a).

By supporting children with their emotional self-regulation, we help them to install a set of brakes and an accelerator pedal so they can manage their emotional pace and flow through the day.

Self-regulation is closely linked to executive function, which includes skills like focusing attention, controlling impulses and remembering information. These abilities develop through practice and repetition. A child's ability to self-regulate can be influenced by their early experiences, emotional wellbeing and motivation. In the EYFS, these skills are key to personal, social and emotional development and they help children to learn and engage with their environment, their peers and the educators.

Some traditional thinking in early years about 'ages and stages' has been challenged by research into executive function skills. For example, Piaget's theory (1952) held that children aged 2–7 years were egocentric thinkers who could not see things from other people's perspectives, and did not have logical ways of thinking. Modern theory tends to describe child development more as overlapping waves than a series of distinct stages. Rather than seeing young children as incompetent, illogical thinkers, Usha Goswami, Professor of Cognitive Developmental Neuroscience at the University of Cambridge, explains that 'children think and reason largely in the same way as adults. However, they lack experience, and they are still developing important metacognitive and executive function skills' (Goswami, 2015, p. 25).

Supporting the development of these important skills can improve children's long-term learning and life chances. As the leading researchers Cybele Raver, Clancy Blair and Michael Willoughby argue:

> … children's executive functioning plays a key role in supporting early learning and positive behavioral outcomes in school. … Put simply, children who can remember information, who can regulate their attention, and who can maintain inhibitory control are in better position to take advantage of opportunities for learning than children who struggle with problems of memory, inattention, and impulsivity.
>
> (Raver et al., 2013, p. 292)

In the case study below, childminder Gemma Maclachlan explores how her work supports children's developing self-regulation and executive function skills.

Case Study 4.3

Managing Conflicts and Emotions, by Gemma Maclachlan

When children join my childminder setting, Little Nomads, it's often the first time they've had to manage sharing time, attention and resources with other children of their own age. For lots of them, that is difficult. There are times when they will struggle to manage their emotions and play together. Coming into the setting gives children a valuable opportunity to develop socially and emotionally. It's a time to learn both about making choices and doing your own thing, and also joining in with others. Children learn to be leaders and followers.

Everyday conflicts are also an opportunity for learning. For example, when we went out into the forest recently, Lisa snatched the binoculars off Jason. Instead of just telling Lisa off, I talked to her about the importance of waiting for her turn. Maybe she could have asked Jason about what he was looking at, during this time? I also spoke with Jason about the importance of noticing when someone is waiting and being ready to share.

As well as dealing with conflicts reactively, talking them through and helping children to find solutions, sometimes it is also important for me to set the scene. The next time we went to the forest, I gave the digital camera to Jamal because I judged

(Continued)

that he was the child most likely to share. We all talked about the importance of kindness, of helping other people to feel happy rather than just putting our own needs first. Jamal was open to sharing the camera with the others, and set a positive model. When we got back, we spent time looking at the photos together over lunchtime and talking about what we had found in the woods. That emphasised teamwork – we are not just a group of individuals going out to the woods, we are learning to work together.

Through that teamwork, children become more resilient, more confident about having their own ideas as well as following other people's. They become more reflective, and more confident about trying things out and asking others to help them. Over time, the children become better at managing conflicts between themselves and regulating strong emotions. That has required me to do a lot of modelling, explaining, listening and mediating. Sometimes I model sharing with my assistant: one of us will ask the other politely for something. I spend lots of time listening to children saying how they feel and I also explain to them how others might be feeling. Sharing books like *The Colour Monster* (Llenas, 2015) is a good way of encouraging children to name and talk about their feelings, too.

As the children become more aware of their feelings, and the feelings of others, they are increasingly able to talk about problems, find solutions, manage their emotions, and advocate for each other. They can comfort each other when they are upset or angry, too. Lisa is getting much better at waiting for her turn, and Jason understands that it's important to be aware of other people, not just focus on what he's doing.

Teaching children to become aware of their emotions

Some children find it stressful to be in a group setting. They may have a parent with a mental health difficulty or live in overcrowded housing. Growing up in poverty is particularly corrosive to children's healthy development: as Sir Michael Marmot has commented, 'stress associated with poverty will damage children's brains, it will damage child development' (Marmot, 2022).

This group of children may benefit particularly from learning strategies to recognise and manage their emotions. For example, some settings use Zones of Regulation (Kuypers, 2011) with children. If children feel overwhelmed by their feelings, like sadness or anger, we can sensitively use the four zones to help them reflect on how they are feeling. Are they in the 'blue zone' of low energy, the yellow zone of heightened alertness, the 'red zone' of anger, or feeling calm and ready to learn in the 'green zone'?

By discussing the zone they are in and naming what they are feeling, the child may become more aware of their emotions, and if they are struggling they may feel a little less overwhelmed. This is a way of gradually and sensitively handing some control to children. In contrast, approaches like 'time out' mean that the educators have all the control, and may not be helping children to process their emotions. As children get older, it is increasingly important to help them to talk about and elaborate on their feelings. We might talk with a child about why they are feeling angry, and what happens to us when we are angry. We might share a picture book, like *I Really Want to Shout!* (Philip and Gaggiotti, 2020) and discuss how we might express anger in a socially acceptable way and what we can do to calm ourselves down.

Over time, it can become second nature to the child to recognise their emotions and actively finding a way to feel calmer. This strengthens an aspect of the child's executive function: their ability to inhibit impulsive behaviour.

Early Learning Goal: Self-Regulation

Children at the expected level of development will:

- Show an understanding of their own feelings and those of others and begin to regulate their behaviour accordingly.
- Set and work towards simple goals, being able to wait for what they want and control their immediate impulses when appropriate.
- Give focused attention to what the teacher says, responding appropriately even when engaged in activity, and show an ability to follow instructions involving several ideas or actions.

(DfE, 2025, p. 12)

Children learning to manage themselves

Linked to children's growing capacity to self-regulate is their capacity to develop their independence, self-care and self-management throughout the day. Helping children to become more independent is a central aim of early education and care, requiring educators to consider:

- *The resources we provide for children.* For example, children can develop their skills in using cutlery and pouring their own drink more easily if they can sit comfortably at the table, with their feet on the ground, and do not need to stretch their arms to reach onto a table that is too high for them.
- *The quality of our interactions.* This includes the way we teach children how to wash their hands thoroughly and remind them of the importance of wrapping up warmly on a cold day or putting their sun hat on when they are outside in the summer months.
- *Practice and repetition.* A regular focus on making healthy choices at mealtimes, crossing the road safely, and washing hands before eating, helps children to establish life-long habits for hygiene, safety and health

On the EEF's Early Years Evidence Store, the self-care theme summarises research evidence about effective practices to help children become independent in toileting, toothbrushing, handwashing, making healthy food choices, staying safe, keeping active and resting. Children's confidence develops as they can do more for themselves. Educators can also act thoughtfully to help this development. For example, it might be tempting to think that constant positivity and praise helps to boost children's self-esteem and confidence. In fact, research suggests the opposite. The important work on 'growth mindset' by Carol Dweck (2007) shows how constant praise can lead children to focus on pleasing their educators. Children may become so accustomed to praise that they choose easier things to do, knowing that they will succeed and gain praise. It is more important to help children to develop their confidence in tackling difficult tasks. An effective way to promote this is through feedback, focusing on the child's efforts, highlighting what has gone well, and sensitively pointing out where they might have tried something differently.

We might think about rules in a similar way. It is important to have secure routines and rules: children do not thrive in chaotic settings. But an excessive focus on rules can lead to what researchers call 'situational compliance'. This means that children follow the rules when they know the educators can see them, because they want praise. But when they think there is no one around, children with 'situational compliance' might behave poorly. They are not developing self-control and self-discipline.

It is important to help children to understand the reasons behind rules. Simple rules help everyone to feel safe and secure. This approach helps children to learn 'committed compliance'. For example, children need to know that whether an educator is watching them or not, it is wrong to snatch things off another person. Children's developing understanding of rules is outlined in Table 4.1. It is important to note that children develop at different rates, and some children with special educational needs may need more intensive support to understand and follow rules. Additionally, changes in circumstances, like transition into a new group or class, the arrival of a new sibling, or moving house, can lead to children seeming to regress in their PSED for periods of time.

Table 4.1　Helping children to learn about rules throughout the EYFS

Aspects of learning about rules	Birth to 3 years old	3- and 4-year-olds	4- and 5-year-olds: Reception
Attitudes and dispositions	Begin to show 'effortful control'. For example, waiting for a turn and resisting the strong impulse to grab what they want or push their way to the front.	In addition: Find solutions to conflicts and rivalries. For example, accepting that not everyone can be Spider-Man in the game, and suggesting other ideas. Increasingly follow rules, understanding why they are important.	In addition: Identify and moderate their own feelings, socially and emotionally.

Aspects of learning about rules	Birth to 3 years old	3- and 4-year-olds	4- and 5-year-olds: Reception
Concepts and skills	Waiting	In addition:	In addition:
	Sharing	Listen to someone else and agree a compromise.	Reflect on their feelings and the feelings of others, in different scenarios.
			Respect class rules.
Vocabulary	Wait	In addition:	In addition:
	Turn	Agree	Respect
	Next	Disagree	Strategy
		Suggestion	Reflection
		Rules	Scenario
		Calm down	

Early Learning Goal: Managing Self

Children at the expected level of development will:

- Be confident to try new activities and show independence, resilience and perseverance in the face of challenge.
- Explain the reasons for rules, know right from wrong and try to behave accordingly.
- Manage their own basic hygiene and personal needs, including dressing, going to the toilet and understanding the importance of healthy food choices.

(DfE, 2025, pp. 12–13)

Building relationships

Making friends, tolerating disagreements and relating confidently with a wider circle of people are important. They are also difficult developments for many children as they move through the EYFS. Research suggests that 'physical aggression by humans appears to reach its peak between 2 and 3 years of age. In the following years most children learn alternatives to physical aggression' (Tremblay, 2002, p. iv17).

The implications of the research for our practice are clear. We need to have a carefully planned approach to help children learn alternatives to aggressive behaviour. Approaches that focus on conflict resolution and helping children to understand, as well as follow, rules are powerful.

Children in the EYFS need educators' support and scaffolding to manage the ups and downs of friendships. We can model polite and cooperative behaviour as adults working in teams, and in our relationships with parents. We can usefully spend time talking through difficulties with children. It is also important to avoid 'jumping in' too quickly to resolve any difficulties between children (Whitebread et al., 2005). This can prevent them from learning the skills they need to overcome a conflict or a problem in a friendship.

All children will find these developments hard at some time. Some children will have very significant difficulties. Some young children in the EYFS will have already suffered adverse childhood experiences (ACEs), including:

- abuse and neglect
- living in a household where there is domestic violence, drug or alcohol misuse, mental ill health, criminality or separation
- living in care

(Marmot, 2020, p. 45)

ACEs disproportionately affect children growing up in poverty. We cannot solve these problems on our own in the early years. We need to work collaboratively with other services. We might develop a professional relationship with our local Sure Start Children's Centre, Family Hub or Early Help team. Specialist services also support children who have suffered a damaging experience, like a bereavement. Longer term, we need to make the political choices which will reduce the rate of child poverty in England, which is currently well above the average rate for economically developed countries (Marmot, 2020, p. 44).

Early Learning Goal: Building Relationships

Children at the expected level of development will:

- Work and play cooperatively and take turns with others.
- Form positive attachments to adults and friendships with peers.
- Show sensitivity to their own and to others' needs.

(DfE, 2025, p. 13)

Conclusion

Supporting children's personal, social and emotional development is at the heart of the EYFS. At every phase, high-quality care is vital, so that children have a positive environment for this important learning.

This is essential, difficult and skilled work which places great demands on us. Supervision, or Work Discussion, can help us to develop a positive environment for children's emotional growth.

It is crucial to remember that this area of the EYFS is about learning, as well as care. As adults, we play a key role in helping children to make sense of their emotions. By helping children talk about and elaborate on their feelings, we help them develop vital skills in self-regulation. By helping children manage the inevitable difficulties and responsibilities of life in a group, we are offering them a life-long benefit. The same could be said about managing the ups and downs of friendship. The complexity and the importance of this work are often under-appreciated. But, perhaps above all else, this is what makes the early years so special.

Reflective questions

1 How might you explain the importance of settling-in to a parent who is under pressure not to take time off work?
2 Why is it important to help children understand rules, rather than just follow them?

5

Physical Development

Lala Manners and Melissa Prendergast

-EYFS Statutory Educational Programme-

Physical Development

> Physical activity is vital in children's all-round development, enabling them to pursue happy, healthy and active lives. Gross and fine motor experiences develop incrementally throughout early childhood. They start with sensory explorations and the development of the child's strength, co-ordination and positional awareness. They develop through tummy time, crawling and play movement with both objects and adults. By creating games and providing opportunities for indoor and outdoor play, adults can support children to develop their core strength, stability, balance, spatial awareness, co-ordination and agility. Gross motor skills provide the foundation for developing healthy bodies and social and emotional well-being. Fine motor control and precision help with hand-eye co-ordination, which is later linked to early literacy. Repeated and varied opportunities to explore and play with small-world activities, puzzles, arts and crafts and the practice of using small tools, with feedback and support from adults, allow children to develop proficiency, control and confidence.

(DfE, 2025, p.10)

Introduction

Young children's physical health, development and wellbeing have always been central to early years education and care. From the 18th century philosopher Jean-Jacques Rousseau to the Victorian reformer Robert Owen, children's physicality is recognised as being essential to their growth and development. This is echoed in the work of Froebel, Steiner and Montessori.

It is now our turn to prioritise physical development in our practice. It needs to be a strong thread through all our planning and provision. Physical development is not only crucial for young children's health, but also for their all-round learning. As the International Early Learning and Well-being Study (IELS) research explains, 'there is growing evidence that physical and cognitive development are related, and that cognitive and motor skills are mutually supportive of one another' (Lucas et al., 2021, p. 23). Whilst physical development is a discrete area of learning in the Early Years Foundation Stage (EYFS), the Statutory Framework makes it clear that 'all areas of learning and development are important and inter-connected' (DfE, 2025, p. 8).

When we ensure that children have good levels of physical development, we lay the foundations for later health, wellbeing and physical capabilities. But the truth is that we are not managing to ensure this. Nor are we making meaningful and sustainable progress. Around 95% of children achieve the Early Learning Goal for Physical Development, the highest of any area of learning. Yet levels of physical activity are stubbornly low. The UK's Chief Medical Officers (2019) recommend that children in the early years should spend at least 180 minutes (3 hours) a day doing a variety of physical activities spread throughout the day, including active and outdoor play. This should include at least 60 minutes (1 hour) of moderate-to-vigorous intensity physical activity. Yet research by the Early Intervention Foundation (2022) found that only 19% of children are getting the officially recommended amount of physical activity needed to grow up healthily. Rates of childhood obesity and dental decay are shocking, with one in ten children judged to be obese by the time they reach the Reception year. There is also increasing concern across the early years about young children experiencing difficulties with their mental health (Manners, 2018).

We need to improve educators' understanding of children's physical development and make improvements to provision which go well beyond the requirements of the EYFS and the Early Learning Goals.

What is physical development?

Physical development concerns the growth of the brain and body, and the ability to move in a controlled way, coordinating movements, balancing and gradually developing fine and gross motor skills. This includes changes in body size, muscle strength, balance, coordination and abilities such as crawling, walking, running, grasping and handling objects. The basic motor skills which involve all the different parts of the body are called Fundamental Movement Skills (FMS), consisting of:

- locomotor skills (e.g. running and jumping)
- stability skills (e.g. twisting and balancing)
- manipulation skills (e.g. throwing and catching)

Babies and young children have a natural desire to be physically active, exploring the different ways their bodies can move and driving their physical development. However, children's physical development may be negatively affected by:

- overusing sitting devices (e.g. car seats, baby-walkers and bouncy chairs)
- unsafe or inappropriate environments
- lack of opportunities to move safely and freely
- adults' negative attitudes to physical activity

Children's growth and physical development can also be negatively affected when they grow up in poverty, live in substandard housing, and when they do not get enough sleep or have a healthy diet. As a result of the COVID-19 pandemic and rising rates of child poverty, these factors affect many children in the early years.

It is vital that educators have an overall understanding of child development in this area. Whilst most children will make good progress in developing their FMS, given adequate circumstances, some will need extra encouragement or targeted help with specific physical development skills. The IELS thematic research makes a strong case for the importance of our professional knowledge: 'an awareness and understanding of motor skill development, its risk and protective factors, and the relationships between motor skills and other learning outcomes, may help teachers and other early years practitioners intervene earlier to support children's development' (Lucas et al., 2021, p. 14).

Educators need a deep understanding of children as unique individuals because physical development varies from child to child. We need to know each child's strengths and struggles. We must also invest time in understanding the general pace and direction of children's physical development.

Child development

There are two key principles about children's physical development to remember:

1   Motor and muscular development is *cephalocaudal*. This means that it works from top to bottom, head to toe. Control of the head is achieved before musculature to gain control of the shoulders. Once babies can hold up their head, the spinal muscles then develop to enable sitting aided then unaided. Their legs gain strength once they start to crawl. With practice, they become strong enough for standing and walking. As the muscles around the ankles and feet mature, toddlers begin to run and jump.
2   Motor and muscular control is *proximodistal*. This means that it emerges and extends from the centre to the extremities, inside to outside. For example, muscles need to be strong and stable around the shoulder girdle to support the smaller muscles in the elbows, wrists, hands and fingers.

This developmental sequence informs such things as doing up zips and buttons, handling cutlery, handwriting and using scissors.

Keeping these principles in mind helps us understand why children sometimes struggle with activities, even avoid them. They may be motivated, but if they don't have the necessary strength, balance and coordination, they may need to go back a few steps. For example, if handwriting is difficult, provide a range of activities that strengthen the shoulder, wrist and fingers: hanging from their hands, swinging, carrying and digging.

The role of the adult

Every child's physical development journey is unique. Some children's daily life will include physical skills: helping to look after a pet or livestock, planting, cooking, sewing, cleaning, washing and dancing. For others, their environment cannot adequately support their physical development. This may be due to the conditions they live in, or the lack of access to local amenities like safe places for outdoor play.

We need to address the imbalance between those children whose day involves a range of movements and those for whom it is difficult to be active. We can approach this by:

Threading opportunities for children to move throughout every day:

- When the children arrive and leave, create a daily challenge such as putting a line of masking tape on the floor and thinking of ways to move along it.
- At story time, encourage children to change position: squat, kneel, sit with legs straight or crossed, lie on their back or tummy.
- During transitions, move in different ways: walking on knees, sliding on hands and knees, taking long steps.

Embedding a culture of physical activity and movement in the environment:

- Make time in meetings to discuss how you are ensuring that you encourage physical development, both indoors and outdoors.
- Monitor each child's engagement with physical activity *and* their progression. Some children will require a lot more input from adults than others.

These approaches are underpinned by the evidence-informed practices identified in the Education Endowment Foundation's (EEF) Early Years Evidence Store (EEF, 2024b). Creating a culture that motivates children to move and enjoy physical play supports both physical development and executive function outcomes. Alongside this positive and motivating culture, educators also need to consider the importance of teaching children the specific skills they need for movement, for example, locomotor, object control, stability or fine motor skills. This approach often includes educators giving children verbal and physical direction. The following case study provides a snapshot of how this can be done.

Case Study 5.1

Connecting Language and Physicality, by Melissa Prendergast

We use the ShREC approach (James, 2022) to shape our interactions and teaching. This evidence-informed approach involves

- Sharing the child's attention
- Responding to their play
- Expanding their learning and developing back and forth
- Conversation

ShREC is a way of having high-quality interactions with the child as they move and engage in physical activity.

Share attention: the adult sensitively joins the child in their play.

The adult pays attention to what the child is focusing on, not redirecting them but showing a genuine interest:

> Amina was concentrating hard to try to steady herself on the beam. I went over and watched closely, showing her that I was interested in what she was doing. Amina looked at me and smiled.

Respond: the adult comments on what the child can see, feel or hear.

For physical development, this will usually be words and language associated with movement. This helps develop the child's spatial awareness as they connect words to the movements they are making with their body:

> I said, 'You're using one arm to try to balance.'
>
> Amina looked at me and tried again.

Expand: this is where the 'teaching' takes place.

The adult responds to the child and to their learning needs. Expansion can be used to remind them how they might overcome the challenge facing them. Or it can be used to give feedback about how their strategy is going:

> I said, 'Can you hold your other arm out as well to help you balance?' – I modelled the movement.
>
> Amina was clearly a bit nervous about doing this but had a go. She wobbled.
>
> I responded, encouraging and praising her: 'That's great, you're trying really hard.'
>
> Amina: 'I'm falling off.'
>
> I replied, 'It's difficult at first.' I held out my hand to see if Amina wanted some help. She held my hand and walked along the beam.

(Continued)

> *Amina smiled.*
>
> *I said, 'That's it Amina, you're using both of your arms to balance now. Well done.'*
>
> *Amina replied: 'I'm not falling off!'*
>
> *I said, 'No, you're balancing.'*
>
> Conversation: the interactions go back and forth, either verbally or non-verbally.
> Amina and I used both gesture and spoken language to have our conversation. This developed over the time we spent together as we increased the number of interactions we had.
> Children learn to communicate with their bodies; they learn the language of movement; they develop awareness of their physical capabilities; they learn to move freely and with confidence. This is a joy to see!

Planning for progress in physical development

Planning for physical development should be simple, manageable and sustainable. For example, educators will be put off if the environment is complicated to set up and maintain. Indoor and outdoor areas should provide a range of physical opportunities that children may enjoy independently or in a group. Resources should be accessible and include a mix of large, moveable loose parts for building, and construction and smaller materials for manipulative activities.

The EEF's Early Years Evidence Store is a useful resource when planning for physical development. It identifies three evidence-based approaches that support children's physical development:

1 promoting physical activity
2 teaching the skills needed for movement and handling
3 teaching the skills needed for mark-making and letter formation

The Evidence Store summarises research evidence about the importance of freely chosen play in outdoor, natural environments:

> Children were encouraged to participate in more risky play through climbing natural structures. Likewise, freedom to play with natural elements such as grass, rocks, and branches was supported. These activities all led to improvements in children's physical development outcomes. A common theme across the evidence was ensuring that children were provided with choice and a high degree of independence.

(EEF, 2024b)

It is also important for educators to explicitly teach older children in the EYFS (aged 3 to 5 years old) the skills they need for movement and handling. Focusing on a specific skill can help children build competency in that skill. Children need lots of time, space and encouragement to practise these skills across different contexts to deepen their learning. Educators need to use their professional judgement to decide when to interact and offer teaching, and when to stand back and ensure they do not interfere and spoil children's active play.

Evidence highlights the importance of sensitively timed verbal and physical prompts and feedback. The active role of the adult is especially important for children who come to our settings with limited experiences. In general, children from lower-income families are at greater risk of not developing well when compared to their more affluent peers. Children from disadvantaged backgrounds may benefit when educators offer them targeted support with their movement and handling skills. While some children can use the opportunities we provide independently to develop their skills, others need explicit modelling and teaching.

The Movement Environment Rating Scale (MOVERS) is a helpful tool when planning and assessing the quality of our provision for physical development, supporting self-assessment and improvements in practice (Archer and Siraj, 2017). Using a robust, evidence-informed tool like this helps us to ensure that we are continuously reflecting, improving quality and working towards equitable provision for every child.

Some of the important aspects of physical development are outlined in Table 5.1.

Table 5.1 Physical development and movement throughout the EYFS

Aspects of physical development	Birth to 3 years old	3- and 4-year-olds	4- and 5-year-olds
Attitudes and dispositions	Explore movement and sensory experiences with primary caregiver or independently – inside and outdoors. Support and include those differently abled.	In addition: Plan for more complex movement play. Negotiate and collaborate with others. Enjoy more challenging play outdoors. Begin to reflect on activities and how to refine them.	In addition: Increase independence in self-care. Create more interesting opportunities to be active outside. Persevere to keep practising and improving skills. Be resilient and determined. Explore wider possibilities of using skills in different contexts.

(Continued)

Table 5.1 (Continued)

Aspects of physical development	Birth to 3 years old	3- and 4-year-olds	4- and 5-year-olds
Concepts and skills	**Skills**	**Skills**	**Skills**
	Rolling, crawling, sitting, standing	In addition: throwing, catching, kicking, aiming, passing, batting, hopping, galloping, cycling, swimming, constructing, writing, drawing, painting, cutting/scissors	In addition: skipping, galloping, turning
	Climbing, walking, jumping, running		Balancing, sewing, modelling
	Stretching, swinging		**Concepts**
	Pedalling, scootering, grasping		Precision, accuracy
	Holding, prodding		Rhythm, sharing
	Squeezing, wiping, brushing		Imitating, copying
		Processing instructions	Following, leading, demonstrating, practising
		Combinations/sequences	
Vocabulary	Position:	In addition: enjoy, happy, frustrated, sad, cross, bored, tired, exhausted, free, relaxed, energetic, calm, pleased, disappointed	In addition: dither, meander, rapid, adjacent, topple, wilt, dangle, slump
	On, off, under, above, below, near, far, over, beside, in, out		
	Directions:		
	Around, backwards, forwards, sideways, through		

The importance of multisensory experiences

When children move, they learn about their bodies and what they are capable of. They learn the rules of play and how to get on with others. They manage their emotions, learning to regulate their feelings (Archer and Siraj, 2017).

Multisensory experiences have a central role to play in supporting these developments. Offering a wide range of activities to stimulate the senses requires specific planning. It is not just the five main senses we need to look at, but also the three lesser-known ones. These are *proprioception*, the *vestibular* sense and *interoception*.

Proprioception

What is it? It tells us where we are in space, how our bodies relate to our environment, where we begin and end. Proprioceptive sensors lie under the skin and send information to the brain about where we are and what we are doing. Birds have these sensors at their wing tips to help them fly in formation.

How to support: Encourage whole-body movements such as carrying, digging, pushing–pulling, stretching, jumping, running, climbing, kicking and throwing.

Impact: Proprioception supports children with their handwriting, helping them with forming proportional letters, directionality and spacing between words. It enables children to judge the amount of force needed for a particular task.

The vestibular sense

What is it? The vestibular mechanism is situated in the inner ear and is the oldest of our sensory systems. It is critical for developing balance and helps us know when we are moving or still, upside down or upright. The vestibular system works with the neck, head and eye muscles to stabilise vision and enable us to know where we are going and not fall over. It is also connected to hearing and the processing of language.

How to support: The vestibular system takes around seven years to mature and needs a range of varied movement opportunities. 'Dizzy play', swinging movements, turning, being upside down, spinning, leaning, rolling and toppling help develop this sense. Outside spaces provide the best environment to do these, but smaller indoor spaces can work.

Impact: A well-functioning vestibular sense supports all learning that includes left and right. It also helps keep children calm and alert. It supports children to move over uneven surfaces, use escalators and be confident in open spaces.

As the child's balance develops, their ability to be still, concentrate and listen will increase. Their emotional security is also supported through the relationship between the vestibular system and the limbic system in the brain that generates emotionally based behaviour.

Interoception

What is it? This is when the internal organs of the body send messages to the brain via the skin and blood. It lets us know when we are hungry, thirsty, tired or need the toilet. Interoception starts early and is all about developing the capacity to listen to the body, regulate responses and describe physical and emotional states.

How to support: Sensory and movement play refines this sense, particularly repetitive, rhythmic movements such as pushing and pulling, sweeping, digging. Activities such as exploring hot and cold are also effective.

Impact: The interoceptive sense helps children tune into emotional cues and respond appropriately. It enables them to decide if they are tired because they are hungry, if they need to rest, if they are scared or excited.

Moving for its own sake plays a critical role in supporting physical development. Simply experiencing *the feeling of me* is important for children as they roll on the grass, plait their hair, sway to songs and enjoy the feel of rain or sunshine on their bodies. It is important to value these movements, however random or trivial they may seem.

Being active outdoors

The Finnish framework for physical activity in early childhood, 'Joy, Play and Doing Together', states that 'Children are most physically active during guided play that involves physical activity and has rules, and during free spontaneous play. Among children aged 3–4, free spontaneous play accounts for about 20% of the time, and they play more freely outdoors than indoors' (Ministry of Education and Culture, Finland, 2016, p. 29).

As Jan White reminds us, 'the outdoors offers a perfect companion to provision indoors, working in harmony and providing a complementary environment that enhances and extends what we are able to offer children inside' (White, 2013, p. 3).

We should make sure that children can have access to move about in a space without obstruction. Outdoor provision should include a variety of surfaces to move on: large vertical and horizontal surfaces; places and materials for digging and filling; things to lift, carry, transport and move around; wheeled vehicles; and quiet spaces to recuperate.

Making movement fun

Physical development is not just about movement: it is also about children's 'physical literacy'. Physical literacy is an umbrella term which considers people's attitudes towards movement and physical activity throughout their lives. As well as physical competence, confidence and the motivation to be active, it includes how people think, feel and how they join in with others.

There is a strong link between young children's wellbeing and their movement play, according to a 10-year study conducted by the movement play specialists Jabadao. Their study suggests that children's enjoyment, relaxation, vitality, openness, self-confidence and self-knowledge are all increased through their participation in movement play (Jabadao, 2009).

When children are physically confident and competent, daily routines become manageable and enjoyable: taking coats off, washing hands, sitting in a circle, cutting up snacks, and moving between rooms and activities. Growing independence in self-care is important for supporting children's agency and self-image.

The following case study illustrates the importance of children's attitudes, feelings and sense of fun in relation to physical development.

Case Study 5.2

The Running Project, by Lala Manners

The children in my Reception class became interested in running. I'm not sure why! We looked at animals that run like lions and tigers and thought about why. We then thought about those that don't run much, like cows and sheep.

We moved on to think about human running and the reasons why people run, looking at types of running: park runs, running for the bus, sprinting, marathons, cross-country, parkour. We discussed speeds and distances, watching videos on YouTube.

Next, we explored our own running. Would we run better barefoot, in trainers or wellies? We realised slippers were useless! How fast could we go? What helped or hindered us? How could we improve our running?

We examined how we felt when we ran. Were we puffed-out, tired, happy?

All these involved long discussions.

Finally, we made a collage of the areas we had explored, using lots of cutting and sticking. We celebrated this with a presentation in assembly.

Inclusive practice

It is vital that physical development is inclusive. We need to plan carefully (using advice from specialists) for children who have special educational needs and disabilities (SEND). All spaces inside and outside should be safe and accessible to all.

When cooperating physically, children learn that different bodies move differently and that some children are more confident than others. They will learn when others may benefit from their help and, importantly, become sensitive to when help is not wanted.

Children learn to wait their turn, so that everyone can participate. They learn about sharing spaces and resources when moving together.

Negative behaviour or language related to difference must be addressed seriously. For example, staff must have a consistent way of dealing with spaces that become gender specific; the 'labelling' of less confident or competent individuals and the risk of children whose development has not progressed in a linear way being excluded from active play. It is important to note that research evidence focuses mainly on children who are developing typically, rather than those with disabilities or medical conditions, so educators will need to use their professional knowledge, reflect together on challenges, and monitor provision carefully to ensure that all children feel included.

Gross motor skills

Gross motor skills are whole-body movements. They are the critical building blocks that provide the strength, coordination, balance and agility needed for all other skills.

Practising rolling, crawling, climbing, running, jumping, kicking and throwing pave the way for more complex physical skills. The importance of continuous and varied experience of these skills cannot be overstated. Even when they are fluent and used effectively, children will benefit from repeating and refining them.

How to practise these skills

Inside (shoes off if possible):

- Rolling: ask the children to curl up into a ball by hugging their knees tightly – now rock backwards and forwards, slowly then getting faster. Ask them to lie on their front with long arms and legs – now flip onto their back without losing the shape – flip back onto front again.
- Crawling: try going at different speeds, forwards and backwards, around and under tables and chairs
- Jumping: hold the back of their chair with both hands then jump with feet together on tiptoes, flat feet, feet out and in, forwards and backwards
- Running: put tables together in a line to create a big one – children place one hand on the table and face forwards – ask them to run around the table, keeping their hand on it at all times – change direction
- Ball skills: use rolled up socks or crumpled paper bags to throw, kick, catch, pass and aim
- Obstacle courses: invite the children to construct a course themselves using the available resources like cushions, tables, chairs, carpet, walls, floor, steps

Outside:

- Provide a range of large loose parts, including car tyres and crates for children to lift, carry and construct
- Suggest ways in which the available resources may be used to challenge jumping (across/onto/down), running (in a circle/back and forth), climbing, balancing and swinging
- Encourage group activities that include digging, pushing resources around the space, sweeping up afterwards

Early Learning Goal: Gross Motor Skills

Children at the expected level of development will:

- Negotiate space and obstacles safely, with consideration for themselves and others.
- Demonstrate strength, balance and coordination when playing.
- Move energetically, such as running, jumping, dancing, hopping, skipping and climbing.

(DfE, 2025, p. 13)

Fine motor skills

These are sometimes called manipulative skills as usually they apply to the hands only. However, the mouth, feet and eyes are also significant in developing these skills. Fine motor skill development depends on the development of the gross motor skills.

Hands are one of the final body parts to mature. The range of skills that hands perform becomes increasingly complex and develops over a lifetime: sewing, cooking, writing, knitting, hairdressing, playing card games, board games, modelling, painting, playing a musical instrument.

To strengthen the hand muscles try:

- Playing with sponges in water, playdough, twisting tops off bottles, prodding, squeezing, rolling and pinching appropriate materials
- Peeling small pieces of fruit, adding a pinch of salt or spice to a recipe, finding small objects hidden in a bowl of dried rice, feeding the fish
- Threading material through a lattice or threading pasta and breads on a string
- Creating intricate patterns with small buttons, beads and paper straws
- Peeling off stickers and placing on a sheet of paper
- Sand play with small utensils such as teaspoons and egg cups
- Play 'dancing and talking' fingers – drawing faces on fingertips and having conversations between hands
- Finger drumming

> ## Early Learning Goal: Fine Motor Skills
>
> Children at the expected level of development will:
>
> - Hold a pencil effectively in preparation for fluent writing – using the tripod grip in almost all cases.
> - Use a range of small tools, including scissors, paint brushes and cutlery.
> - Begin to show accuracy and care when drawing.
>
> (DfE, 2025, p. 13)

Thinking beyond the goals

Health and self-care were moved from Physical Development to Personal, Social and Emotional Development in 2021. This is not helpful, as gross motor and fine motor skills impact greatly on the development of self-care. Manipulative skills help with cleaning teeth, holding cutlery and getting dressed. Gaining physical competence and confidence supports children's safety in the wider environment and encourages healthy behaviours around food and drink.

The current goals for physical development are narrow in focus and not very ambitious. To extend their reach, consider the following:

- Invite children to create their own movement sequences, using music to provide a steady beat
- Practise challenging combinations of movements: they can spin or jump and balance on one leg
- Introduce interesting materials to move with: chiffon scarves or coloured ribbons
- Encourage the exploration of different ball skills: batting, passing and aiming

Conclusion

Every child's movement journey is different. It unfolds in its own way. Early movement experiences that are enjoyable and meaningful will provide a wealth of learning and long-term health benefits. Children's physical development in the early years can influence their levels of engagement, enjoyment and proficiency through their teenage years and beyond (Ridgway et al., 2009).

Yet despite knowing how important physical development is, and despite the crisis in young children's health, we are not yet doing enough in the early years to make a difference. The expectations for physical development in *Development Matters* are too modest and the Early Learning Goals lack ambition. We need to ensure that physical development is properly valued so that children can benefit from improved health, fitness and a life-long enjoyment of physical activity.

Reflective questions

1   What practical measures do you take to ensure all children are active throughout the day?
2   How do you ensure physical development is valued by parents and staff?

6

Literacy

Sinéad Harmey

EYFS Statutory Educational Programme

It is crucial for children to develop a life-long love of reading. Reading consists of two dimensions: language comprehension and word reading. Language comprehension (necessary for both reading and writing) starts from birth. It only develops when adults talk with children about the world around them and the books (stories and non-fiction) they read with them, and enjoy rhymes, poems and songs together. Skilled word reading, taught later, involves both the speedy working out of the pronunciation of unfamiliar printed words (decoding) and the speedy recognition of familiar printed words. Writing involves transcription (spelling and handwriting) and composition (articulating ideas and structuring them in speech, before writing).

(DfE, 2025, p. 10)

Introduction

Mohammed-Jawad bursts into his classroom and runs up to hang his coat on his peg – proudly pointing to his name, he declares 'that's my one'.

Seeing children recognise their name for the first time is one of the joys of being an educator in the early years. It used to be thought that children move from a 'pre-reading' to a 'reading' stage. Another perspective, an emergent literacy one, is that the journey to becoming a reader and a writer is more fine-grained and that children emerge into literacy from birth. Children are in a continual process of becoming literate: aware that print contains meaning and that speech matches print. We see this in lots of subtle ways in early years classrooms.

What do we mean by literacy? The Statutory Framework for the Early Years Foundation Stage (EYFS) (DfE, 2025) describes literacy as reading and writing:

- reading consisting of two dimensions: language comprehension and word reading
- writing involving transcription and composition

This framework helps us think of the components involved in skilled reading and writing. But it can be difficult to match that definition with literacy learners in early years settings. As an early years teacher and researcher, I find it more helpful to define literacy as a process that involves learning that symbols in print make meaning:

- I can read these symbols and listen to someone else's message
- I can write these symbols, and they carry meaning (even if the symbols do not quite look conventional yet)

As Mohammed-Jawad joyfully demonstrated, these symbols arranged in this way mean something – his name.

This chapter builds on the idea that literacy is a meaning-making activity, and that oral language is foundational. First, I consider how oral language feeds into literacy. Then, I consider how to support emergent readers by fostering a love of books and building foundational reading skills. Finally, I examine emergent writing and how to support it.

Literacy builds on oral language

Written text is thoughts and language in print. Understanding language, or language comprehension, is essential for reading and writing. It starts from birth and the development of language 'underpins all seven areas of learning and development' (DfE, 2025, p. 9). Chapter 3 in this book focuses on language and communication. In this section, I want to focus on:

- how literacy and oral language are interconnected
- how we can support children's literacy development through the development of oral language

Research supports the idea that strong oral language skills are linked to later reading ability (Law et al., 2017). Some of the aspects of oral language that support literacy include the development of:

- narrative skills
- vocabulary

- print knowledge
- phonological awareness

I focus next on narrative skills and vocabulary; print knowledge and phonological awareness will be discussed later in the chapter.

Narrative skills

Narrative skills are the ability to tell a story, describe or retell events, or provide instructions. There are many places in the early years curriculum where we can support the development of oral narrative skills. Stories span cultures and form the backbone of poems, rhymes, story books, drama and play. Most stories follow a 'story grammar' – a setting, event, characters, with (typically) a beginning, middle and end. Children's narrative skills develop by providing opportunities to listen to and engage in stories, poems and rhymes. When educators retell stories with a light-touch emphasis on the 'grammar' of the story, they support the children to develop narrative skills. Planning to support children to expand their own stories will also support these skills.

Narrative skills can develop further via opportunities to tell stories through:

- engaging in sustained conversations with peers and adults
- using props and puppets
- pretend play

Narrative skills, however, go further than fiction and storytelling. The day-to-day routines of the setting provide opportunities for children to sequence and retell events. Later in children's education, the ability to describe and sequence events will be part of subjects like science, geography and music.

Vocabulary

Knowing and using a wide variety of words is another essential component of literacy development and underlies language comprehension. The rate at which young children accumulate vocabulary is astounding and many children will learn words incidentally in the context of language-rich environments (Christ and Chiu, 2018). Children who have a limited vocabulary, however, are less likely to just 'pick up' as many words. Educator support can accelerate children's word learning through deliberately promoting vocabulary acquisition (Justice, 2002). It is useful to think about vocabulary not just as words, but also as *types* of words. Beck et al. (2013) provide a useful framework for this and describe three tiers of words that older children in the EYFS need to learn:

- Tier 1: basic everyday words used often (book, bear, door)
- Tier 2: words which are commonly found in high-quality story books but not commonly used in ordinary conversation (impressed, wonder)
- Tier 3: content-specific words used infrequently (photosynthesis)

For younger children, Christ and Wang (2011) recommend considering how we can provide many opportunities for children to hear advanced words and think about how we can teach word meanings incidentally and deliberately across many areas of learning throughout the day. When thinking about the curriculum in the early years, it helps to consider how we will embed the teaching of different types of words across areas of learning. We can do this intentionally through modelling, expanding on what children say, labelling, repeating and rephrasing. It is important that we provide repeated opportunities to use and hear words through sharing stories and poems and in small-world play. This supports the development of a rich and varied vocabulary.

Intentionally planning to develop narrative and vocabulary skills fits well with interactive reading in the early years (Grøver et al., 2023). Interactive reading is defined as a shared reading context where the adult intentionally encourages the child to 'become an active participant in reading' (Education Endowment Foundation [EEF], 2023a). This could be through talking with the child about the storyline or illustrations. Questions that encourage rich and extended conversations (not a 'yes' or 'no' answer) are particularly helpful in developing vocabulary and narrative skills. For example, in planning to read *We're Going on a Bear Hunt* (Rosen, 2000), there are huge opportunities to develop language through interactive reading of the text and, indeed, in other opportunities throughout the day. You could:

- support children to retell the story in sequence
- encourage a retelling of the story in their play
- embed talk around the story in multiple areas of learning, from maths (counting) to physical development and to art
- re-read books with attention to the illustrations. There are rich language opportunities within and beyond the text – for example, why is the boy carrying the stick?

Ultimately, the Early Learning Goals for Language Comprehension (below) will be supported by a sustained and intentional focus on narrative and vocabulary skills. Regular sharing of books across a wide variety of topics and genres will expose children to a varied 'diet' of words.

Early Learning Goal: Comprehension

Children at the expected level of development will:

- Demonstrate understanding of what has been read to them by retelling stories and narratives using their own words and recently introduced vocabulary.

- Anticipate – where appropriate – key events in stories.
- Use and understand recently introduced vocabulary during discussions about stories, non-fiction, rhymes and poems and during role-play.

(DfE, 2025, p. 13)

Emergent reading

The Early Learning Goals for Reading (DfE, 2025) are the end goals of the EYFS. In this section, I consider what a supportive literacy curriculum needs to include to help children to reach this goal, and go beyond it. I am framing literacy as a meaning-making process that starts at birth, which can be supported by:

- fostering a love of books
- providing meaningful opportunities to engage with print
- learning how print works
- developing phonic knowledge

Fostering a love of books

As adult readers, we are guided by our motivation when choosing what we read and how we read it:

- Can you remember the last book that you could not put down?
- What was it about that book that captured your attention?
- Can you remember how this felt compared to the last text you 'had to read'?

At these moments, you were impacted by two factors: motivation and engagement. Your ability to maintain attention and your unwillingness to put this book down stemmed from your motivation to read. You had a goal – to get to the end of the book! You were engaged or involved in the reading process (Wigfield and Guthrie, 2000). You maintained your attention because you were engaged in the story and made connections with it. Apart from the personal enjoyment that reading brings, it is well established that reading motivation and engagement are linked to later academic achievement. This makes sense when we consider that the more children read, the more they have opportunities to develop reading skills and learn new words and knowledge.

It is useful to think about motivation and engagement when considering how to foster children's love of books. Children who are motivated to read will pick up books that they are interested in and seek out favourite stories to be read to them. Children who are engaged enjoy listening to stories. They pay attention and share ideas. They talk about books that they are reading and that are being read to them.

We can help children to develop a love of books by paying attention to how motivated they are to read and how engaged they are in book-reading activities.

The social reading environment plays an important part in promoting and fostering a love of books. Think back to where you read that last book you read for pleasure. As adults, we usually seek somewhere comfortable to read books and the same goes for children.

- Where can children read in your setting?
- Is it comfortable and inviting?
- Are the books in good condition and can children easily see and access a range of titles?

We can help children to develop a love of books by reading aloud a variety of children's literature. This helps inform children's motivation to read independently. Reading aloud provides opportunities to learn about stories and engage with print. It also promotes informal book talk through:

- a culture of recommending books to each other through display areas
- involving parents and carers to encourage a culture of reading within and beyond the setting

Learning how print works

Reading starts the moment we look at print. But, accessing print requires some key conceptual understanding about how print works, or 'concepts about print', as *Development Matters* explains (DfE, 2023, p. 79). First, children need to understand that print has meaning and has different purposes. Fostering a love of books and creating multiple opportunities to engage in meaningful writing activities support this. There are also more technical things to learn about how print works. Written English follows certain rules, which we need to understand. We write in English from top to bottom and start at the top left of a page. Then writing moves left to right, before going to the next line and starting at the left again. To read a book, we start at the front and turn the pages to the left until we reach the back of the book. Letters make up words and words make up sentences. To read a word, we need to start at the first letter and move left to right. It is all quite complicated really!

It is important to teach children in Reception:

- the 'meta-language' (the specific vocabulary and terminology used to discuss and analyse language) we expect them to understand and use, for example letter, first letter, sound, book, page, title, sentence
- the literacy behaviours they need to control to read (where to start and which way to go)

This teaching supports emergent reading and should be part of the literacy curriculum.

We can help children to develop their conceptual awareness about print during interactive reading (see Justice and Ezell, 2004). This is illustrated in the following case study.

Case Study 6.1

Print Referencing in Action During Interactive Reading

The educator, Naomi, is reading *Open Very Carefully – A Book With a Bite* by Nick Bromley (2014):

Naomi: OK everyone, sitting comfortably? Today we're going to read this book – it's called 'Open Very Carefully – A Book With a Bite'!

Alex: A crocodile!!

Naomi: That's right, Alex – you saw a crocodile on the cover of the book! Let's open this book very carefully (turns the page) … here on the first page I see a beautiful lake.

Amy: With a mother duck and baby ducks.

John: Ducklings.

Naomi: Yes – I can see them too – mother duck and three yellow baby ducklings and a little grey duckling with a red hat. Let's see what's happening. Where should I start reading?

Jamie: Up the top.

Naomi: Yes, right up here on the top left-hand side – I'm going to start here (points to the first word) and then go this way (gestures left to right under the first line of text). Once upon a time, there was a mother duck with three pretty ducklings and one... Wait a minute... what's that...?

In this exchange, Naomi is building engagement with the story by talking about the pictures. She is helping the children to learn new vocabulary by expanding on what they are contributing and by print referencing.

- Talking about pictures allows children to build a 'mental model' of the story that they are about to hear and supports comprehension
- Print referencing draws children's attention to how print works

---

Print referencing is an effective strategy to develop conceptual awareness about print. It provides a kind of meta-language for children to use: the cover of the book, the first page, where I start reading. Building in print referencing, as Naomi does, demonstrates the kind of things children need to be able to do in order to use letter–sound knowledge. We expect children to know where to and how to look at print whilst we are teaching them more complex phonic skills. Deliberately teaching conceptual awareness about print as part of the literacy curriculum in the early years lays the foundations for this.

To read letters and words, children need to match speech sounds (phonemes) to symbols (graphemes). This demands phonological awareness – the ability to perceive and manipulate sounds in words (Cain, 2010). Supporting the development of phonological awareness is an essential component of any literacy curriculum, as difficulties in this area are linked to later difficulties in reading. To support phonological awareness, engage children in activities like:

- recognising words that sound the same
- saying words that sound the same
- identifying and segmenting syllables
- playing with individual sounds through songs, word games and rhymes

Phonics instruction supports children's understanding of the link between what they hear and what they see. Evidence suggests that the teaching of phonics should be 'explicit and systematic' (EEF, 2018) for children in Reception. There is less evidence about the impact of phonics instruction with younger children (aged 3–4). Children need to learn how to decode words, analyse word parts and recognise words. There is strong evidence that 'once children know a few consonant and vowel sounds they can start to blend those letters into simple words' (Foorman et al., 2016, p. 14) and indeed read simple sentences by the end of Reception.

Early Learning Goal: Word Reading

Children at the expected level of development will:

- Say a sound for each letter in the alphabet and at least 10 digraphs.
- Read words consistent with their phonic knowledge by sound-blending.
- Read aloud simple sentences and books that are consistent with their phonic knowledge, including some common exception words.

(DfE, 2025, p. 14)

Emergent writing

Writing starts when a child picks up a tool and makes marks that express some sort of meaningful message. The message, however, might not be obvious to the reader. Writing is a very complex process. It requires bringing together a huge amount of knowledge and skills, both cognitive and physical. It is a physical act requiring fine motor control and self-regulation. It involves knowledge about letter–sound relationships and spelling patterns.

It involves composition – so it could be thought of as the bringing together of ideas and shaping those ideas in written form. In this section of the chapter, I consider how we can support children with:

- the physical act of writing (transcription)
- the act of composition (writing a message)

I also consider how writing can support reading and language more generally.

The Physical act of writing

The fine motor control required to write letters develops first through the coordination of larger muscle groups. This happens across the early years curriculum, for example in Physical Development and Expressive Art and Design. As educators, we have all seen the intense look of concentration as children grip writing tools in an effort to reproduce symbols. Rowe and Wilson (2015) studied children's writing from age 1 to 3. They found that children's early mark-making may seem random, but that children follow developmental trajectories:

- using forearm movement to make big purposeful marks
- repeating patterns like lines and circles
- producing semi-conventional letters

We can support the physical strength needed to write from early on. In a project I co-developed called *Write from the Beginning* (Harmey et al., 2024) we focused on two areas during playful interactions between children, parents and educators. These were:

- developing strong hands for writing
- sharing stories

Case Study 6.2

Write from the Beginning: Developing Strong Hands for Writing

In our project, we explored playful opportunities to develop strong hands and share stories. Adam's educator, for example, noticed how he was having difficulty with holding and grasping tools during art. As a result, we focused specifically on playful opportunities for him to engage in lots of activities to build his core (body) and shoulder strength. We used strategies like bear crawling, walking on all fours, climbing, and crawling to music and songs. All of these activities

(Continued)

develop (a) core strength, (b) strong shoulders and (c) bilateral control (the ability to use both sides of the body in a coordinated and sequenced manner, for example both hands). These large-scale activities feed into later smaller movements (Mackenzie and Scull, 2018). Think of it like a tree. If the trunk and large branches are not stable, the finer twigs do not have support. We also provided lots of opportunities to develop fine motor control by playing with playdough (pinching, rolling, squeezing, squishing) while sharing stories and singing songs. All of these activities are foundational to developing the strength needed to write using a pen or pencil in the future.

We can further support early interactions with print by providing lots of opportunities to make marks using a variety of media and tools. Tools like sticks, large paintbrushes and sponges, together with media like chalk and paints, provide opportunities for grasping and making marks. Cutting with scissors helps develop hand strength. *Development Matters* describes how sensory play with sand, flour and mud can support the development of gross motor control. Writing is part of children's play – for example, shopping lists, sending notes and letters at the post office and writing menus. Providing a clipboard, whiteboards, notebooks and paper all encourage the child's motivation to write. Together with appropriate handwriting instruction, this provision will put them on the path to write recognisable letters, some correctly formed, by the end of Reception (EEF, 2018, p. 14).

Over time, children can develop emergent writing skills by using a variety of media like felt-tip markers, pencils, chalk, tempera paint sticks, charcoal and smaller paintbrushes. As children move towards producing more conventional letters, it is helpful for educators to use meta-language which supports writing – words like up, down, round and back. This helps children to write accurately and develop conceptual awareness about print. As we teach children to write in Reception, we might focus their attention on:

- where to start
- which way to go
- how to group letters into words
- leaving spaces between words

The act of composition

The prime purpose of writing is to make meaning. Providing the opportunities to practise the act of transcription will help children to understand that writing is a meaning-making process. As I sit here writing this chapter, I am thinking about the message I want to convey. I am thinking about how to organise that message into recognisable symbols so that you, the reader, can understand what I am thinking.

In today's society, however, it is also worth thinking about text as being multi-modal. We express meaning in text. But we can also use pictures and symbols, using either traditional tools (pens and pencils) or digital means (photos and apps). Indeed, using pictures in tandem with writing is supportive for emergent writers as it helps children to organise their ideas.

There are many opportunities for educators to model how ideas can become print by modelling and scribing for the child. In our *Write from the Beginning* (Harmey et al., 2024) project, parents worked with me to engage in playful interactions around writing. After sharing *Walking Through the Jungle* (Lacome, 2012) we invited children to write with tempera paint sticks on sheets of paper we had taped to the wall. In the following case study, I explore how a parent supported her son to write his message.

Case Study 6.3

Composing Together

Nunu and her son Ahmed were working together. Ahmed drew a big blue elephant. Nunu worked to annotate his drawing by inviting him to tell her about his picture: 'tell me what this is... what is happening here? 'It's elephant', said Ahmed. Nunu responded and expanded his statement ever so slightly by saying 'Oh it's a big blue elephant'. 'A big blue elephant', responded Ahmed and Nunu wrote the phrase for him on his page.

Shared writing can become part of the daily routine, with the educator handing over increasing control to the children. For example, the educator might start by annotating a picture before handing the pen to a child and asking them to add letters or punctuation they know and can write. As children begin to write on their own, their first attempts may be phonically plausible but inaccurate (for example: cr for car or byk for bike). This is absolutely fine. Children who use invented spelling are 'flexing their muscles'. They are using their growing phonological awareness skills and linking sounds

Early Learning Goal: Writing

Children at the expected level of development will:

- Write recognisable letters, most of which are correctly formed.
- Spell words by identifying sounds in them and representing the sounds with a letter or letters.
- Write simple phrases and sentences that can be read by others.

(DfE, 2025, p. 14)

to letters. Ouellette and Sénéchal (2017) found that invented spelling in kindergarten (Reception) is linked to later success in spelling and early reading.

All the opportunities described in the last two sections bring children to a point where they will have the physical ability to write recognisable letters and words, and write simple phrases.

Speaking, reading and writing: Interconnected and not separate

I have written about oral language, reading and writing separately in this chapter. You might think that I am suggesting that we should teach these three aspects of literacy separately. Not quite. There is evidence that there is a need for discrete and intentional teaching of certain elements of literacy – for example, phonics and vocabulary teaching. But there are distinct benefits to considering how the elements support each other. How might this look in practice? Take, for example, the following case study as Lizzie, Mohammed-Jawad's educator, works with him to caption a painting.

Case Study 6.4

Integrating Reading, Writing and Language

Lizzie sits beside Mohammed-Jawad as he finishes painting. On the page is a big yellow sun and some green stripes at the bottom.

Lizzie:	Tell me about your painting, Mohammed-Jawad.
Mohammed-Jawad:	It's sun and park.
Lizzie:	Oh nice – and is that the grass there at the bottom of the picture?
Mohammed-Jawad:	Yes, it's sun and grass.

Lizzie takes a strip of card and says, 'where shall I start?' and Mohammed-Jawad points to the left. She writes the sentence as she says it – 'It's sun and grass'.

Lizzie:	Now we'll put your name here. You know the first letter, so you start for me.

Mohammed-Jawad takes the pen and writes the M for his name.

This exchange exemplifies how language becomes text. It illustrates the interconnected nature of literacy. Mohammed-Jawad provided the meaning, and then worked with his educator to turn the spoken sentence into text which can be read. This became an opportunity for learning about how print works. Inviting children to add letters to text allows them to start making these connections.

The literacy curriculum should offer opportunities for children to make these connections across reading, writing and speaking. Books authored by children bring the connection between speaking and writing even closer. We can share these pieces by reading them aloud to the class and put them in the library for children to read independently. This demonstrates to children that literacy is about making meaning, and that they can be authors. In my work with struggling writers, the first place I often start with is small caption books that include the child's name.

Conclusion

The developmental trajectory in becoming literate is rapid in the early years. If we only look at the Early Learning Goals we can forget that children need a solid foundation of language. They need to integrate a range of physical and cognitive skills. The road to reading and writing simple sentences and understanding texts is built on these foundations. Reading and writing require motivation, engagement and self-regulation. Above all, as the first sentence of the EYFS Statutory Educational Programme says, literacy is about enjoyment (DfE, 2025). Motivation and engagement provide children with positive dispositions towards literacy. They need this to persist with becoming expert readers and writers.

In Table 6.1, I outline how early learning might look in the EYFS across different phases. In the vocabulary section, I refer to the meta-language which might be helpful at each phase, assuming that reading and writing themselves are vehicles for developing vocabulary across the wider curricular areas.

Table 6.1   Literacy throughout the EYFS

Aspects of literacy development	Birth to 3 years old	3- and 4-year-olds	4- and 5-year-olds: Reception
Attitudes and dispositions	Enjoy stories/songs/rhymes. Enjoy sharing books. Seek out favourite stories. Pay attention to songs/rhymes/stories. Enjoy drawing/making marks. Confidently share ideas about reading/writing.	In addition: Engage in storytelling and sequence events. Confidently converse and express what they need. Engage in more extended conversations. Plan writing and persist to try and form some shapes while writing.	In addition: Engage in extended stories/learn new vocabulary. Reflect on likes and dislikes (e.g. stories). Seek out opportunities to write messages. Engage in more extended writing episodes.

(Continued)

Table 6.1 (Continued)

Aspects of literacy development	Birth to 3 years old	3- and 4-year-olds	4- and 5-year-olds: Reception
Concepts and skills	Say some words/songs/rhymes. Repeat words and phrases in songs/rhymes/stories. Ask questions about books. Share ideas about books. Talk about writing/drawing. Add meaning to marks by talking about writing. Hold a book and turn pages. Notice some features of print.	In addition: Understand some concepts about print. Sequence stories/narratives. Recognise words with the same initial sound or that rhyme. Clap syllables. Write some letters and some or all of their name. Use some print to represent meaning. Use a variety of language structures.	In addition: Recognise, name and write some letters. Blend sounds in some short words. Read/write their name and read some exception words. Read simple phrases. Form letters correctly and revise. Re-read what they have written. Match sounds to letters. Write short sentences using a capital letter and a full stop.
Vocabulary	Book, name	Front/back of book, page, first, next, last, turn, start/end	Letters, words, phoneme, grapheme, digraph, left/right, full stop, capital/lower case

Reflective questions

1   The development of narrative skills and vocabulary is essential in supporting children's language comprehension. How can we integrate this into interactive reading opportunities?

2   Are the social reading environments of the classroom inviting?

3   Are children motivated to use the social reading environments independently?

4   The Early Learning Goals separate reading and writing into components. Are there components that receive more/less emphasis in your curricular provision? What areas need more emphasis?

5   What opportunities are there to link together reading, writing and speaking?

7

Mathematics

Fliss James

┌─ EYFS Statutory Educational Programme ─┐

Mathematics

Developing a strong grounding in number is essential so that all children develop the necessary building blocks to excel mathematically. Children should be able to count confidently, develop a deep understanding of the numbers to 10, the relationships between them and the patterns within those numbers. By providing frequent and varied opportunities to build and apply this understanding – such as using manipulatives, including small pebbles and tens frames for organising counting – children will develop a secure base of knowledge and vocabulary from which a mastery of mathematics is built. In addition, it is important that the curriculum includes rich opportunities for children to develop their spatial reasoning skills across all areas of mathematics, including shape, space and measures. It is important that children develop a positive attitude and interest in mathematics, look for patterns and relationships, spot connections, 'have a go', talk to adults and peers about what they notice and not be afraid to make mistakes.

(DfE, 2025, p.10)

Introduction

Early mathematics is astoundingly important for children's development. Positive early experiences and achievement in mathematics lay the foundations for future learning: research evidence indicates that children's early maths understanding is the strongest predictor of later school achievement and success in entering the workforce. Fascinatingly, babies are born mathematical: research shows that very young children have an instinctive sense of quantity, pattern and spatial relationships. From an early age, children develop their ideas about maths through play, exploration and routines. Children have a natural desire and curiosity to learn and find out about their world. Many of the things children wonder about are bursting with mathematical ideas!

Maths anxiety

It is common for adults to express negative feelings and a lack of confidence about maths. Unfortunately, poor school experiences are often the cause.

Early years educators need to be mindful of expressing negative feelings about maths. Myths about maths abound: there is no evidence of a 'maths brain' or that particular people are 'wired up for maths' or are 'maths people'. It is important that we shift this false narrative. It is time to empower all adults and children to be able to engage with the wonder and creativity of maths.

Early maths is incredibly important, and all young children have a right to thrive in meaningful, challenging and enjoyable maths teaching.

Maths is all around us

The world we live in is highly mathematical. Do you ever stop and look at the patterns and shapes that surround us? There are many examples in the natural world, from the spirals in seashells to the arrangement of sunflower seeds.

Our daily lives are filled with maths: from the moment we wake, we encounter mathematical ideas. Getting up on time, making breakfast and navigating our way to work all involve mathematical thinking. It is important to develop an understanding of the mathematics that is embedded in everyday life.

The importance of mathematising

Children engage with mathematical ideas in their play from a very young age:

> In their free play, children naturally engage in mathematics. Observations of preschoolers show that when they play, they engage in mathematical thinking at least once in almost half of each minute that they are playing.

> (Clements and Sarama, 2017)

Yet, despite this natural mathematical play, we know that young children need *our input* to make sense of these ideas. Children's interests, actions and experiences are important, but they are not enough in themselves. They are a starting point. Children need adults to help them build on mathematical knowledge and make connections.

So how can we do this? The term 'mathematising' has arisen in the literature to make abstract mathematical ideas 'real' for children. When adults mathematise experiences for children, they help them to 'see' the maths. Through engaging children in meaningful back-and-forth conversations, adults can encourage children to recognise and talk about maths in everyday situations. Use of open-ended questions can prompt children to make connections, reason, reflect and apply their knowledge. It is vital to understand that without the sensitive, responsive, intentional action of adults, these mathematical ideas do not develop into concepts that children truly understand.

Effective mathematics teaching in the early years

The Education Endowment Foundation's (EEF) guidance report *Improving Mathematics in the Early Years and Key Stage 1* identifies three important aspects:

- adults' own understanding of mathematics
- children's mathematical development and how they learn
- effective mathematical pedagogy

(EEF, 2020a)

Firstly, sensitive and supportive relationships are vital. Adults need to know children well and foster a culture that supports and celebrates children's curiosity, problem-solving and reasoning skills.

Adults also need to understand how children typically develop mathematical concepts and skills. It is also vital that adults are aware of how the following factors influence development:

- higher-level thinking skills: executive functions, self-regulation and metacognition
- language skills
- motor skills
- previous experiences, interests, enjoyment and attitudes

(EEF, 2020a)

Adults need to plan experiences that challenge young children's mathematical knowledge. This is neatly described in the New Zealand Education Review Office report *Early Mathematics: A Guide for Improving Teaching and Learning*:

Without a balance of deliberate teaching and spontaneous learning, a 'hands off' approach does not benefit children's learning. When teachers do not deliberately or intentionally extend children's interests and build on their learning over time, children are disadvantaged.

(Te Tari Arotake Mātauranga/New Zealand Education Review Office, 2016, p. 24)

Practitioners need to have a strong understanding of maths so that they can identify the maths the child is engaging with, tune in and extend it. To quote the Erikson Early Math Collaborative:

This knowledge will also help you recognize the kinds of structured activities that do the best job of making these ideas real for young children, which means you will be able to make them fun without losing the important concepts under the 'glitter and glue'.

(Erikson Early Math Collaborative, 2014, p. 6)

Understanding how children learn mathematical ideas will help you to work out what a child does and does not understand. You will be equipped to know what they need to learn about next.

Intentional pedagogy and teachable moments

As educators, we need to understand effective and developmentally appropriate early mathematics pedagogy, which is key to ensuring that children develop mathematical thinking, knowledge, concepts and behaviours. At the core of effective high-quality early childhood education and care is the idea of 'intentional pedagogy' (Epstein, 2007).

Effective educators combine positive relationships with meaningful learning experiences, so that they can integrate explicit instruction with sensitive, warm interaction. They provide responsive, individualised feedback and intentional engagement – while maintaining a setting that is orderly and predictable, but not overly structured or formal (Howes and Tsao, 2013). Because of the huge disparity in the skills of the young children attending ECEC [Early Childhood Education and Care] settings, supporting their learning and development is complex and challenging.

(Siraj et al., 2018, p. 18)

Teachable moments involve spotting and capitalising on opportunities to promote mathematical learning in everyday play and routines. As Clements and Sarama (2018, p. 3) state, 'teachable moments, handled well, can be wondrous and satisfying'.

Yet, relying on teachable moments is not enough. We must seek out and take advantage of meaningful, spontaneous situations. Many educators do not spend enough time observing children to tune into such opportunities. Additionally, many educators do not have the necessary mathematical concepts, skills and vocabulary at their fingertips.

Teachable moments are important but need to be part of a 'hybrid approach'. We also need to dedicate time for children to learn mathematics and integrate it throughout the day:

> Math can be integrated with children's ongoing play and activities, but this integration usually requires a curriculum and a knowledgeable adult who creates a supportive environment and provides challenges, suggestions, tasks, and language. Combining free play with intentional teaching, and promoting play with mathematical objects and mathematical ideas is pedagogically powerful.
>
> (Clements and Sarama, 2017)

From a review of the best available research evidence, the second recommendation in the EEF guidance report (EEF, 2020a) explains how to integrate maths throughout the day. Routines are highlighted as a purposeful way to help children learn and apply mathematical ideas.

Educators can deliberately support children's mathematical development through a range of meaningful and engaging contexts: songs, rhymes, play with puppets, games and picture books.

Case Study 7.1

Engaging Daily with Mathematical Concepts

A team of educators in a Reception class have been learning about how to intentionally maximise routines to enable children to have daily moments when they can explicitly engage with mathematical concepts and language in a purposeful and meaningful context.

Hannah approaches the snack table and smiles at the educator, Michele, who warmly encourages her to join the other four children already seated.

Michele: Hi Hannah, there is one seat left, there are 5 spaces at the table. We have got brown bread, cream cheese, cucumber and some grapes for snack today.

Hannah: I want grapes.

Michele: Yes, you can have some grapes. I need some help to cut them up. First, we need to work out how many plates we need so everyone can have some snack.

(Continued)

Hannah: I do it… 1, 2, 3, 4…

Michele: Thanks Hannah, you counted your friends to help us work out how many children are here. You counted 1, 2, 3, 4… we need to count you too!

Michele models using her fingers to show the quantity.

Hannah: 1, 2, 3, 4, 5. 5!

Michele: 5! Yes, 5 children altogether. So that means we need 5 plates. Hannah, can you make sure that everyone has a plate, we need 5 altogether.

Hannah: I want to do the cups too. I can count 5 cups.

Michele: Thanks Hannah, that's really helpful. There are 3 blue cups here (showing three fingers) … I wonder if you can see how many more we need so that we have 5 altogether?

Hannah pauses, another child who is using their fingers and looking at the other children around the table to solve the problem, exclaims 'I know, 2 more… 3… and 4 and now 5!'

Maths through picture books

There is an increasing body of evidence indicating that using picture books can be especially effective in providing engaging contexts for exploring mathematical content and concepts. Carefully selected picture books afford rich opportunities to promote reasoning, ask questions and involve educators and children in sustained back and forth conversations that extend mathematical thinking and understanding.

With a multitude of books to choose from, it is important to be discerning. We need to choose books that are appealing for children and encourage them to make connections and relate events in the book to their own lives. Importantly, research carried out by Carrazza and Levine (2024) found that children's understanding of number progressed more when the books they engaged with involved meaningful storylines that incorporated purposeful counting as opposed to using basic counting books. This shows that narrative and context matter when using books to stimulate children's mathematical development.

Once we have chosen a book, the way we use it with children is key. Merely reading to children as a 'captive audience' is not enough to foster mathematical thinking and reasoning. Instead, we need to consider how we can maximise the rich opportunities that the book provides by interacting with children.

Research shows that one of the most effective ways to exploit the power and value of picture books is an interactive, dialogic approach (Clements and Sarama, 2018; van den Heuvel-Panhuizen and Elia, 2012). The key ingredient of an interactive approach is how the educator purposefully engages with the children. Interactive reading requires both a shift in mindset for the educator and in the power balance between them and the child. Crucially, this means engaging in sustained, back-and-forth, multi-turn conversations which encourage children to talk about what they are interested in and the skills and concepts they are exploring. Through conversation, children can practise language and receive immediate feedback from a more knowledgeable other. Educators can use the four evidence-informed strategies of the ShREC approach (James, 2022) to establish shared attention by making comments about the book like 'I wonder' and 'I notice', follow the child's lead and sensitively shaping the discussion.

Top tips for choosing books

- Choose books that spark joy, curiosity and connect to children's interests and lives. Representation and inclusivity matter.
- Consider the mathematics in the book:
  o   Is it developmentally appropriate?
  o   Is the content presented in a meaningful way?
  o   Is it correct?
  o   Are there connections between different concepts?

Top tips for interactive reading

- Think about the social and emotional atmosphere – warmth, sensitivity, enjoyment.
- Tune in, share attention and follow the children's lead. Be responsive and flexible.
- Notice and label the mathematical ideas in the book.
- Provide clear explanations of mathematical content and new vocabulary encountered.
- Pose open-ended questions but remember, while these are powerful it is important not to ask too many – it is a delicate balance.

How does children's understanding of number and counting develop?

Subitising

Developing a strong sense of number and counting in the early years is essential. An important aspect of number sense is *subitising*. Educators working with young children need to understand the concept, which is described in *Development Matters* and in the EYFS Statutory Framework.

The word *subitise* comes from the Latin 'to arrive suddenly' (Gilmore et al., 2018). *Subitising* is the ability to quickly recognise and say the number of things in a group without counting. For example, if there are 5 cherries on a plate, subitising is when the child knows there are 5 without counting them one by one. Research shows that subitising is one of the main skills that very young children should develop. Attuned and knowledgeable interactions are essential to develop subitising (Baroody, 1987; Baroody et al., 2008; Sarama and Clements, 2009).

There are two kinds of subitising:

- *Perceptual subitising*: when you 'just see' how many items there are in a very small collection, you are using perceptual subitising
- *Conceptual subitising*: this involves seeing the parts and putting together the whole. For example, when looking at a domino, you might see two groups of 4 as one 8.

(Clements and Sarama, 2021, pp 18–19)

Subitising supports counting and lays the foundations for arithmetic. It helps children develop important ideas such as understanding 'how many' and how numbers are composed.

When children subitise, it is important that we acknowledge this. An example of this would be a child showing an amount using their fingers and saying '3', and the educator responding by asking the child to 'count them to check'. In this instance, educator has unintentionally discouraged the child's subitising.

Everyday experiences and routines offer purposeful opportunities to develop subitising. There are some simple, practical ways in which educators can intentionally develop this vital skill. This case study below describes how educators can use tidy up time to help children develop subitising.

Case Study 7.2

Promoting and Supporting Subitising

A team of educators wanted to promote subitising in their setting and were inspired by some ideas from professional development. Firstly, they intentionally focused on using number words up to five in their interactions with the children during tidy up time. For example, an educator might say 'there are 4 large blocks left to tidy up' rather than 'it's tidy up time, put away the blocks'.

Mathematising this experience started to have an impact quite quickly. The children started to notice and talk about quantity (as well as using their fingers), making comments like 'I got 2 cars to put in the box', 'there are 3 crayons under the table', 'I put the 4 cups in the sink'.

The educators encouraged the children to see the amount rather than just the object. This enabled children to start to build up a concept of number and connect number words with specific amounts.

Secondly, the team reflected on their learning environment. They thought carefully about how to organise resources into small groups to support subitising explicitly. They ensured that the labels included groups of objects and not just numerals. This further enhanced the educators' deliberate talk about small groups of objects, supporting subitising rather than counting.

Number words and numerals

Another aspect of number sense involves understanding that numbers – both the words and the numeral – are used in different ways. Numerals are visual symbols: they are abstract. Words for small numbers are among the first words that children learn, and numerals come a little later. The full meaning of number words and numerals is acquired over a longer period.

Cardinal numbers

Numbers can be used to represent quantity: 2 for two things. We want children to develop an understanding that we use numbers (both words and numerals) to name specific amounts. Many young children will recognise the numeral 2 without understanding that it represents two things. Knowing that the word two and the numeral 2 cannot be used with any other quantity is an important development. This is called *cardinality* and is the building block for counting, addition and subtraction. Children need lots of time and practice to develop competence in this.

Ordinal numbers

These are used as labels for putting things in order, and refer to a position in a sequence. For example: first, second, third.

Nominal numbers

These do not give us information about quantity, but function purely as labels. For example, door numbers or telephone numbers. These numerals are not about 'how many'.

Referential numbers

Numerals can also be used as a reference point. When we talk about time or temperature, we are using number words and numerals to refer to something that we have a shared agreement of. For example, 'Let's meet at 5 o'clock'.

Counting

Children love to count: it is a big part of their day-to-day life. It is the first recognisably mathematical activity that children engage in and something that adults tend to place a lot of emphasis on. Counting is often a social experience for very young children. Adults encourage children to use rhymes, stories and songs to promote their counting. Yet, the point of counting – that is, to find out how many – is often *not* established in these experiences. Counting *is* deceptively complex! It is, therefore, essential that adults have a detailed understanding of how children learn to count.

We can explore this by looking at the *counting principles*. Gelman and Gallistel (1986) identified five principles that underpin young children's counting:

1   The *one-to-one principle*: one number word from the counting sequence is named for each object

2   The *stable-order principle*: number words must be said in the same order every time

3   The *cardinal principle*: the final number word tells you how many objects have been counted. It signals the end of the count.

4   The *abstraction principle*: any collection of 'things' may be counted

5   The *order-irrelevance principle*: the order in which the objects in a set are counted does not change the total. The total is always the same.

Cardinality

A significant stage in the development of children's counting is when they understand the connection between counting objects in a collection, and the total number of objects in that collection. The Erikson Early Math Collaborative (2014, p. 185) describes the principle of cardinality as the 'cornerstone of competent counting'. At first, children may not realise how many objects there are in a collection even after counting them. Children must learn that the last number word tells them how many things have been counted. It is a complex process, involving more than stating the last number word. To be able to count a collection of objects, children need to know the count sequence as well as pointing to or moving the objects. They need to know the last number word provides them with the total in the collection.

For us to understand if a child has grasped the principle of cardinality, we must have a sound understanding of what it means. Often when children are asked to count how many children are in a group, educators focus on:

•   the correct sequence (stable order principle)
•   one number word for one item (one-to-one correspondence)

It is less common for educators to draw the children's attention to the last counting word and ask, 'how many?' Yet, it is *this* part of the process that is essential. We can emphasise the importance of this by explaining why we are counting: 'We are counting the children because we want to know how many are here today.'

We need to offer both planned and spontaneous opportunities for children to count, indoors and outdoors! When we ask children to count, there must be a genuine reason to do so. Unless the context is purposeful, it can be confusing for children. Indeed, it can make them reluctant to count. The whole point of counting is to find out how many – so it is important to ensure that children know why they need to do so.

Operations

By the end of the EYFS, we aim for children to be able to count confidently, have a deep understanding of the numbers to 10, the relationships between them, and patterns within those numbers. Young children have a sense of quantity from a very early age. They explore concepts of more, less and same; they add and take away things throughout their play and day-to-day routines. For a child to understand number operations, they need to know how to use numbers to describe relationships and solve problems. This includes:

- how sets or collections can be changed by joining and separating
- comparing and ordering
- the relationships between numbers – that larger numbers contain smaller numbers

It is important that educators are intentional, planning meaningful and purposeful opportunities for children to learn about joining, separating, comparing, and about parts and wholes of sets. To support children to add and subtract with automaticity, children need a clear understanding of the parts of numbers and how they relate to other numbers. Children need to grasp the idea that the quantity of five, for example, is not just a collection of ones. Five can also be understood as a group of two and a group of three. A focus on conceptual subitising can help children to build a strong visual sense of quantity and a deep understanding of part/whole relationships. Engaging children in sustained back-and-forth conversations, in which children are encouraged to talk about their strategies to solve number problems, can be especially powerful.

In the Reception year, there should be a focus on the composition of number to 10:

- Focus on composition of 2, 3, 4 and 5 before moving onto larger numbers
- Provide a range of visual models of numbers: for example, six as double three on dice, or all the fingers on one hand and one more, or as four and two with 10 frame images
- Model conceptual subitising: 'Well, there are three here and three here, so there must be six.'
- Emphasise the parts within the whole: 'There were eight eggs in the incubator. Two have hatched and six haven't yet hatched.'
- Plan games which involve partitioning and recombining sets. For example, throw 5.

Early Learning Goal: Number

Children at the expected level of development will:

- Have a deep understanding of numbers to 10, including the composition of each number.
- Subitise (recognise quantities without counting) up to 5.
- Automatically recall (without reference to rhymes, counting or other aids) number bonds up to 5 (including subtraction facts) and some number bonds up to 10, including double facts.

(DfE, 2025, p. 14)

Early Learning Goal: Numerical Patterns

Children at the expected level of development will:

- Verbally count beyond 20, recognising the pattern of the counting system.
- Compare quantities up to 10 in different contexts, recognising when one quantity is greater than, less than or the same as the other quantity.
- Explore and represent patterns within numbers up to 10, including evens and odds, double facts and how quantities can be distributed equally.

(DfE, 2025, p. 14)

Subitising, counting and number operations are not the only aspects we should focus on in the early years. It is equally important to ensure children are given rich opportunities to learn other mathematical topics including shape, spatial reasoning, pattern and measures.

There is no longer an Early Learning Goal for shape, space and measures. Yet, as the EYFS Statutory Educational Programme states, it is essential that the curriculum enables children to learn mathematical knowledge in these key areas:

> In addition, it is important that the curriculum includes rich opportunities for children to develop their spatial reasoning skills across all areas of mathematics including shape, space and measures. It is important that children develop positive attitudes and interests in mathematics, look for patterns and relationships, spot connections, 'have a go', talk to adults and peers about what they notice and not be afraid to make mistakes.

(DfE, 2025, p. 10)

It is critical to note that the Early Learning Goals are *not* the curriculum for the Reception year. They are 17 checkpoints to help us summarise what a child knows and can do, and where they might need more help. We need to ensure that children experience a rich early years curriculum, not a narrow focus on the end goals.

Spatial reasoning

Spatial reasoning is very important for mathematical development and our everyday lives. We use spatial reasoning when we get dressed, pack a bag, read maps or build flat-pack furniture. It is key for problem-solving. There is an increasing body of research that suggests spatial reasoning is foundational for all mathematics:

Spatial reasoning supports learning at all levels of mathematics education, from early years to university level. A spatialised curriculum is engaging, reduces attainment gaps, and could mitigate the development of a negative view of mathematics.

(Farran et al., 2023)

The Early Childhood Maths Group explain what spatial reasoning involves:

Spatial reasoning involves our interpretation of how things, including ourselves, relate to each other and our spatial environment and includes interpreting images and creating representations.

(Gifford et al., 2022, p. 5)

Importantly, spatial reasoning involves more than geometry – it helps us to make sense of numerical relationships and symbols that are represented spatially such as number lines. For example, to understand mathematical concepts such as place value, children need to be able to distinguish between left and right (Farran et al., 2022).

It is essential to give young children time, space and freedom to explore the world physically. When you observe a baby, you will see how they try to reach and grasp things dangled in front of them. This is part of learning how to locate objects in space. As children's physical skills develop, so do their spatial abilities. Crawling, cruising and walking are ways young children develop an awareness of space. As they figure out how to move from one area to another, they negotiate obstacles. As children get older, they need opportunities to run, roll, jump, crawl and hide. They need to experience different heights so that they can begin to learn about different perspectives.

Educators play a vital role in helping children to learn spatial language. Using gestures helps children learn spatial words. When educators use precise language and explanations in back-and-forth conversations, they enable children to develop a deep knowledge and understanding of mathematical concepts.

Case Study 7.3

Spatial Reasoning and Directional Language: The Obstacle Course

Zara is an early years educator in a nursery class. She is currently training to be a teacher and is learning more about how important physical development is for young children's mathematical thinking and learning. Zara's setting is in a densely populated area of London; many of the children live in homes that are overcrowded

(Continued)

and have limited access to gardens and outdoor spaces. The nursery has a large outdoor area, and Zara is keen to create more opportunities for the children to develop their gross motor skills and their spatial reasoning. The setting does not have fixed climbing equipment; instead, the educators create obstacle courses for the children using a range of open-ended materials. However, if educators are not intentional in their planning and teaching, sometimes this experience can be forgotten about. Zara thinks carefully about specific children she wants to involve in constructing the course so she can deliberately encourage the children to share their ideas.

Case Study 7.4

How Language Extends Mathematical Thinking

Three-year-old Fatima spends part of every day in the block area. Over the last half term, her constructions have become increasingly complex and detailed. Fatima's key person has noticed her interest in the blocks and dedicates time to sensitively engage in her play. She knows that using precise language is important to extend Fatima's mathematical understanding. As Fatima constructs, her key person pays attention to what she is focused on.

Fatima comments, 'I got a square!'

Her key person responds by commenting, describing what she is doing to mathematise her play and expand her language: 'Yes, it is a square, you used four blocks to make a big square.'

Fatima says, 'it's going to be a castle!'

They engage in a back-and-forth conversation about how to build the castle. Fatima's key person intentionally uses specific language and models her thinking out loud. At tidy up time, she helps Fatima to replace the blocks by drawing her attention to the shadows (stencilled outlines of the different blocks) on the shelves which guide children to putting each block back in its correct place.

Fatima's key person says, 'We need to turn this block sideways so it can fit. This block is curved, let's look for the matching shadow.'

The next day, to extend her thinking, she suggests Fatima make a plan before she starts creating her construction.

Pattern

Children experience patterns in their daily lives, particularly through routines. Patterns help them to predict what is going to happen next. Developing an awareness of pattern helps young children to notice and understand mathematical relationships.

The Erikson Early Math Collaborative (2014, p. 83) defines pattern as: 'any predictable sequence found in physical and geometric situations as well as numbers'.

Often, when we consider pattern, we think about regular repeating patterns that are visual, such as stripes on clothing. Generally, these are the first patterns children notice.

What makes a pattern a pattern?

Patterns require a rule. A regular pattern contains an element that repeats continuously. This is called the *unit of repeat*.

If children are given many and varied opportunities to find out about patterns, they will come to learn that patterns involve a rule. When children understand the rule in a particular pattern, they can start to predict and then make generalisations.

How to support young children's understanding of pattern

Children need lots of opportunities to see how patterns exist in the world around them as well as in maths. An engaging way to support this understanding is to go on a pattern walk. Exploring the local environment to spot patterns is a great way to mathematise the patterns around us.

Children need to learn that patterns involve a rule. Though children need opportunities to copy and extend patterns, it is important to note that being able to copy a pattern does *not* necessarily mean that the child understands the rule. Children need experiences that help them to learn the rule. One way to do this is for the educator to break the rule of the pattern deliberately, and then support the children to notice and understand it.

Educators often focus on showing children simple, regular repeating patterns. These repetitive patterns are important for children to understand the building blocks of numerical patterns. Yet, we also need to expose children to many and varied patterns. Patterns can be visual, auditory, temporal and involve movement. Visual patterns are much easier compared to movement patterns such as a dances, or auditory patterns such as drum beats or claps.

Educators need to plan and thinking intentionally, drawing children's attention to patterns that exist in the world, in their own play and in maths itself. Children's developing understanding of pattern, and how educators can support this, is outlined in Table 7.1.

Conclusion

Children need rich, stimulating playful experiences that connect purposefully to their interests and everyday lives. They need sensitive, responsive educators who will support

Table 7.1 Pattern throughout the EYFS

Aspects of learning about pattern	Birth to 3 years old	3- and 4-year-olds	4- and 5-year-olds: Reception
Attitudes and dispositions	Enjoy exploring the world, through open-ended resources indoors and plenty of time outdoors. This requires a well-organised, rich, sensory environment. Children need access to materials, freely combined with sensitive adult interactions.	Plan and think ahead about playing and exploration. Reflect on choices: 'I notice you have created a pattern that repeats with the sticks and leaves.' Keep trying when things are difficult: when the rule of a pattern is broken, persevere to correct it.	Reflect on what they are learning and how this links to what they have learnt before. Adults might ask questions like: 'What were you thinking when you chose to add the shiny gems into your pattern?' 'What did you learn from the book about the patterns in shells/leaves/flowers?'
Concepts and skills	Notice patterns and arrange things in patterns.	Talk about patterns using everyday language. Create and extend regular repeating patterns. Identify where the rule of repeating pattern is broken and correct it. Describe a pattern of events.	Continue, copy and create repeating patterns. Add in additional elements to regular repeating patterns to make them more complex.
Vocabulary	Same Different Say the words for items in treasure baskets and heuristic play	Pattern Notice Copy Stripy Spotty Design First Then After	Continue Repeat Recognise Rule Extend Sequence Mistake Correct Discuss Explain

their thinking and learning both spontaneously and in carefully planned intentional ways. All children can be powerful maths learners. The input they receive, and the experiences they have, influence their mathematical thinking and learning. We know that specific types of input are crucial for children's early mathematical development:

- hearing and using mathematical language in sustained back-and-forth conversations
- physical play

- use of manipulatives
- seeing and using gestures (including using fingers for representing quantities and counting)

The evidence is clear: educators play a critical role in building young children's brains. Children learn more in the first five years of their lives than at any other time. What happens early, matters for a lifetime. We have a big responsibility to enable children to feel confident and to enjoy maths! The dispositions and attitudes we instil, and the opportunities we provide, will have a lasting impact on children's future development and life chances.

As Clements and Sarama state:

Early math learning, from birth, is critical for all future learning ... and living. Early math promotes math, but also social, emotional, literacy and general brain development.

(Clements and Sarama, 2021, p. 15)

Reflective questions

1   Can you think of a time when you helped a child to 'mathematise': to notice and reflect on the maths in their play or in an everyday routine?
2   Can you make a list of genuine, purposeful reasons for children to count?
3   How could you increase opportunities for children to develop spatial reasoning skills?

Understanding the World

Julian Grenier, June O'Sullivan, Liz Pemberton and Aaron Bradbury

EYFS Statutory Educational Programme

Understanding the world involves guiding children to make sense of their physical world and their community. The frequency and range of children's personal experiences increase their knowledge and sense of the world around them – from visiting parks, libraries and museums to meeting important members of society such as police officers, nurses and firefighters. In addition, listening to a broad selection of stories, non-fiction, rhymes and poems will foster their understanding of our culturally, socially, technologically and ecologically diverse world. As well as building important knowledge, this extends their familiarity with words that support understanding across domains. Enriching and widening children's vocabulary will support later reading comprehension.

(DfE, 2025, p. 11)

EYFS Statutory Framework

The EYFS seeks to provide ... equality of opportunity and anti-discriminatory practice, ensuring that every child is included and supported.

(DfE, 2025, p. 7)

Introduction

The urge to understand the world is a powerful one, through the early years and beyond. From their earliest days, children are investigating and learning through their first-hand explorations and through their relationships with others.

Babies and young children engage in a non-stop cycle of looking, touching, climbing, smelling and tasting everything around them. A baby playing with a Treasure Basket will put things in their mouth and feel them with their hands and fingers, returning to some favoured objects and setting aside others. A toddler in nursery looks back at their key person, checking it is okay before skipping across the room to grab hold of something that looks exciting. Their confident exploration depends on the sympathy and reliable support of their special adult. From a very young age, children can distinguish between living and inanimate objects. So many children love animals, being outdoors, touching and smelling the earth or sand, enjoying trees and other plants. These deep feelings towards the living world play an important part in helping children to feel happy, healthy and calm.

Children in the early years:

- constantly explore and learn about their family culture and the cultures all around them
- become increasingly aware of the wider world of shops, parks, libraries and places of worship
- spend time with people from families other than their own and notice how people are different
- need confident and sympathetic support to explore the physical world, keep them safe from danger, and to reassure them when something different is still okay
- need to be able to talk about the differences they notice between people's hair textures, skin colours and languages
- need confident, positive attitudes towards diversity to thrive in 21st century England, a dynamic and diverse society
- are growing up during the climate change emergency and need to learn how they can become part of the solution to this crisis, and not part of the problem

We can already see why this area of learning is so important to children in the early years. This early learning will also build strong foundations for subjects that come later in their education.

The revised Early Years Foundation Stage Statutory Framework (EYFS) (DfE, 2025) and *Development Matters* (DfE, 2023) put a greater emphasis on the foundations of science, history and geography. They also place more emphasis on teaching and learning about equality and diversity.

It is important to note that children in Reception do not learn history, science or geography as subjects. It does not make sense to design a primary school geography curriculum that begins in Reception, for example. However, it does make sense to consider how the EYFS area of learning called 'Understanding the World' can give children foundational concepts and vocabulary which will help them learn geography, history and science when they are older.

Strong foundations to support later learning in science

Children are inquisitive – young children are often described as being 'into everything'. They have a strong disposition to explore and learn about their world. As young children mix different substances together, they may feel, notice and talk about the changes. That will be true whether they are mixing mud, leaves and water together in the mud kitchen, or flour, yeast, salt, oil and honey to make bread. We can understand activities like these as early experiences of learning chemistry. As children push toy boats under the water, they are experiencing forces. This will be part of their later learning in physics. Children planting cress seeds on cotton wool or searching for woodlice under logs are learning about living things – biology.

To maximise children's early scientific learning, we need to think about the importance of a richly resourced, stimulating environment. In my experience, this is a strength in many early years settings and in schools. If you are working with children aged 3 to 5 years old, you might use the Early Childhood Quality Rating Scale – Emergent Curriculum (ECQRS–EC) environmental rating scales (Sylva et al., 2025) to check quality and set priorities for improvement.

Adult interaction is crucial. We need to think about how we help children to develop their early scientific skills in observation, and their early understanding of key concepts. This requires thoughtful, intentional pedagogy. As the New Zealand government's Te Ihuwaka Education Evaluation Centre argues, we need to 'take a deliberate, scientific lens to the learning opportunities available. This will support children with the opportunities to develop the knowledge, skills, dispositions, and working theories that serve as the foundation for ongoing learning in science, and for developing scientific literacy' (Te Ihuwaka/New Zealand Education Evaluation Centre, 2021, p. 7). If educators do not feel confident about their own scientific knowledge, sustained, high-quality professional development will be a priority.

The child as a 'natural scientist'

It is important for educators to encourage babies and young children in open-ended exploration of the world, including a range of natural and manufactured materials. This will build on their natural curiosity. We can supplement this by going to places which some children may not have visited before, like a forest or a beach.

However, it is important to step beyond a simplistic view that because children are born to explore, they are 'natural scientists'. As educators, we need to be intentional and think ahead about what we want children to learn, and we need to consider the key vocabulary that will be part of this learning. When it is snowy, the children are likely to talk excitedly about skidding and falling over. We could build on this by introducing words like 'slippery', 'smooth' and 'rough'. To consolidate that vocabulary, we might later set up an experiment where we slide a block of wood down a smooth surface, and down a rough surface, and talk about what we noticed and how the different surfaces look and feel. This sort of activity and investigation communicates key concepts and models the key vocabulary in a natural way, so that children enjoy learning it.

As the New Zealand government review on Science in the Early Years comments:

> When teachers introduce scientific concepts, using the correct terminology for those concepts, they promote children's scientific thinking and knowledge. This helps children share their thinking and explore ideas. It helps move their thinking from 'everyday' concepts to 'scientific' concepts. Using scientific terms is likely to help children understand that they are 'doing science'.

(Te Ihuwaka/New Zealand Education Evaluation Centre, 2021, p. 8)

In addition to first-hand experience, books can be an excellent way of helping children to learn early scientific concepts. For example, it is common for children to imagine that heavier objects will fall faster to the ground than light objects. In their excellent study, Venkadasalam and Ganea (2018) show how this common misconception can be challenged with high-quality picture books (both fiction and informational). Children who enjoyed the books also learnt that weight does not affect the speed of an object's fall.

It is also important to challenge a second child development myth, that as children got older, they move from a kind of 'naïve scientist' stage to being rational science learners. Research by Usha Goswami (2015) suggests this is false. Young children certainly develop 'naïve theories' about the world through exploring objects, using all their senses. Most of those 'naïve theories' are helpful: when we let go of an object, we know it will fall to the ground. However, when we learn Newtonian physics, we gain a richer account and learn that if we drop a ball from a moving train, it will not fall straight down, but instead fall forwards – because the moving train imparts a force.

However, even when we 'know' this through science teaching, it is still very difficult for us to imagine that the ball will not fall straight down. In fact, we never replace our naïve theories with a more rational scientific knowledge: instead, we learn to inhibit them in favour of what we have been taught. That sort of cognitive inhibition requires strong executive function skills. Those skills develop most strongly across the whole early years curriculum: through challenging outdoor play, learning nursery rhymes and playing games like 'Simon Says', for example. This is an example of how an excessive focus on 'subject teaching' in the early years will not give children the best foundations for their later learning in school.

Equity: Ensuring that every child has a fair chance

According to a report prepared by Oxford University for the Royal Society, children from low-income backgrounds 'make poor progress in science at every stage of their school career'. International research suggests that addressing science achievement gaps requires more intensive efforts in the early years. So, we need to take steps to tackle inequality and ensure that all children get a rich early education in science.

What might this rich early scientific curriculum look like in practice? Table 8.1 shows one way we might think about early learning about science in the different phases of the EYFS. It is also important not to downplay the importance of pleasure and the sheer enjoyment children show. Joy and enthusiasm are at the heart of learning in the early years. The examples of vocabulary are just some of the words educators might use in regular, natural conversation with the children.

Table 8.1   Science throughout the EYFS

Aspects of learning about science	Birth to 3 years old	3- and 4-year-olds	4- and 5-year-olds: Reception
Attitudes and dispositions	Enjoy exploring the world, through open-ended resources indoors and plenty of time outdoors. This requires a beautifully organised indoor environment where children can access materials freely, together with sensitive adult support and enthusiasm.	In addition: Plan and think ahead about playing and exploration. Reflect on choices: e.g. adults might say, 'I'm interested that you chose the fine brushes to paint the daffodil.' Keep trying when things are difficult, e.g. using equipment that requires greater dexterity like using pipettes to suck up and squirt out water in the water tray.	In addition: Reflect on what they are learning and how this links to what they have learnt before. Adults might ask questions like: what were you thinking when you chose to roll over the big log to find woodlice? What did you learn from the book about butterflies?
Concepts and skills	Holding, tipping, filling, emptying, mixing	In addition: Close observation, sometimes with magnifying equipment. Caring for plants and animals. Fitting three or more cogs together so that when you turn one, they all turn.	In addition: Exploring objects safely using all their senses – smell, touch, hearing, sight and taste. Creating close observational drawings and paintings. Describing some common plants and animals.

(Continued)

Table 8.1 (Continued)

Aspects of learning about science	Birth to 3 years old	3- and 4-year-olds	4- and 5-year-olds: Reception
Vocabulary	Wet	In addition:	In addition:
	Dry	Fill	Push down
	Stamp	Empty	Push up
	Splash	Float	Upthrust
	Puddle	Sink	Close observation
		Bark	Vibration
		Seed	Transparent
		Magnify	Shadow
		Investigate	The names of the seasons
		Wind-up	
		Cogs	The names of some common plants and animals in the local environment
		Mouldy	
		Push	
		Pull	
		Attract	
		Repel	
		Melt	

Learning about sustainability, by June O'Sullivan

The EYFS is the ideal time in a child's education to introduce sustainability, but it requires teachers and educators to have a vision of a world in which our children will thrive for generations to come.

What is sustainability?

Sustainability is built on three pillars (economic, social and environmental) which are interconnected through the UN's 17 Sustainable Development Goals (SDGs) (United Nations, 2016). These goals provide a blueprint for a sustainable future, with an achievement target deadline of 2030. These goals were built from the Brundtland definition of sustainability, which suggested we need to 'meet the needs of the present without compromising the ability of future generations to meet their own needs' (Brundtland, 1987, p. 24). This placed a focus on preserving things. Sen (2013) later recognised that to do this we need to become agents of change who can reshape the world when given opportunities to think, assess, evaluate, inspire, agitate on issues at appropriate times. He suggested we need to 'prompt the capabilities of present people without compromising capabilities of future generations' (Sen, 2013, p. 11).

Both approaches suggest we have to make sensible decisions about how we live, protecting the Earth's resources in a way that treats all communities fairly. This means becoming sustainability informed – in other words, understanding why, when and how to act sustainably at home and at work.

The UN's 17 Sustainable Development Goals are:

- No poverty (SDG 1)
- Zero hunger (SDG 2)
- Good health and wellbeing (SDG 3)
- Quality education (SDG 4)
- Gender equality (SDG 5)
- Clean water and sanitation (SDG 6)
- Affordable and clean energy (SDG 7)
- Decent work and economic growth (SDG 8)
- Industry, innovation and infrastructure (SDG 9)
- Reduced inequalities (SDG 10)
- Sustainable cities and communities (SDG 11)
- Responsible consumption and production (SDG 12)
- Climate action (SDG 13)
- Life below water (SDG 14)
- Life on land (SDG 15)
- Peace, justice and strong institutions (SDG 16)
- Partnerships for the goals (SDG 17)

Promoting sustainability across the whole organisation

Introducing sustainability to young children might seem surprising, but early childhood is when foundational thinking, being, knowing and acting develop. During the period when relationships with others and the environment are becoming established, education can empower children to shape a better world. Whilst children are influenced by the environment, culture and people around them, they can also become agents of change once they begin to understand the consequences of their behaviour.

Sustainability requires an interconnected and compassionate organisational strategy that incorporates governance, leadership, operations and pedagogy. This strategy recognises the interconnection between responsibility, economy and natural resources, underpinned by fairness. If we consider ourselves as guardians of our children's future, a strategic approach is important.

For staff working in a social enterprise nursery organisation like London Early Years Foundation (LEYF), sustainability is addressed through:

- a cross-subsidy fees structure, allowing access to government-funded places without additional charges
- operating nurseries in disadvantaged neighbourhoods
- leading and teaching using a Social Justice Pedagogy

- supporting staff and apprentices with access to sustainability training
- building community partnerships to drive social impact
- understanding how we interact with the environment so we can tread lightly on the planet

A pedagogy for social justice is underpinned by compassion, holistic child development and fostering harmonious relationships. It provides a natural framework for teaching sustainability to young children. It shapes their relationships with the world, connecting them to nature and developing the knowledge, skills and values needed to nurture a sustainable future. Sustainability is not a distinct subject or part of an environmental curriculum topic: it is integral to a broad and inclusive quality education (Bokova and Figueres, 2015; O'Sullivan and Sakr, 2022). It needs to run through the governance, leadership, operations and pedagogy of every setting.

Learning about sustainability in the EYFS

A good starting point in the EYFS is the specific area of Understanding the World, which helps children make sense of their physical world and their community through opportunities to explore, observe and find out about people, places, technology and the environment. Learning about sustainability also enhances the entire early years curriculum, promoting critical thinking, problem-solving, discussion and project work.

Teaching sustainability aligns with how we teach everything else in the early years. We can build on children's interests and their sense of enquiry, both in their setting and beyond, and consider how we can scaffold and then extend their learning. This model can also be a starting point for staff who are uncertain about sustainability and not sure where to begin. At LEYF, we begin with a compassionate pedagogical conversation, which can often elicit quite emotional responses as staff feel anxious that they are not more knowledgeable and sustainable in their life choices. But it is important to recognise your starting point and work from there. Begin by looking at your daily routine and resources, and you will be surprised how that starts a volley of constructive actions. For example, you might:

- think about how you plan deliveries and how you reuse delivery boxes
- involve the chef, who can source food locally and cook seasonally, so children understand where their food comes from and how it is connected to the seasons
- build partnerships with more sustainable suppliers

LEYF works with many sustainable suppliers through its community partnerships. For example, Green Bottoms dispose of nappies and wipes in a more sustainable way. They collect the waste and turn around 60% of it into energy and fibre pellets which are turned into noticeboards, acoustic panelling and even mixed into asphalt for road surfacing. Bikeworks offer a bike lending service to children from families who cannot afford a bike, to encourage them to cycle in local parks and improve their physical health at the same time. Fashion Enter is a social enterprise which uses end of roll fabrics, reducing the huge waste created by the fashion industry. This means sheets, aprons, shoe covers, bags and other resources are made in a way that can save the planet from unnecessary waste. City Harvest redistributes food which would otherwise be wasted and well-trained chefs can integrate this into their menus. At LEYF, better training for chefs has led to better-planned meals, with correct portion sizes for the children's ages and menus using more seasonal food. The reduction in food waste, together with the partnership with City Harvest, has saved over £21,000 on food costs per year, and this money has been used to subsidise more places for children from low-income backgrounds.

You might also examine the issue of single-use plastic and agree a target for reduction:

- Do you need plastic aprons?
- Can you get recycled bags for taking home dirty linen?
- Do you need to use plastic gloves for serving lunch, when handwashing is more hygienic?
- Do you need to have soap in plastic containers?
- Could all staff have a reusable water bottle?

The list is endless once you start looking around you. Small steps lead to big changes.

You might also think about how you behave in your daily practice. Do you turn off the lights and minimise water waste? These are simple ways which engage children and start sustainability conversations with them – and with parents and staff. Becoming sustainable is all about leading change, it is a journey to change hearts and minds. If you are overwhelmed about where to begin, organisations like Planet Mark can help set motivating SMART targets.

As they learn about the impact of our actions on the planet, children will want to help. Think about buying your books from the charity shop and going to the library more often: this instils a sense of reuse in children. Teach the staff, parents and children to reduce their consumption, recycle and repurpose. Make friends with local businesses, who often have resources they no longer need which can offer the children creative opportunities. Florists will donate discarded flowers, which become petal showers, soap, perfume and many other sensory experiences. Picture framers often have insets which provide children with a new way to display their paintings. Hardware shops are a source of resources for 'loose parts' play. Connecting with the local garden centre often results in free plants, and local councils will often donate bulbs that have not been used. Children like to become guerrilla gardeners, making seed bombs to plant in little green corners or on unloved green spaces. They are instinctively connected to nature and learn very quickly about compost heaps, wormeries and bug hotels to support local biodiversity. Join the local tree planting schemes or allotments. Share some of the food you have grown by visiting the local elderly home or making friends with your local community organisations and the food bank.

Nurseries, schools and other children's settings are community catalysts, connecting people and fostering social justice. Ensuring that children are visible on the streets is hugely beneficial for them and the community. Take children for walks, on the bus, to visit the local cafe and use the park. Organise a litter pick with the children – they really dislike litter because they are closer to the ground than we are. All of this aligns to the social pillar of sustainability. You just need to think differently and be prepared to build a social network locally. Children are the best community envoys and have a real sense of social justice.

Sustainability requires educators to have a vision of a world in which our children will thrive for generations to come. To do this, we need to connect and join a community of practice such as Action for Sustainability in Education (www.linkedin.com/groups/12992229) where colleagues from across the world interested in sustainability share ideas, research, new information and build a network. We do not have all the answers to sustaining our planet, so we need to start to think differently. We will have greater success if we teach our children about their planet from the earliest age.

Early Learning Goal: The Natural World

Children at the expected level of development will:

- Explore the natural world around them, making observations and drawing pictures of animals and plants.
- Know some similarities and differences between the natural world around them and contrasting environments, drawing on their experiences and what has been read in class.
- Understand some important processes and changes in the natural world around them, including the seasons and changing states of matter.

(DfE, 2025, p. 15)

Strong foundations to support later learning in history

Children are always curious about aspects of the past which they can relate to. For example, I remember putting up a display which showed all the children's teachers and early years educators as babies and young children. This prompted a great deal of discussion and amusement. Similarly, families often share photos and videos with their children, as a way of helping them understand the family's past, culture and some precious moments.

Early education is all about children gradually understanding the wider world, beyond their immediate experiences. We can help children build on their understanding of 'family history' and learn wider concepts about past and present by carefully introducing them to a small amount of new knowledge. This needs to be enough to stimulate their curiosity and enable future learning, without overwhelming them with too much abstract information about kings and queens, and other historical figures from the past.

For children aged 3 and 4, simple timelines can show a series of events in order. Those timelines might be about the order of the routines of the day, illustrated by photographs or symbols.

For example, you might put the following routines in order: coming in, registering yourself, brushing your teeth, deciding where you want to play first, and so on. You might also create timelines about children's growth from babies, to toddlers, to being 4 or 5. You might have a set of photos showing the school or setting from its earliest days. Children's early understanding of the past will be simple and imprecise. They might know there was an important woman from the past called Mary Seacole who nursed injured soldiers, yet also still expect to see her in real life. They might be fascinated about dinosaurs and know they lived a long time ago, but will not have a full understanding of what this means – and nor would we expect them to.

Children can meaningfully explore the past through books, stories, poems and rhymes. This is most likely to be appropriate in the Reception year. We need to think carefully about diversity when we make these choices. It is important to include examples which focus on different parts of the world and different traditions. We also need to ensure we feature the stories of important women: it is all too easy only to share books about 'great men' in history.

Children are fascinated by visits to old buildings and sites. Trips to see castles, other ruins, old churches or houses with thatched roofs will prompt much observation and discussion. Young children do not need a detailed understanding of historical periods or other information at this stage. They might focus their observation and discussion on what aged bricks, stones and glass look like, for example. As part of a museum trip, it might be possible to make connections between the exhibits and some children's family history.

Early Learning Goal: Past and Present

Children at the expected level of development will:

- Talk about the lives of the people around them and their roles in society.
- Know some similarities and differences between things in the past and now, drawing on their experiences and what has been read in class.
- Understand the past through settings, characters and events encountered in books read in class and storytelling.

(DfE, 2025, pp. 14–15)

Strong foundations to support later learning in geography

Children's earliest learning in geography is practical and closely linked to their everyday lives. As Gopnik et al. (1999) explain, even very small babies have a sense of space and movement. Babies and toddlers remember how to find their way round places they know well, like their home and their early years setting. We all have a sense of space and place from our earliest days, and it establishes the first building blocks of our understanding of geography.

Young children are often fascinated by everything they see. They might want to stop and linger, looking into shop windows, touching tree trunks and talking about the cats and dogs they see around. It is generally us, the educators, who want to rush along. Unhurried walks around the local neighbourhood and small trips to shops, parks and libraries are important. They help the youngest children to develop their sense of place.

As they approach their third birthday, some children may like to tell us about their sense of place through narratives as they draw or paint. They might say 'this is mummy in my home' or rapidly draw a bold line across the paper, saying 'I'm running in the park'. Chris Athey (1991, p. 188) observed children making their own maps to represent familiar places like the nursery garden. These types of drawings show objects in fixed locations relative to other objects, like the nursery slide being next to the sandpit.

Children's connections to different environments

Many 3- and 4-year-olds can tell us about their local environment. Benjamin, aged 3, was walking to Forest School when he stopped and told his educator, 'this is dangerous'. He was remembering what she had said the week before about not crossing the road near the bend. He pointed to the zebra crossing as a safe place to cross.

Children who have been abroad on holiday can often tell us what they liked. They can talk about how the place, language and food were different to what they are familiar with. Holiday photos shared online, and postcards, can stimulate these sorts of discussions. Many children have family living in different parts of the world. Through their first-hand experience of visiting relatives, or through video calls and photos, they can talk about similarities and differences. For children without experience of the world beyond England, videos and books can create spaces for conversations and ideas which would otherwise be closed off to them.

In Reception, children build on their earlier sense of space and place through learning a more precise vocabulary of position. Some examples of this are: close, near and far, left and right, behind and in front, on top and underneath. We might engage with young children who are figuring out how to show the location of the 'treasure' on a map they are drawing. We might also talk with the children about their positions at different stages of a dance routine.

Young children hold mental maps of familiar places and will often show those places in drawings and by making early versions of maps. Building on these experiences, we can introduce older children in the EYFS to simple maps and teach them how to use them. I remember visiting a school where a Reception teacher had created a set of installations outdoors. These were all based on the story of Goldilocks. Small groups of children found Goldilocks' house. Then they went onto the house of the three bears. Finally, they went to the woods and saw a cut-out of Goldilocks running away. The children needed some help at the beginning to work out how to follow the map, but soon got the hang of it.

Research suggests that children 'start to acquire geographical knowledge about their own country by 5 years of age' (Barrett et al., 2006, p. 72). At this early stage, children may be able to show some different countries if asked to draw a map of the world. They will not have an accurate sense of shape, size or position. For that reason, it is unlikely that young children will understand formal maps. Instead, what is most likely to make sense to children in the Reception year is talking about the different places they know: what different places look like, what they do there, and what happens whilst they are there (Barrett et al., 2006, p. 61).

A space becomes a place

The foundations of geography are personal: they depend on children's experiences. A space becomes a place because of the emotions we attach to it and the knowledge we have about it. Young children can talk readily about familiar places: my home, my nursery or my street, for example. They may be able to talk about shopping areas and places of worship, too. Children will additionally have many experiences of linking places to people. They may talk about seeing relatives, shopping trips with family members, or where they go to worship. In my experience, there are also children who have not been to many places. In London, they may never have ridden on a red bus, been on the Tube, or seen the River Thames. Even a small trip out, like a ride on the bus to a local market, can be a source of days of conversation, play, drawing and model-making. These foundational experiences enable children to make connections between people, activities and places.

Similarly, learning about weather is founded on direct experience. It is important for children (in appropriate clothes) to feel the rain falling on them or the wind blowing in their faces. If it snows, children can feel the compression of fresh snow under their feet as they leave snow prints behind them. There is a rich tradition of outdoor learning in the early years, including approaches like Forest School. These first-hand experiences provide children with much to talk about, using early geographical vocabulary. Educators can support this by using simple terms like sunny, windy, rainy and snowy. Vocabulary that may be less familiar includes words like hail, stormy, gale, downpour or blustery.

Learning about diversity

Children learn more from birth to 5 years old than at any other time in their lives. That includes the values and attitudes they need for life in modern England. As early years educators, we can set the scene for children to develop positive attitudes about diversity and difference. For example, that means challenging stereotypes about what boys and girls, or men and women, can do. Research suggests that from 3 months of age, babies notice the physical differences that define ethnic groups (Kelly et al., 2005), so it is important to encourage children's curiosity as they notice and talk about this. We can celebrate racial and cultural diversity through our attitudes and our selection of books and play resources. It is important to tackle prejudice, like racism and sexism, directly and with sensitivity. This is not just behaviour that is 'not nice': it can cause long-lasting distress and damage. Dialogue with all families is also important: research suggests that parents appreciate guidance from educators about how we might appropriately challenge stereotypes when talking with young children (Fawcett Society, 2020).

None of this should imply that we 'teach diversity' to young children as a separately planned item. Instead, this work is all about regular discussions, challenging assumptions and getting the right books and resources. The aim of this and the following sections is to raise everyone's awareness and encourage discussion and debate. This will help us work together for a fairer future for every child.

Case Study 8.1

Building Knowledge and Valuing Diversity, by Rohan Allen

Rebecca Cheetham Nursery School, located in the vibrant and diverse community of Newham, East London, serves children aged 2 and up and their families. Guided by an approach that starts with the child, the nursery's curriculum emphasises the importance of children 'building knowledge'. This knowledge-building approach includes deepening and widening children's understanding about valuing diversity and differences.

At the heart of this approach is a commitment to understanding each child's family, culture and faith. This foundation enables educators to engage in meaningful conversations about life at home, including family celebrations and traditions.

For instance, early years educator Farhana invited a small group of children to explore similarities between Diwali, Lunar New Year and Christmas. Through thoughtful questioning, she encouraged the children to identify shared elements, such as Jamila's observation that 'they all have lights – the Divas, fireworks, the Christmas star and Christmas tree lights'. These discussions not only spark curiosity but also lay the groundwork for mutual respect and understanding.

The nursery enhances children's knowledge with carefully chosen books and thoughtfully planned play opportunities. During Christmas, small world figures of the Nativity scene help children learn about the story behind the festival. In January, for Lunar New Year, red envelopes and pretend money offer hands-on experiences tied to the celebration.

Outdoor spaces also support this learning, with a small playhouse adapted for pretend play around different festivals. For Eid, children can try on traditional clothes or sample festive foods, broadening their understanding of the festival.

As children grow in confidence and communication skills, they begin to articulate their understanding in nuanced ways. Mila, for example, reflected on celebrating both Christmas and Eid in his family:

> I celebrate Christmas and Eid. Mummy does Christmas she celebrates, and daddy celebrates Eid. They both look different because Eid doesn't have a Christmas tree. But they both have presents. Eid has jewellery and people wear Mendi, and mummy wears Mendi and jewellery. My daddy goes to the mosque, and my mummy goes to the church.

Such moments illustrate how children integrate their experiences and share their learning in meaningful ways.

Rebecca Cheetham Nursery's approach demonstrates the power of relationships, play and dialogue in fostering inclusion and curiosity. By starting with what children know and extending their understanding, the nursery equips them to navigate a diverse world with empathy and respect.

Gender equality

Many of the toys young children play with and the media they see on television and online are very gendered. Shops may have different shelves for boys and girls. As a result, some children in early years settings may have rigid ideas about gender. The following tips are adapted from the suggestions of the Fawcett Society (2020, p. 108) to help combat gender stereotyping:

1   Encourage children to engage with a range of activities by offering play options that actively challenge gender stereotypes and demonstrating that activities and spaces are inclusive to all. If the home corner is available for everyone to use but only the girls use it, educators can challenge this by actively engaging all children in that space. Similarly, all children can be invited and given space to play football.

2   Be supportive of children when they take part in activities that run counter to gender stereotypes. All children should be encouraged to engage in risk-taking play and caring activities. Keep a watchful eye for other children's reactions to their peers who challenge gender stereotypes and ensure that any bullying related to non-conformity is addressed.

3   Educators should offer children a wide range of worldviews – include stories with diverse lead characters based on gender, ethnicity and other characteristics, so that they don't just see the 'default male'. Try counting the number of male and female characters in the books and materials used in the setting – if characters, and lead characters, aren't equally present, can you find books where they are? Are female and male characters shown equally in different roles? Are male firefighters or builders, and female teachers or mothers, more common?

4   Have conversations about gender with children and challenge any stereotypes they try out. Educators can ask children to explain why they think a particular thing is 'for girls' or 'for boys' and use examples to challenge any stereotypes, like photographs of women playing football for England.

5   Similarly, educators can have conversations with colleagues about gender stereotypes. We should be willing and ready to challenge colleagues who repeat gender stereotypes. This can be as overt as telling a colleague you disagree when they tell children something is a 'boy' or 'girl' activity, or as subtle as suggesting a less stereotypical book if they often select a traditional fairy tale to read to the children.

6   Ensure that all children are given equal space and time in our settings. Research suggests that girls are given less attention – think about who we call on to answer and who gets our attention during carpet and group times. Look regularly around the setting to see whether staff are talking and playing more with girls than with boys.

Disability equality and neuro-affirming practice

Over 25 years ago, I was on the edges of one of the most inspiring projects I have seen in the early years. In Haringey, London, disabled children with the most complex conditions had been cared for in a hospital-based nursery for many years. The council planned to move the children to Rowland Hill Nursery School in 1997. During the early stages of the project, there was huge anxiety and there were even concerns that some children might die without hospital-based care. I was privileged to see the children move out of the hospital and flourish, with meticulously planned care and education at Rowland Hill. I also saw how all the children benefitted, learning to communicate with peers using sign language and visual symbols, for example, and being able to talk matter-of-factly to their parents about disability. Inclusion provides many opportunities for children to learn about disability, reinforced by curriculum thinking which enables them to:

• play with resources which show disabled people in an ordinary, everyday way
• enjoy books which include disabled people in regular activities and events

The author and researcher Kerry Murphy argues that learning about diversity means challenging traditional, deficit-based views and moving beyond seeing developmental differences as problems to be fixed. Instead, we can understand these differences as valid aspects of a child's identity, focusing on their strengths and unique developmental pathways, 'rather than thinking that we need to fix a child or cure them of their neurotype' (Murphy, 2025). Whilst Murphy's work is primarily aimed at educators, it is important that we teach children to have a richer and more affirming understanding of neurodiversity. For example, instead of ignoring an autistic child who is stimming (self-stimulating behaviour), or telling them to stop, as educators we can explain to children that 'stimming can often signify engagement, joy, musicality, play and communication' (Murphy, 2023, p. 13).

Murphy also challenges myths such as the misconception that autistic individuals lack empathy. Instead, we should help all children to understand, as appropriate to their age and development, that 'all humans have strengths, traits, differences and needs that need to be understood and supported' (Murphy, 2023, p. 10).

Racial equality, by Liz Pemberton

Case Study 8.2

The Importance of Talking about Race

Kemi is a confident and self-assured child. Her smile is huge and her imagination is expansive! She has beautiful, tightly coiled Afro hair separated into two sections with multi-coloured bobbles, and she is holding an imaginary microphone.

One hand is grasping her 'mic', the other hand is waving in the air. Her eyes are tightly closed as she bellows out her high notes with enthusiasm and passion, oblivious to anybody else around her.

Max is an energetic child who often plays alone but has always had an affinity with Kemi. He is racialised as white and has the hood of his coat on his head with his arms outstretched inside of the main body of his coat, pretending to be an aeroplane.

Both are 4 years old and they are in the garden at their nursery.

Something catches Max's eye as he whizzes around Kemi. His attention focuses on her outstretched hand waving. He pauses and then asks loudly: 'Kemi, why are the insides of your hands pink and the other side is brown?'

Kemi stops suddenly, looking momentarily confused by Max's question, and she inspects her outstretched hand by bringing it closer to her face.

Before she can form the words to respond, Ethan, the nursery practitioner, who has overheard, interjects: 'Max, that isn't a very nice thing to say; say sorry!'

This case study tells us about how we can send out dangerous messages on the subject matter of 'race' in the early years.

As an educator, there are many ways in which Ethan could have responded to this incident. It may (or may not) surprise you that there *is* a right and a wrong way to do this if we are to think about this as a perfect opportunity to lean into a conversation with children about race. Debbie Epstein says that 'the anti-racist educator needs to have an ear for the opportunities provided by children's own comments and questions' (Epstein, 1993, p. 324), and Max's question is a perfect example of such an occurrence.

Birth to 5 Matters, the early years guidance document, explicitly states that 'talking about race is a first step in countering racism' (Early Years Coalition, 2021, p. 22) and this is sage advice. We must do this as Epstein tells us, by having an ear for the opportunities to do so. How do we do this if racial literacy is so poor within the sector and there is a seeming reluctance to want to engage in dialogue about the impact of racism for children during their earliest years?

For many parents of racially minoritised children, the sad reality is that 'the talk' – a colloquial term coined in the US which is almost seen as a rite of passage for Black parents to pre-warn their children about the inevitable day when their racialised identity is perceived as a negative thing or as a threat – is always looming. But this may not necessarily be the case for white parents of white children when it comes to them having the conversation about the injustice of racism in the same way one would talk to their child about the concept of not being violent by having 'kind hands', or introducing the idea of consent to children with regard to touch as an introduction to the wider subject matter of sexual abuse.

Max's passing inquisitive comment about the colour of the palms of Kemi's hands illustrates how children, in the words of *Development Matters*, 'notice differences between people' (DfE, 2023, p. 103). To respond to it in the way that Ethan did has a negative ripple effect, and as educators we must be aware of this. Undoubtedly his response was what he believed to be appropriate, and we would like to think that those of us who are responsible for the care and education of children would never intentionally respond to their needs inappropriately, but within this exists a challenge, the challenge to accept correction.

When matters pertaining to race in the early years are mishandled by practitioners in a nursery environment, it is not uncommon for intention to be used as a pacifier. By this, I mean the excuse of one not meaning any harm by it. This is supposed to excuse the impact of what could indeed be very harmful to the child who is on the receiving end. We must be aware of this. If we start to prioritise one's intention over the impact of a statement that may harm a racially minoritised child, it feeds into a dangerous cycle of upholding a system that effectively says, 'if I didn't mean it, then it doesn't matter'. We wouldn't apply that same theory if a child unintendedly bumped into another child, knocking them to the floor. If that child subsequently hit their head, they would still have suffered an injury and we wouldn't dismiss that child's pain because the other child didn't mean it. There would be a process of learning and accountability, an apology and a reminder to the child about their spatial awareness as they were running.

Ethan's dismissal of Max's statement would not only attach a feeling of shame to Kemi's understanding about the colour of her skin, but it may convey a deeper and even more harmful message to Max, the white child. That message is that conversations about race are 'not very nice'. What if this happens repeatedly throughout Max and Kemi's nursery and school experience? What is the cumulative impact for both children when it comes to their understanding about race and racism? Neither child's skin colour is going to change, and given that we live in a racist society, this is a very dangerous situation.

In 2020, I created the '4 Es of anti-racist practice' (Table 8.2). If we extend this learning opportunity for Max and Kemi by 'showing interest, expanding conversations and using diverse resources', there will be a very different outcome and impact for all the children. An informed response from the educator would have left Kemi feeling affirmed and proud of the colour of her skin and Max educated about the reasons why skin colours come in a range of shades.

Table 8.2 The 4 Es of anti-racist practice

Step	Anti-racist practice
Step 1	EMBRACE all children's racial, cultural and religious/non-religious backgrounds, especially when they are different from your own.
Step 2	EMBED a culture of belonging and value amongst early years teachers and children.
Step 3	ENSURE that your practice is culturally sensitive and places the child as the expert of their cultural, racial and religious identity.
Step 4	EXTEND learning opportunities for the child by showing interest, expanding conversations and using culturally relevant resources.

If you were a white child who was raised to think that talking about skin colour was unkind or impolite, you can perhaps see why now, as an adult responsible for the care of children, you find it so uncomfortable to talk about race.

So, where do we go from here?

We can draw on *Development Matters*, which suggests we should 'model positive attitudes about the differences between people including differences in race and religion' (DfE, 2023, p. 103), to support Step 4 (extend) from my framework (see Table 8.2). But before we start to think about the array of multi-cultural posters that we have on our nursery walls or in our classrooms, and all those skin-coloured paints that we use, we should reflect on that deep inner work that we must do on ourselves first. That way, we can develop our ability to respond to those uncomfortable feelings that arise when the topic of race is brought into the arena by the children that we are caring for and educating.

Flex your anti-racist muscle

I want to begin by posing some reflective questions for you to ask yourself and answer honestly. These are not responses that you are required to share with anybody, but they will start a process of unlearning and start the preparation for what I like to call an anti-racist workout. See these questions as the pre-stretch and me as your personal trainer getting you ready to flex your anti-racist muscle:

1   What are you bringing to your practice from your own lived experiences about race?
2   In your practice, how do you encourage a balance of child-initiated and practitioner-led provocations that can lead to exploring things around race, ethnicity and culture?
3   Are you confident with the language that you should be using when it comes to explorations of the concept of race, ethnicity and culture?

When you start to unpack the answers to these questions in your own mind and start to connect them to your everyday interactions with all children, you will start to be able to consider your own positionality as an early years educator. Perhaps you are a white teacher, and your concept of your own racialised identity is something that you have never considered. That in and of itself is something to look at more deeply because it would suggest that because you have deracialised yourself as a person and as an educator, you have also deracialised the children that you care for. Adopting an 'I don't see colour' approach is part of the problem.

Development Matters suggests that we should 'encourage children to talk about the differences they notice between people, whilst also drawing their attention to similarities between different families and communities' (DfE, 2023, p. 107). That cannot only apply when we are talking about the differences in the colour of the children's coats, or their eyes, as we saw with the example of Max and Kemi. Children see the colour of their skin, even if we would like not to because it makes us feel uncomfortable.

The best response that Ethan could have given would have been to:

1   Assess Kemi's reaction, detect whether there are any feelings of confusion, upset or dismissal and also give her the opportunity to respond before he took the lead. It may have been the case that Kemi's response is 'it's because I'm Black and Black people have lots of shades!' She might have said 'I don't know': it isn't anything she would have ever considered before, given that this is her normal. Either way, we must give children the opportunity to be the expert on their own racial identity. You cannot assume that their own families have not equipped them with racial literacy and a strong sense of self pertaining to their own racial identity. You will only find out if you provide space and opportunity for this to happen.
2   If Kemi has no response or a response that indicates that she is embarrassed or upset, process this response and understand that this is indicative of a society that constantly 'others' Blackness as something to not take pride in. Widen the spectrum of the conversation so that it is inclusive of everybody in the playground. What you want to reinforce to both children is that, in fact, there are differences with everybody, including skin tone and colour, even amongst the white children (if the setting is predominantly white).

3   *Building Futures: Believing in Children* (DfE, 2009) focuses on provision for Black children in the EYFS. It notes that 'the learning environment should be a place where children feel confident, so that they are willing to try things out. Seeing themselves and things familiar to them will help them feel confident and secure' (DfE, 2009, p. 25). In my webinar, *Inclusion in Role Play for the Under 5's*, I stress the need to ensure that the home corners, hairdressers and shops in your space should feature a range of hair products and diverse food. You can use empty containers and packets from the supermarket, and different eating utensils such as chopsticks, as permanent features in these spaces. Be sure to explain to the children why these objects are in the respective areas in the setting. It is important that the children are introduced to the various items. So, use additional supporting resources such as books that can help introduce these things to the children in a culturally sensitive way.

The topic of 'race' is a huge one, but it isn't one that should be approached with trepidation or reluctance in the early years. If we continue to perceive this as a 'no go' area for young children, then we do more harm than good in the long run. Let us be as excited about learning and engaging as we expect our children to be because it is only then that we can truly help our children contribute to the momentum of change that we want to see in the world.

LGBTQ+ equality, by Aaron Bradbury

As early years professionals, we can make real change by educating children about the acceptance of LGBTQ+ people (those who identify as lesbian, gay, bisexual, transgender, queer, or any other minority sexuality or gender identity). In his ecological systems theory, Bronfenbrenner (1977) explored oppressive practices including poverty, racism and sexism. We could include homophobia, transphobia and other forms of LGBTQ+ phobia here, and how we support ever-changing family structures in the 21st century.

We should encourage all early years settings to engage with a diversity of families, not just those in our immediate communities. Early Years Foundation Stage Statutory Framework (DfE, 2025, p. 7) is explicit about the importance of equality of opportunity and anti-discriminatory practices, 'ensuring that every child is included and supported'. We may have heard it said that we are inadvertently talking about sex if we promote LGBTQ+ inclusion in the early years. This is false. When discussing gender and sexuality, we are exploring and celebrating identities, love and family, as well as the way people are positioned within our society, and the love and respect we need to develop for one another. We do this in an age-appropriate way. For example, with children under the age of 5 we might discuss different family arrangements, but we do not have involved conversations about sexual choice (Price and Tayler, 2015).

What should we be doing in the early years to promote LGBTQ+ representation?

We can make a start by reflecting on the following questions:

- Do we support members of the team who are open about being LGBTQ+ at work?
- Do we support the families of children whose parents identify as LGBTQ+?
- Does our curriculum represent a diversity of family structures and give voice to each unique child who we know has LGBTQ+ parents?
- Are we reading and keeping up to date with research and discussions about LGBTQ+ work in early childhood?
- Have we created a supportive and inclusive environment for all children, one that affirms all LGBTQ+ identities, in recognition of the children's current and future selves?

As early years professionals, building meaningful partnerships with all parents and carers is crucial. Exploring relationships and each other's attitudes and practices to these is part of a progressive curriculum. It is important that all families, including those that identify as LGBTQ+, are treated differently and uniquely. We don't treat all heterosexual families the same, do we?

We can put this into practice by asking parents or carers questions such as:

- What name(s) does your child call you?
- How would you like us to refer to you when we speak to your child?
- How would you like us to describe your family to others?
- How would you like us to respond to questions about your family?

Creating a welcoming environment

It is important to create an environment that is welcoming and nurturing for members of the LGBTQ+ community. Here are some of the ways we can do this:

1   Intake forms: change the space for the name of the 'father' or 'mother'. Use 'parent' or 'guardian' instead.
2   Make diverse images more visible, in a child-centred way. This will help children to explore their different cultures and family structures.
3   Have posters representing a range of families on display in the entrance and around the setting.
4   Think about your use of pronouns. Pronouns are a part of everyday speech and we often assume the pronouns people use for themselves. Have you made the effort to ask colleagues and families what pronouns you should use for them?
5   Arrange for professional development that addresses these topics, which can be hard to approach without expert input.

We should not forget that our work is all about educating, caring for and providing children with a nurturing environment in which they can thrive. The notion of a *loving pedagogy* is emphasised by Grimmer (2021). This includes engaging with the representation of LGBTQ+ people.

Crucially, we must examine our personal values and beliefs, and the power they have. Who decides on what is right and wrong? Are we stifling children's development because our own values get in the way?

By becoming more open to, accepting of and loving to everyone in our society, we can begin to share the beauty of the world. We can celebrate diversity in its widest sense.

Early Learning Goal: People, Culture and Communities

Children at the expected level of development will:

- Describe their immediate environment using knowledge from observation, discussion, stories, non-fiction texts and maps.
- Know some similarities and differences between different religious and cultural communities in this country, drawing on their experiences and what has been read in class.
- Explain some similarities and differences between life in this country and life in other countries, drawing on knowledge from stories, non-fiction texts and – when appropriate – maps.

(DfE, 2025, p. 15)

Conclusion

The area of learning called 'Understanding the World' has a lot packed into it. It includes the foundations of science, history and geography. It also includes the crucial early learning about diversity children need for life in the 21st century.

Sometimes, the structure of the EYFS is misunderstood. Educators think that children should learn the prime areas first, with the specific areas coming afterwards. A more helpful image is weaving. We weave the prime and specific areas together, creating a unified curriculum. Much of the learning children do as part of understanding the world builds on their earliest interests and feelings of curiosity. As children explore their world, they want to tell us what they notice. Over time, this helps them to build their vocabulary. As they see new places, they are broadening their horizons. They build a store of cultural knowledge: what happens in a theatre, what you see in a museum, how public transport works, how you get a freezing sensation when the tide rolls over your bare feet. Wider experiences and broader vocabularies help children to feel more confident to talk about what they know, beyond the 'here-and-now' of their everyday lives. This will also help children when they are older and learning to read. When you see the word 'castle' in print for the first time, you can focus on sounding it out. Once you have done this, you do not also need to puzzle over what it means if you have visited a castle and know the word.

Events in the news are always telling us how important scientific literacy is. We see how important it is for everyone to treasure and care for our local environment and for the whole world's ecology. We see how urgent equality issues are. For all these reasons, understanding the world is a crucial part of the early years curriculum, and relevant to children at every age.

Reflective questions

1 Professional development is central to effective practice. Understanding the world has been neglected in the early years for many years. How will you take your learning forward about the foundations of science, history and geography? If you lead a team, how will you do this for everyone?

2 Understanding our culturally diverse world is key to children living in 21st century England. How will you go beyond a general acceptance of different children and embrace a more positive set of attitudes to promote diversity and challenge prejudice?

Expressive Arts and Design

Anni McTavish and Melissa Prendergast

EYFS Statutory Educational Programme

The development of children's artistic and cultural awareness supports their imagination and creativity. It is important that children have regular opportunities to engage with the arts, enabling them to explore and play with a wide range of media and materials. The quality and variety of what children see, hear and participate in is crucial for developing their understanding, self-expression, vocabulary and ability to communicate through the arts. The frequency, repetition and depth of their experiences are fundamental to their progress in interpreting and appreciating what they hear, respond to and observe.

(DfE, 2025, p. 11)

Introduction

Seven-month-old Ines is exploring the handle of a dumpling spoon. Grasping the smooth bamboo, she lifts and mouths the sieve-shaped end. She seems fascinated by the shape and texture of the spoon. With her key person nearby, Ines is finding out about the materials in her world. She is developing her confidence, her curiosity and her abilities to explore things around her.

Young children need time to investigate the properties of materials as well as creating and making. We need to offer them an enticing selection of media to explore mark-making and painting on different scales. We need to make sure that they get the chance to experiment with sounds, listen to a range of culturally diverse music, and see styles of dance from around the world. Along with songs, nursery rhymes and poems, they need to hear a variety of stories and tell their own through dramatic role play and dance. The arts are rich and offer endless opportunities for self-expression and learning. As Kress (1997) notes, before children learn reading and writing, they express themselves and learn about the world by drawing, singing and dancing. McArdle and Wright (2014) describe the arts as 'children's first literacies'.

These 'first literacies' have significant benefits in the following areas:

- *physical development*: exploring media and tools helps develop fine motor skills and hand-eye coordination
- *social skills*: sharing, taking on different roles, helping each other, and evaluating and appreciating each other's work
- *cognitive development*: using language specific to the arts; exploring and connecting ideas and objects to symbols; making choices about subject matter, materials and processes used in art
- *expressive qualities*: developing agency to communicate ideas and feelings; appreciating the ideas and feelings of others
- *imagination, creativity and experimentation*: testing techniques, processes and materials in meaningful ways
- *problem-solving skills*: selecting colours and media; deciding on the music that best fits a dance

In this chapter we consider how to offer an ambitious and enjoyable curriculum for Expressive Arts and Design (EAD), focusing on the visual arts, music and the performing arts. We explore how each of these areas can provide opportunities for young children's wider learning and development. We weave case studies into the chapter, illustrating our points in practice. Finally, we end with a section on providing a culturally diverse arts curriculum.

Thinking about your curriculum

The Office of Standards in Education (Ofsted, 2024) suggest that the EAD curriculum incorporates three main areas:

- the visual arts, including drawing, painting and sculpture
- music, including singing
- the performing arts, including dramatic role play and dance

A broad and balanced curriculum will give children opportunities to create their own art and develop their imagination and creativity. This will involve play, independent exploration of materials, opportunities to appreciate the arts, and learning specific skills like paint-mixing or cutting with scissors. Learning key skills and techniques will give them further opportunities to express themselves imaginatively through the arts. When planning the curriculum, it is necessary to think about how you will support every child's thinking and creativity. Instead of thinking that some children are 'naturally creative', and others are not, we need to plan intentionally for each child's creative development – especially, perhaps, for those who do not demonstrate a 'natural' flair.

Benson (2012, p. 44) identifies four aspects to guide curriculum planning:

1   *Space and time*: give children unhurried time to think, explore ideas, work in different ways, make changes and return to activities.
2   *Relevance and motivation*: take note of children's interests and curiosities, providing hands-on, open-ended, multisensory experiences.
3   *Ownership and control*: encourage children to make decisions, take considered risks and evaluate their own learning.
4   *Interaction with others*: promote children's questions, supporting them to collaborate and benefit from working with others.

In the following case study, we can see these four principles in action.

Case Study 9.1

Looking, Seeing and Giving Feedback

In a Reception class, the educator (Adam) shares three contemporary portraits with a group of children. They discuss what they see: particularly looking at line, colour and shape. With Adam's guidance, they comment on what they like and do not like, ask questions about the things they notice and point out the similarities and differences between the portraits.

Adam asks the children to spend some time looking at themselves in small mirrors. Then he invites them to share their thoughts about the lines, colours and shapes they see. They have a lively discussion. Adam introduces some art-specific vocabulary as they talk, including the names of primary and secondary colours and terms like 'tone' and 'shade'.

Adam asks the children to draw an outline of the shape of their face onto paper – he sits with them and draws his too. They discuss what they see – Adam repeats what the children say, making sure to use positive phrasing and offering constructive feedback.

(Continued)

Next, they all add noses, mouths and eyes to their drawings. Again, Adam leads a discussion about their portraits, inviting the children to speak about what they notice. Some children want to amend their portraits a little when they see what the others have done. Adam does this too. They all use each other's feedback positively.

Activities such as this help children develop their abilities to look and see in detail, notice similarities and differences and become aware of shapes, lines and patterns.

The activity is a social one – the children begin to evaluate (and amend) their work, guided by an attuned and sensitive adult. Being able to do this at such a young age will stand them in good stead for future learning – responding to feedback is an important thread in all aspects of education.

As the Reception year goes on, Adam introduces other visual arts media, including collage, weaving and sculpture. These also provide plenty of opportunities for problem-solving, designing and making. This enables children to expand their understanding of media and materials and build their knowledge of the right tools and resources for the job.

Benson (2012) argues that creative thinking is best supported when the educator facilitates and guides children, as opposed to 'just letting the children explore', or directly instructing them on what to do. It is important to value the learning processes that children go through to complete and develop their work, rather than just the product. Thirty identical Mother's Day cards will not provide any opportunity for children to develop their creativity. Evangelou et al. (2009, p. 59) highlight research findings that children are more interested in process than product when they draw and make music. They suggest that 'responding to children's work effectively may be more about understanding the processes they have been through to achieve the work than about endorsing the final product'.

This focus on process is also highlighted in Eglinton's framework (2003), a helpful guide to developing a holistic curriculum comprising of three elements:

1   *Practical: exploring, making and doing.* This could be using clay to make a sculpture.
2   *Aesthetic development: connecting with beauty.* This might be visiting a beautiful building and then talking about how it makes you feel.
3   *Encounters with real art: seeing, hearing, exploring artists' work.* This may be listening to music or watching a street dance performance and making your own creative response (e.g. devising your own dance).

An activity might cover all three aspects but is more likely to include one or two.

The following case study illustrates two of these aspects: the *aesthetic* experience of gathering leaves, conkers and grasses and the *practical* experience of making and doing.

―Case Study 9.2―

Exploring Colour-Mixing Techniques

During the autumn, a team of childminders take their children to gather leaves, conkers and grasses. The children and the educators have a good look and select the items they want to use for their art. The children talk about what they find and like – the educators encourage them to say why they like some more than others, affirming what the children say and helping them to develop confidence in their choices.

The children then use the leaves, conkers and grasses as they explore colour and colour-mixing techniques. They mix their own colours and paint with large brushes on a variety of surfaces, including paper and cardboard. As their skills develop, the children begin to use a wider range of tools including shaving brushes, fine brushes and small sponges for detail and texture. The educators teach them about 'stippling': the technique of dabbing paint onto paper to create a picture using lots of small dots. The educators model different techniques, narrating what they are doing. The children have a go themselves, with the educators guiding them through the activity.

Later in the day, the educators follow up this work by reading *Leaf Man* (Ehlert, 2014) and *Pumpkin Soup* (Cooper, 1999).

The visual arts

We see very young children making marks with their fingers in spilt food or juice. We see them drawing on misted glass. We see them creating sculptures in the sand or snow. These visual representations can give children opportunities to make meaning: they are a form of communication. When thinking about the EAD curriculum, we need to provide an environment which encourages children to express their ideas in creative and imaginative ways.

Anning and Ring (2004) studied children's drawings for over three years. They noticed how the home environment seemed more conducive to children drawing than early years settings. Parents were more attuned to their children: they drew alongside their child and listened to them talking about their drawing.

Anning and Ring noticed that the same child could be keenly drawing at home yet avoiding it in their setting. They suggest that there were two reasons for this. Some educators were worried about interfering with children's drawings. Others saw the main function of drawing as a stage towards writing, and this hindered the child's opportunities and freedom.

The following case study illustrates the benefits of children and adults drawing together and contributing feedback to each other. The children share their ideas and thinking: they are equal partners in the drawing process.

Case Study 9.3

Drawing: A Joint Effort

Maya draws a card for her mum, adding two small 'x's' inside. She asks the educator, Jasmin, for help with drawing a heart for her card. Jasmin models drawing a heart shape on a piece of paper: first drawing one side, then the other. She narrates what she is doing. Jasmin asks Maya if this is what she wants. Maya nods energetically, smiling. Jasmin explains that she and Maya could draw a heart each together: Maya's on the card and Jasmin's on the paper. Maya is thrilled with her heart! Jasmin comments on how it makes her card look special.

Next, Maya heads outside to see what is happening with a group of children who are drawing on the tarmac with chalks. Soon after, Maya finds Jasmin with a child who is missing home. Jasmin suggests, 'perhaps we can draw your house?' The child watches quietly as Jasmin starts to draw. He then begins to take a more active role, pointing out where to put 'the sink' and 'my cooker'. Maya joins in, touching the roof of the house, saying 'Spider-Man can go up high!' Maya asks Jasmin to draw a Spider-Man. Jasmin then asks both children if they could draw some clouds or the sun shining – both children draw the sun.

If educators are overly anxious about interfering, or see drawing only as a lead-in to writing, they might limit the child's artistic scope and autonomy. Sometimes it is important to get involved, with sensitivity, drawing with children and talking about what we are doing. It is also important to value drawing for its own sake.

Early Learning Goal: Creating with Materials

Children at the expected level of development will:

- Safely use and explore a variety of materials, tools and techniques, experimenting with colour, design, texture, form and function.
- Share their creations, explaining the process they have used.
- Make use of props and materials when role playing characters in narratives and stories.

(DfE, 2025, p. 15)

Music

Before birth, the foetus can hear sounds and begin to distinguish their mother's voice. Early musical activities such as vocalising and responding to sounds form important foundations for later language, literacy and mathematics. The infant's fascination with the human voice suggests that it is the ideal instrument for developing young children's musicality.

The flexibility of the voice allows for a range of sensitive musical responses. From a soft lullaby to a jaunty finger-rhyme, musical exchanges can help to model conversational turn-taking, and be an important tool in building warm, loving relationships.

Burke (2018) proposes four areas of musical learning and development:

- hearing and listening
- vocalising and singing
- moving and dancing
- exploring and playing

These are detailed with excellent examples in *Musical Development Matters* (Burke, 2018) and in *Development Matters* (DfE, 2023).

Regular occasions for relaxed musical play can lead to creative music-making, also known as invented song-making. This enables children to be *musical creators*, rather than *recreators* of other's music or songs. Evangelou et al. (2009, p. 64) summarise concerns that 'a tightly framed musical curriculum, for example with an exclusive focus on group music making and performance, can give little opportunity for music generation'.

The following example shows how the educator's attuned responses encourage a child's exploration and composition. The educator follows the child's lead, facilitating back-and-forth communication.

Case Study 9.4

ShREC and Music-Making

The educators in this setting use the evidence-informed ShREC approach (James, 2022). This is a series of four strategies that support quality interactions with young children.

Asia, who rarely speaks at nursery, is watching a group of children play a wooden xylophone. Jayden, her key person, is paying attention to this, noticing Asia's curiosity. Once the group of children leave to do something else, Asia picks up the mallet and taps softly on the bars, looking over at Jayden nearby. Jayden comes over, acknowledging Asia's music-making, and taps back a response. Encouraged, Asia plays more, using firmer pressure. 'You're making music Asia', says Jayden. Asia experiments, trying out different tempos. She plays some more music, looking and smiling.

Jayden takes a photo to add to Asia's special book, so they can talk about it later.

In this case study we see the adult *sharing attention* with the child, showing that she is interested in what she is doing. This is the *Sh* of ShREC. The adult then *responds* to Asia by tapping back. This is the *R* of ShREC. Seeing that Asia reacts well to this, the adult then *expands* on Asia's communication by introducing a few words. This is the *E* of ShREC. Asia replies to this by playing the xylophone more confidently. Thus, we see a back-and-forth *conversation* using music and the spoken word. This is the *C* of ShREC.

Singing

Many parents and carers find singing an instinctive way to communicate with and soothe a baby.

Singing plays a crucial role in early years music. As Nicola Burke explains in *Musical Development Matters* (2018, p. 1), 'all vocal communication is comprised of musical elements such as pitch, rhythm and timbre, demonstrating that musicality is an intrinsic part of being human'. In addition, singing is integral to the following aspects of the EYFS curriculum:

- *Creativity and imagination*: singing encourages creativity and imaginative play. Children can make up their own songs or engage with stories and themes through singing, sparking their imagination.
- *Confidence building*: for young children, learning songs and performing them in front of others can boost their self-confidence and provide a sense of achievement.
- *Cultural awareness*: through songs, children are introduced to diverse cultures, traditions and languages, helping them develop a broader understanding of the world.
- *Language development*: singing helps children develop their language skills by introducing them to new vocabulary, sounds and sentence structures. It encourages verbal expression and pronunciation in a fun and engaging way.
- *Cognitive development*: singing activates both hemispheres of the brain at the same time. It can also improve children's memory, attention and problem-solving skills. Singing helps children grasp patterns, rhythms and sequences, supporting their cognitive development.
- *Social and emotional development*: singing in a group promotes social interaction, cooperation and sharing. It fosters a sense of belonging and community, which is an important aspect of emotional development. It can also help children express and understand emotions through the lyrics and music.

Incorporating singing into the early years curriculum can support multiple aspects of a child's development in a joyful way. When educators take time to find out about special songs from home, this can help young children foster a connection between their family and their setting. Singing these songs in the setting can help the child to settle and feel a sense of belonging.

The ability to distinguish sounds and recite and learn rhymes will help to boost children's phonological awareness. This is an essential skill for later reading (EEF, 2018, p. 12). Children should have a rich diet of songs and rhymes – developing a core list of songs and keeping it at hand will help you to keep track. You can start with simple songs and rhymes and gradually progress to more complicated ones. You can then extend the learning by linking these songs and rhymes to high-quality books. For example, you could link 'Ten in the Bed' with the picture book by Penny Dale (1990) and 'I Know a Teddy Bear' links with *Brown Bear, Brown Bear, What Do You See?* (Carle, 1997).

Using a 'singing grid' is a practical way of developing singing as part of your curriculum. As well as being fun and challenging, it is a creative way of supporting children to make choices and connect with their interests. To make a 'singing grid':

1   Place a large sheet of paper or fabric on the floor and divide it into four or six squares.
2   Put an object in each square that represents a song or rhyme – for example, a toy bus to represent 'The Wheels on the Bus'.
3   Invite the children to pick up an object.

As they build their confidence, language and song repertoire, the choice of songs and rhymes can become more complex by using:

• a song to develop number
• a song or chant linked to the seasons
• a hello or greeting song using all the languages in the group
• an object that invites a response, such as a small 'jumping' rabbit.

The performing arts

Imaginative play

Pretend play generally begins between 1 and 2 years. We get used to young children imitating adult behaviours they see around them. We see them putting their favourite soft toy to bed and pretending to make a nice cup of tea. A home-like space with cushions to sit on and small saucepans with pretend food is a good place to develop this type of play. Children will also imitate other things they notice, leaping around on a broomstick to be a horse, or getting on all fours to be a dog.

In 'small-world play', children play imaginatively by engaging with miniature figures, toys or objects to create an imaginative, scaled-down world. Young children benefit from having plenty of familiar objects to use in their small-world play.

As children move on to symbolic play, they can use one thing to stand in for another. They may use a cardboard box for a car or a leaf for money. Not only are they being imaginative, but they are showing us that they understand how symbols work. Later in their education, symbol use will be an integral aspect of reading, writing, science and mathematics.

A curriculum that nurtures early drama will include opportunities for role play. Real-life experiences such as visiting the shops, a builder's yard or the doctor's can be useful in prompting role play. The children can use these real-life experiences to create something new out of them in their play. In turn, this helps children's broader development. Children who take part in more role play become better at seeing a situation from another person's point of view (Evangelou et al., 2009, p. 60).

Imagination and imaginative play are enhanced through:

- exploring home experiences
- meeting and chatting with visitors about their jobs and skills
- having a selection of high-quality story books and poetry
- having adaptable resources, such as: cardboard boxes, blocks, lengths of fabric, hats, scarves, belts, bags, pots and pans
- small objects like shells, clothes pegs and conkers

Early drama needs story and characters. Approaches like 'Helicopter Stories' and 'Tales Toolkit' can support children to develop their skills and confidence in story-making.

The Tales Toolkit approach is a structured method for helping young children develop storytelling skills through using a set of visual prompts, including character, setting, problem and solution. This structure guides children in creating their own narratives (Jones Bartoli, 2018). This approach is suitable for children from the age of 2 to the end of the EYFS.

The Helicopter Stories approach, which is suitable for older children in the EYFS, builds on the work of Vivien Gussin Paley. The educator spends time with each child in the setting individually, listening to their story. Then they write down the story word-for-word. Once all the stories have been written down, the children come together around a 'stage' marked out with tape and act the stories out. For Paley, pretend play is one of the most important aspects of early childhood: '"Pretend" often confuses the adult, but it is the child's real and serious world, the stage upon which any identity is possible and secret thoughts can be safely revealed' (Paley, 1990, p. 7).

Both approaches provide a straightforward format that enables children to develop their ideas into stories with a structure.

In this next case study, we see the children engaged in creating a story together, negotiating rules and problem-solving. The adults have the delicate role of encouraging the play and sensitively intervening when it gets out of hand!

Case Study 9.5

The Drama of the Crocodile

A group of 3- and 4-year-olds are engaged in a drama game inspired by *The Enormous Crocodile* (Dahl, 2016). They use a large green cushion to represent the crocodile, and chase back and forth, pretending to eat each other up. But the crocodile is caught instead.

The game becomes noisy and a bit wild, with some children getting overwrought. The educators, not wanting to stop the game, need to find a way of helping the children find a diversion from simply chasing each other.

The next morning, the children arrive to find the crocodile stuck in a swamp across the other side of the room. They begin a rescue mission, using blocks and planks to traverse the swamp. They rescue the crocodile, and the children start the game of chase all over again!

One of the educators intervenes: 'Why is this crocodile chasing you? What does it want?' A conversation between the educator and children ensues. The children suggest that the crocodile is VERY hungry. They decide that the best thing to do is to make a shop selling crocodile food. They bake special crocodile biscuits to sell.

Later, the children create a book, using photographs of the game, and the simple refrain of 'Snap! Snap! Snap!' This quickly becomes the favourite story for group times. The educators organise copies of the book to be shared with parents.

Although the children had no first-hand experience of swamps or crocodiles, this dramatic play was hugely engaging. The story was allowed to evolve over time as the children interacted with each other and the adults, negotiated, problem solved as a team and expressed their fears in a safe context.

Dance

As their coordination develops, young children enjoy exploring sounds, rhythm and movement. They bounce, wriggle, jump and join in with clapping and action rhymes. Mollie Davies explains that:

> The body, the instrument of action, is central to the classification of movement. Giving colour and form to the 'playing' of that instrument are three important and interrelated categories:
>
> - dynamics which relates to how the instrument moves
> - space which refers to ways in which the body inhabits and uses space
> - relationships which identifies ways in which the body acts and interacts
> - with people and objects.

(Davies, 2003, p. 3)

Listening to and engaging with music from a range of different genres and cultures supports children to move expressively and create their own dances. Using instruments and adaptable materials such as lengths of fabric, ribbons or scarves enhances this.

It is key for educators to facilitate this, exposing children to different types of music and dance, ensuring there is plenty of time for free exploration, and guiding children to learn new movements, techniques and dance steps and new vocabulary to describe what they are doing.

> ## Early Learning Goal: Being Imaginative and Expressive
>
> Children at the expected level of development will:
>
> - Invent, adapt and recount narratives and stories with peers and their teacher.
> - Sing a range of well-known nursery rhymes and songs.
> - Perform songs, rhymes, poems and stories with others, and – when appropriate – try to move in time with music.
>
> (DfE, 2025, pp. 15–16)

Reflecting and celebrating cultural diversity

Creating a culturally inclusive arts curriculum is about making sure that all children, regardless of their background, feel represented, valued and empowered through the arts. Some of the things to consider and be mindful about are:

- *Learning from families and the community*: Work with parents, carers and community members to bring diverse cultural knowledge into the setting, such as inviting family members to share their skills or traditions through art workshops. Activities such as collective mural painting or group dances can be great for fostering inclusivity and cultural exchange.
- *Art forms and artists*: Introduce children to art forms and artists from different cultures, including visual arts, music, dance and drama. Showcase works of art that reflect diverse communities, histories and lived experiences. This helps children see themselves in the curriculum, as well as learn about others.
- *Materials*: Ensure that art supplies, toys and visual materials represent a broad range of cultures. Use natural materials and traditional craft items from various cultures, like African textiles, Asian ceramics or Indigenous crafts.
- *Celebrate cultural heritage*: Incorporate activities that reflect the diverse cultural backgrounds of the children in the setting. For example, you can share children's particular cultural traditions through planning art projects.

Celebrating cultural events like Lunar New Year, Diwali and Black History Month can be educative and incorporate many aspects of the arts curriculum. However, it is important that these events are not the *only* thing you do or your main emphasis. This would position cultural diversity as a separate entity rather than something which runs through the day-to-day curriculum.

The National Society for Education in Art and Design (NSEAD, 2021) raises important questions to consider when planning an Anti-Racist Art and Design curriculum.

- Does your curriculum include artists, makers and designers from a range of ethnically diverse communities?
- Do you include a broad range of art, craft and design?
- Do you proactively consider issues around gender, race, sexuality, disability and class in all your planning? How?
- Do you involve local artists and makers, or other arts-based communities? You might use a local artist's work to inspire an exploration of new media and materials or invite an artist to visit.
- Do you plan visits to galleries, museums, performances or other special outings? When you plan these, do you consider how this might represent your communities?
- Do you make links to your local community, its history and potential for art and design? For example, several settings based in an area renowned for ceramics developed a studio space to work with clay. Study visits were planned to see the local potteries, exposing the children to valuable, real-life experiences.

Another aspect to consider is artistic display. This can be the work of children, artists or members of the community. It is important to consider the sorts of messages that displays give. Good displays will showcase the processes of children's learning and represent the whole community in the setting. The two are inseparable.

Conclusion

Children need a broad range of rich experiences and plenty of time to explore and use resources in their own way. They also need educators to teach them key skills and vocabulary. Both approaches will help them to become more independent, more able to put their ideas into action, more reflective and more evaluative of their own creativity and others'.

Creating and appreciating the arts can offer lifelong enrichment and joy. A strong foundation in the early years sets the stage for continued engagement with and appreciation for the arts. As educators in the early years, it is essential to keep this in mind when designing the curriculum.

Educators have the unique opportunity to foster children's imagination, creativity and connection with the arts. This is an opportunity not to be missed.

Some of the important aspects of arts and design are outlined in Table 9.1.

Table 9.1 Art and design throughout the EYFS

Aspects of children's development: art and design	Birth to 3 years old	3- and 4-year-olds	4- and 5-year-olds: Reception
Attitudes and dispositions	Enjoy exploring objects, materials and malleable play. Develop curiosity and creativity through the natural and made world, e.g. exploring leaves, conkers and shells to investigate colours and textures. Using scarves and ribbons to explore movement and music.	In addition: Plan and think ahead about playing, exploring and sometimes making. Reflect on choices: e.g. adults might say, 'I can see you've mixed two different types of green. Which colour do you think you might use?' Keep trying when things are difficult, e.g. when the glue doesn't work, trying tape instead.	In addition: Reflect on what they are doing and creating; building on previous experiences and learning. Collaborate with others, sharing skills, ideas and materials. Develop stories in their imaginative play and represent ideas through a wide variety of art including music, singing and dance.
Concepts and skills	Touch, grasp, mix, press, make marks. Use simple tools – crayons, brushes, scissors. Move and respond to music.	In addition: Compare, combine, manipulate. Use tools such as a holepunch, a fine brush, a large needle and thread. Explore and express ideas and feelings. Combine different media and materials, e.g. paint and collage.	In addition: Layer, transform, choreograph. Use a glue-gun or a pottery wheel. Represent ideas and thinking with a range of media and materials. Describe what they feel or see in response to an artwork, image or object.
Vocabulary	Soft, smooth, rough, sticky, pencil, chalk, crayon, paint, brush, scissors, tape, string, stapler, sculpture, painting, colour, dots, lines	In addition: prickly, media, materials, weaving, beautiful, imagine, shape, pattern, texture, two-tone, spin, jump, glide, tiptoe	In addition: mixed media/multi-media, form, space, balance, mood, atmosphere, names of the primary and secondary colours, gallop, bounce, flow, symmetry, pointillism

Reflective questions

1   Reflect on the three areas of art and design: the visual arts, music and the performing arts. Which area is well established in your setting? Which requires more work?

2   Consider the three elements of the arts: practical, aesthetic and encounters with art. Are these balanced in your curriculum?

3   How many times in the last 3 months have you drawn on the knowledge and expertise of families to develop children's artistic and cultural awareness?

10

Understanding Assessment and Curriculum

Jan Dubiel

Introduction

Creating opportunities and experiences for children to engage with our curriculum is at the heart of our work in the early years. Ensuring that we put this into action well drives the decisions we take at both a strategic and day-to-day level. We build on children's individual needs as well as holding wider aspirations. We try to ensure that the curriculum is progressive, accumulative and appropriate. Many of the decisions we make require an effective approach to assessment, taking care to be authentic and accurate.

Putting the curriculum into action

To put the curriculum into action, we need to understand the nature, purpose and practice of assessment. We must recognise the key role of assessment, to be confident about:

- what elements of the curriculum we need to deliver
- how we can most effectively achieve this

Assessment includes checking what children know, understand and can do. More broadly, it helps us to take account of children's interests and their capabilities as learners (the characteristics of effective learning). With this information, we can:

- reflect on the best ways of interacting with children and teaching them
- plan for the next steps in their learning
- monitor their progress
- take action when children might have barriers to their learning

Equally, the Statutory Framework for the Early Years Foundation Stage (EYFS) states:

> 2.1. Assessment plays an important part in helping parents, carers, and practitioners to recognise children's progress, understand their needs, and to plan activities and support.
>
> 2.5. Ongoing assessment (also known as formative assessment) is an integral part of the learning and development process. It involves practitioners understanding children's interests and what they know and can do, and then shaping teaching and learning experiences for each child reflecting that knowledge. In their interactions with children, practitioners should make and act on their own day-to-day observations about children's progress and observations that parents and carers share. However, there is no requirement to keep written records in relation to this.

(DfE, 2025, p. 18)

We could describe assessment as 'knowing the children that you work with so that you can support their learning and development'. Though this may sound simple, it belies greater complexities. In this chapter, I will explore these complexities and articulate the role of assessment in relation to the curriculum.

It is worth clarifying that assessment is an ongoing, continual process rather than a specific event. Our 'knowing of children' builds over time. Every activity, observation, every moment of interaction enables us to refine and add to our understanding of each child. Really 'knowing the child' is distinct from the periodic collection of data.

This continual process of assessment checks:

- whether the child securely understands curriculum content
- whether the child has insecure knowledge and needs further support
- *how* the child is learning: engaging with new knowledge, skills and learning behaviours

Effective understanding and use of assessment is at the centre of effective practice.

In order to 'know the child' and work professionally with that information, we need to consider the specific elements of assessment. The following sequence of questions can help us to develop our understanding of the nature and purpose of assessment:

1   What information do we need?
2   How do we get the information?
3   How is that information used?
4   How is the information recorded and documented?

What information do we need?

Educators are responsible for supporting each child's learning and development. The question of 'what the child needs to learn' is, of course, highly contested, and shaped by the child's society and culture.

In order to support children's learning, educators need a pedagogical repertoire that consists of:

- direct teaching
- carefully considered interaction
- support
- challenge

The fusion of curriculum content (the 'what') with appropriate pedagogical approaches (the 'how') forms the core of our work as educators. To optimise this, we need to be clear about:

- the nature and content of the learning that will take place
- how children will consolidate and extend their learning
- how we will help children progress towards and achieve the planned outcomes in our curriculum

This is an important process. Educators must be clear about the information they need to achieve this. The EYFS sets out an overview of curriculum intentions. This is contained in the Educational Programmes and the Early Learning Goals for the end of the Reception year. Additionally, the statutory characteristics of effective teaching and learning identify critical 'Learning Behaviours' that enable children to develop, build on and use their knowledge and skills. *Development Matters*, which is non-statutory, suggests pathways for achieving those intentions. But the information educators need is more complex and intricate. Working with groups of children requires a deep knowledge and understanding of each individual child as a learner. It also requires wider understanding of the development of children's knowledge, skills and behaviours. This enables educators to understand children's individual learning journeys, and how best to support these. The principal purpose of assessment is to support each child's learning. We need to identify the most appropriate and significant information that we need.

We need to take account of the child's personality, propensities and strengths as a learner. We need to think about what motivates and interests them, and conversely what demotivates them. This enables us to judge how well the content of the curriculum 'lands' with the child.

We need to consider:

- What specific interests motivate and engage the child in their learning?
- Are there specific resource areas (indoors or outdoors) that they gravitate towards?
- What is the child's level of development and attainment in the Prime Areas of the EYFS?

- What is the child's level of development and attainment in the Specific Areas of the EYFS?
- How do they demonstrate the characteristics of effective teaching and learning?
- What types of interaction do they respond to?
  - o Parallel adult presence and support?
  - o Specific challenge and provocations?
- Do they typically engage in individual or group self-led activities?

How do we get the information?

Effective assessment requires precision and authenticity. The information we collect about the child must be accurate, and we must represent it truly in our assessment. Invalid information (or data) is at best valueless and, at worst, misleading.

Authentic assessment ensures that perceptions of a child's learning, attainment and achievement are 'real'. It genuinely reflects what we know is important (rather than what is easy to measure).

The information we collect drives the decisions we make about how we support children's learning. Traditional approaches to assessment can often be diluted versions of those used with older children. Such methods rely on 'testing' to obtain information.

A working definition of 'testing'

A *test-based assessment* is one in which a series of pre-set questions and/or activities are provided for a child to answer or respond to.

This may be achieved in several ways:

- by the child providing an oral answer
- by manipulating an object
- by pointing to an object or an image on a screen

An identical set of questions or activities is administered to each child in the group. For each question, there is a wrong or right answer or response. The child is scored accordingly. Each child gets a score.

However, this does not account for the nature of young children. Adults and older children understand tests: that the aim is to get as many 'right answers' as possible. Young children do not know this. They do not know that the 'right answer' will have been decided. They often see the questions as an invitation to give a creative or individually perceived response. This may, or may not, provide the information being sought.

The tradition of observational assessment remains strong in early years education. This involves educators in observing children, primarily in self-led activities. Educators make a judgement about the child's level of development based on the knowledge, skills and understanding the child demonstrates.

However, understanding and practice have evolved. We realise now that we need a more sophisticated approach to obtaining accurate information. 'Educator-led observational assessment' involves us in making accurate and meaningful judgements about children's attainment. We do this through observation and also through interaction with the children. We challenge children during their self-led activity, provoke responses and frame questions. This helps us to gain a clearer and more authentic picture of the child's capabilities. The child demonstrates how secure their learning is, by leading the activity. The educator can use their professional judgement, rather than just 'standing back'. That way, they can be confident of their conclusions.

How do we use the information to support children's learning and development?

Once we know that the information we have collected is accurate and authentic, we can focus on how we will use it.

Gathering assessment information enables us to understand and know the child. Then we can support, challenge and extend their learning and development. This process depends on our parallel understanding of the curriculum and how this progresses, in both sequence and depth.

Formative assessment has always been at the core of effective early years practice, and it is a key element of the Statutory Framework for the Early Years Foundation Stage. Fusing this information with our knowledge of the curriculum is complex. It requires us to be both highly reflective and confidently intuitive about the decisions and actions that we take.

We use much of this information during the day-to-day interactions that occur. We might instinctively respond to a comment a child makes, or to an observation of a behaviour or a communication. This is underpinned by our knowledge of the curriculum and our understanding of how children make progress. Additionally, it requires our intricate knowledge of each child. We need to understand their individual approach and how we can support or challenge their learning.

The influential REPEY (Researching Effective Pedagogy in the Early Years) study (Siraj-Blatchford et al., 2002) identifies 'individualised' assessment as a key route to quality outcomes for children. This approach relies on precise knowledge of the child. It also requires familiarity with progression in the curriculum:

> Our findings suggest that the most effective (excellent) settings ... achieve a
> balance between the opportunities provided for children to benefit from
> teacher initiated group work and the provision of freely chosen yet potentially
> instructive play activities. The evidence actually suggests that there is no one
> 'effective' pedagogy. Instead the effective pedagogue orchestrates pedagogy by
> making interventions (scaffolding, discussing, monitoring, allocating tasks),

which are sensitive to the curriculum concept or skill being 'taught', taking into account the child's 'zone of proximal development', or at least that assumed in the particular social grouping.

(Siraj-Blatchford et al., 2002, p. 43)

The REPEY research further identifies the importance of learning that was initially child led, but then supported by an adult. This is described as 'child but adult extends' (Siraj-Blatchford et al., 2002, p. 54). As Figure 10.1 shows, an equal balance of activities which are child-initiated, adult-initiated and initiated by the child but then extended by an adult, is most effective for children in the EYFS before the Reception year. The research suggests that this ensures the best outcomes for children. These approaches all need intuitive and responsive use of assessment knowledge, combined with an understanding of curriculum progression.

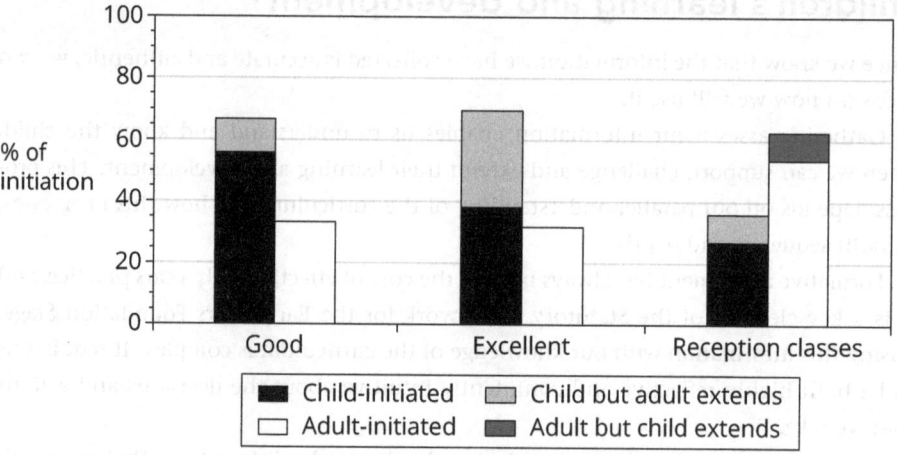

Figure 10.1   Initiation of high cognitive challenge activities within each setting type

(Siraj-Blatchford et al., 2002, p. 54)

Case Study 10.1

Helping the Troll

James, Ornella, Piotr and Kareem have chosen to use 'small-world' resources to retell the story of the Three Billy Goats Gruff. They enact the sequence of events using the appropriate language and change the tone of their voices to represent the different characters. They negotiate roles so that each of them has a turn at being each of the characters in the story. Ornella says that she feels sorry for the troll and that it's sad that he gets pushed into the water. 'What if he can't swim like my sister? He could drown!' she adds.

The children talk about the goats and how they need to get to the grass because they are hungry, and the troll is stopping them. Kareem suggests that if the troll was knocked into a boat instead then he would be safe. James goes to get one from the Water Resource Area that the troll can fit into. The children agree that this is kinder – and safer for the troll – and they retell the story incorporating this plot change.

Observing this episode, the educator gleans a range of information. The ability to retell the story, use appropriate language and negotiate roles demonstrates the children's attainment in the Prime Areas of Language and Communication and PSED, and the specific area of Literacy. However, what is also significant is the way in which the children demonstrate a range of 'Learning Behaviours' which form part of the characteristics of effective teaching and learning. The children build on their existing knowledge but then apply it to a new dimension – born from empathy and emotional literacy. This process of extending the narrative is a potent example of how the children's Learning Behaviours enable ongoing development.

The educator might consider how this can be extended to further support the children's learning and development. For example, scribing the re-worked story for the group to share with the rest of the class would contextualise the role of text as a means of recording the story.

Equally, the educator might consider sensitively judged interactions during the episode itself, exploring further plot twists and the reasons for them.

Summative assessment

The primary purpose of assessment is to provide us with accurate and meaningful information. This helps us to support children's learning effectively. As previously discussed, formative assessment is a powerful tool for improving teaching and learning. It is reactive and responsive to the child and the situation.

Summative assessment is when we collect all the information – the data – together, to create a valuable overview of group and cohort progression. It can also help us to identify the impact that practice has had on learning and development. This serves two purposes. It enables us to identify gaps or patterns in progress, particularly for specific groups of children. It also enables us to make a judgement about which aspects of the curriculum are most effective, and where we need to make improvements.

The delivery of the curriculum lies at the heart of what we do, so we need to ensure that it has been delivered successfully.

Assessment data might be collected through home-grown or commercially produced systems. The information itself comes from educators' observational assessments, as described above. Summative assessment information is a by-product of the everyday approach to knowing children and supporting them. Summative assessment should not be a self-contained, standalone process. Guidance like *Development Matters* might help to inform our judgements. But the information will originate from our evolving knowledge of the child.

It is worth exploring some of the challenges this poses, including:

- the nature of child development, which is more like a series of overlapping waves than a clear sequence of steps
- the broad, interrelated nature of the early years curriculum

Summative assessment provides a useful function. But it is dangerous to simplify assessment information so that it fits with a particular system or expectation. An appropriate curriculum for young children is holistic and includes elements that are difficult to quantify in a simplistic way. Many of the most important elements of the EYFS are particularly challenging in this respect.

Understanding progress in this light is one such significant challenge.

The conventional view of progress in this context has been established by logging the child's development against a series of statements. For example, the previous EYFS Profile described children's attainment as 'emerging, expected or exceeding' in relation to each Early Learning Goal. Many other assessment systems followed that lead. They applied those three levels to the overlapping age-bands within the previous version of *Development Matters*. The intention was to show an authentic notion of progress, using the same statements that were intended to inform teaching and provision. The result was often confused and incoherent. In some cases, assessment using the bands became a simplistic 'tick-list'.

The revised *Development Matters* has just three bands: Birth to 3, 3- and 4-year-olds and Reception (4- and 5-year-olds). This might appear to reduce the ability to demonstrate progress. In fact, it provides a more appropriate opportunity to evaluate the impact of the curriculum and how secure the child's learning is.

To understand how well a child is progressing through the curriculum, we need to find out how confidently and automatically they can use the knowledge, skills and behaviours they have learnt. We cannot find this out through simple tick-lists: we need to view learning developmentally. Educator-led observational assessment enables us to make a more refined and meaningful judgement. This, in turn, will identify the best ways of supporting the child and describe the impact of teaching and provision.

We might use *Development Matters* to check whether a child has securely learnt the skills and concepts they need to count accurately up to 5:

- Develop fast recognition of up to 3 objects, without having to count them individually ('subitising')
- Learn the count sequence: recite numbers up to 5
- Say one number for each item in order: 1, 2, 3, 4, 5
- Know that the last number reached when counting a small set of objects tells you how many there are in total ('cardinal principle')
- Show 'finger numbers' up to 5
- Link numerals and amounts: for example, showing the right number of objects to match the numeral, up to 5

We might then assess the child's learning as follows:

- **Entering**: the child is not yet securely counting to 5. We need to offer more support so that they become secure and fluent.
- **Secure supported** indicates that the statement describes the child who is secure in their counting, with support from an adult or in response to an adult provocation or request. The child has acquired the knowledge, but they are not yet using it independently. This provides us with the opportunity to create occasions within the setting that will enable them to do this.
- **Secure independent** indicates that the child's understanding is secure. They can demonstrate this *without support or provocation from an adult*. They can use their knowledge in a fluid and automatic way.

By reconceptualising our understanding of progress, we can illuminate the importance of 'deep' learning in the curriculum. This still allows us to generate useful data for the purposes described above.

How is the information recorded and documented?

Educator-led observational assessment:

- requires an intuitive professional confidence to tune into a child's learning
- enables us to understand how the curriculum is being embedded
- guides us in shaping appropriate and professionally considered responses
- helps us to support the child's continued development

We can also use this information to summarise individual attainment, and the attainment of groups of children. This demonstrates progress and makes us accountable for the impact of the provision.

The 'knowing of children' remains core to effective EYFS practice. Using this information to ensure that children make secure progress continues to be its key purpose. This type of assessment is an essential part of effective practice. However, in some cases, the concept of assessment has become confused with a perceived need for physical 'evidence' of children's learning.

There are rich traditions of documenting children's learning and development, helping educators to celebrate and understand the nature and trajectory of a child's progress. The renowned pre-schools of Reggio Emilia in Italy use documentation as a powerful way of framing their curriculum. They also use documentation to communicate the strong values that define their approach to childhood and pedagogy (Edwards et al., 2011). Margaret Carr's innovative work develops the concept of 'Learning Stories'. These support, celebrate and articulate children's development and success through pictorial and annotated documentation. Learning Stories can develop the professionalism of early childhood educators (Carr, 2001). These approaches build on a strong philosophy: the physical outcomes are an expression of this, and not merely a time-consuming activity.

Historically, during the development of the EYFS, there has sometimes been an over-reliance on physically recording evidence for the purpose of justification. Educators were wrongly told to gather multiple examples of 'evidence' to support their judgements for the EYFS Profile. Poorly managed moderation processes, in some areas, drove this. Commercial tracking systems encouraged educators to evidence their decisions of children's attainment against statements from *Development Matters*, using photographs or text. These misguided approaches separated assessment from a philosophy that celebrates learning and development. On occasions, it became an unwelcome and time-consuming additional dimension to the educator's role.

The current EYFS acknowledges that paperwork, tracking data and digital recording of children's learning can lead to unnecessary workload. This is especially the case where educators feel that this is an expectation. In some cases, this culture has inadvertently interfered with interaction and effective teaching. Educators might lose the momentum in a powerful episode of dialogue as they reach for a means of recording the moment. The Statutory Framework for the EYFS has long been aware of this anomaly, and it clearly asserts that:

> 2.2. Assessment should not involve long breaks from interaction with children or require excessive paperwork. When assessing whether an individual child is at the expected level of development, practitioners should draw on their knowledge of the child and their own expert professional judgement. Practitioners are not required to prove this through collection of any physical evidence.
>
> (DfE, 2025, p. 18)

Assessing the child is part of the professional role of the educators. So is the interpretation of the assessment to indicate a particular level of development. External parties who wish to gain information about children's progress in the EYFS need to acknowledge that this information is complex. Any dialogue about this should begin with a conversation with the educators, not a review of documentation. The newly produced exemplification for the EYFS Profile (DfE, 2022a) adopts this approach. It consists of educators talking about the children they work with, the observations and the conclusions they have drawn. They discuss how this describes each child's achievement and attainment in the context of the EYFS Profile.

Involving parents

As educators, we have general knowledge and expertise about child development, but parents are the experts in their own children. When educators and parents understand

and trust each other, they can work collaboratively and ensure the best outcomes for every child.

By sharing and discussing assessment information, we can learn from parents about the unique development of each child. This is true for ongoing formative assessment, and the two summative assessment checks: the Progress Check at Age 2 and the Early Years Foundation Stage Profile.

Research evidence tells us that the early home learning environment (HLE) is an important factor in children's success at school and in life. Educators in the early years are well placed to help parents understand their child's needs. We can support parents to enhance their child's development at home. This can have life-long benefits:

- The HLE is an important factor in the development of early speech, language and communication. This not only impacts on a child's development in the early years, but can persist until their GCSEs and A-Levels.
- The HLE is related to children's social and emotional development in the early years. The benefits continue until age 16.
- The quality of the HLE is as important to intellectual and cognitive development as parental factors such as occupation and education. This suggests that what parents do with their child is just as important as who they are.

(DfE, 2018)

Conclusion: Principles of assessment in the early years

1   *Record what helps you to understand the child.* A child's learning and development can be complex and idiosyncratic. The nature of assessment is pivotal to understanding and then supporting and extending children's learning. For that reason, authentic and accurate assessment is vital. On some occasions, it may be necessary to ensure that a child's activity is captured in an accurate and comprehensive way. This may require some physical recording (writing an observation or photographing the child). The decision for this is the educator's alone, on the basis that it will support their professional knowledge.

2   *Record what is significant for an individual child.* When children make specific and notable advances in their development, you may want to note this as an important point in their journey. Again, the educator makes this decision. They will be able to decide what is or is not significant for the child.

3   *Record what you are going to forget.* In the intense ebb and flow of typical EYFS provision, a plethora of children's activity can overwhelm our memory. Brief moments of significance compete with each other and are then immediately overwhelmed by new ones. In this context, sometimes a brief aide memoire, a note to self, or a picture taken quickly, can capture the moment. This helps us to remember its significance later.

Reflective questions

Thinking about the purpose of documentation and recording in the EYFS:

1   How can this support, rather than detract from practice?
2   How can we make it a useful tool, rather than a hindrance?

11

Helping Children Who Are Learning English as an Additional Language to Access the Curriculum

Tania Choudhury

EYFS Curriculum Guidance

English as an Additional Language

Speaking more than one language has lots of advantages for children. It is the norm in many countries around the world. Children will learn English from a strong foundation in their home language. It is important for you to encourage families to use their home language for linguistic as well as cultural reasons. Children learning English will typically go through a quiet phase when they do not say very much and may then use words in both languages in the same sentence. Talk to parents about what language they speak at home, try and learn a few key words and celebrate multilingualism in your setting.

(DfE, 2023, p. 22)

More than one in five children in an English school is learning English as an additional language (DfE, 2024a), with the proportion varying by school type from 19% in secondary to 31% in nursery. In total, this is around 1.8 million children, a number that has roughly doubled in the last 15 years.

England's rich diversity of languages and cultures is reflected in the children attending early years settings and schools. It is imperative that educators do all they can to enable these children to get equal access to the curriculum.

In this chapter I will focus on four main areas that we need to consider:

1   What we know about learning English as an additional language (EAL): the myths and gaps in our understanding; what research suggests
2   Experiences of young children of Bangladeshi-heritage: the typical stages of bilingual development; how children use (and don't use) their home language
3   How educators can support young children to learn English as an additional language: the importance of scaffolding children's language acquisition
4   EAL and SEND (special educational needs and disabilities): the critical issue of distinguishing these two areas

I will illustrate each of these areas with case studies.

What we know about learning english as an additional language

It is important to start off by noting that the term 'EAL' is broad. It simply means that a child is encountering a language at home other than English.

For instance, Adam – whose mother is fluently bilingual in English and Urdu – is categorised as EAL. So is Fatemeh, who has just arrived as a refugee from Iran, chatting away in Farsi and not knowing a single word of English.

Many children are classified as 'EAL', but it is the child's ability to speak and understand English that will play the most significant role in how well they can access learning in the EYFS. Developing proficiency in English is a gradual process that requires time and consistent support. It is crucial to keep in mind that language skills do not develop overnight, and patience is needed as children work to become proficient in English.

Many children arrive in early years settings without understanding or speaking much English. Even so, they can still be on their way to proficiency by the end of the Reception year. Proficiency in English is a strong predictor of later success in school, so it is important that we offer effective support to young children. This will help them to make friends, play and learn; and it will help them succeed later in school, too.

There are two myths to challenge in our understanding of EAL. The first of these is the idea that young children will 'soak English up like sponges'. This is not true. In fact, learning a new language is very hard work for young children, as much as it is for adults. It will not happen 'naturally' just because children are in a language-rich environment.

The second myth is the belief that children should switch to speaking English at home, once they start in an early years setting or in school. This advice is often handed out to parents. A setting that practises this is referred to as a 'subtractive bilingual environment': where the emphasis on learning the second language results in less use, less practice, and even forgetting the first language over time.

This can have serious and negative consequences for children (Hodgkiss, 2021). It might, for example, cut them off from wider family members: uncles, aunts and grandparents who speak the child's first language, but not English. If the child's parents and other family members do not speak English well, the child might be left with no strong language models at home.

This type of 'subtractive bilingual environment', where the child is unable to develop proficiency in either language, can affect the child's sense of belonging and emotional wellbeing, implying that their first language is of a lower status than English and perpetuating a narrative that minority groups are inferior. It could lead to parents feeling that the school perceives them and their culture in a negative light.

This contrasts with an 'additive bilingual environment', in which the child is encouraged to develop proficiency in both their native language and their second language. In this kind of environment, both languages are valued, nurtured and developed, supporting the individual in becoming proficient in both languages without losing one over time. The following case study shows how celebrating Sara's home language encouraged a positive relationship between the early years setting and her family, and in turn, how this impacted Sara's learning.

Case Study 11.1

Partnership with Parents, by Melissa Prendergast

The home learning environment is a powerful predictor of children's learning and development (Sammons et al., 2015). At Sheringham Nursery School and Children's Centre we prioritise the development of strong partnerships with parents. Valuing children's home languages is a key aspect of this work and is essential for the success of our relational and intentional pedagogy.

When Aiden, one of our educators, carried out a home visit to get to know his new 2-year-old key child, Sara, he noticed how much she enjoyed interacting with others – including him! Sara comes from a large family and is immersed in Somali at home and within her community. During the visit, Sara spoke to Aiden in Somali and this spurred him to learn some key words. Aiden understands the importance of nurturing children's home languages, so he sourced some high-quality picture books in Somali and English to lend to the family, for Sara to share at home with her parents.

The trusting relationship that Aiden built with Sara and her family right from the start enabled them to feel proud of their home language. They felt confident to prioritise speaking in Somali and no longer worried that they needed to focus on using English alone.

(Continued)

Aiden supported Sara's mum to contribute to her 'special book', adding photos of things they did at home. Sara's mum wrote comments in Somali and her sister translated them into English.

When Sara turned 3 years old, she moved rooms. Aiden worked on making the transition smooth – Sara's special book and the high-quality picture books in English and Somali were important aspects of this. Initially, while Sara was familiarising herself with a new space and establishing new relationships, she was very quiet. Her new key person, Mariam, noticed that she had a good understanding of English and would use gestures to communicate, for example at the snack table:

Mariam: Today we've got some crunchy crackers and soft cream cheese. Let's get some plates ready ... we have four friends here so that means we need ... Sara looked around then flashed up four fingers to show to Mariam she knew the quantity.

Mariam: Yes Sara! You looked carefully around the table and noticed that there were four friends. That means we need four plates.

Typical stages of bilingual development

Research by Patton Tabors sets out the typical stages of learning English as an additional language:

- Children may start by continuing to use their home languages in the second-language situation. This is mostly likely to occur with younger children. For example, a 2-year-old Portuguese child kept saying 'la casa' to staff, during the first hour he spent in nursery without a parent. At pick-up time, his father explained that he was asking to go home.
- Children follow this with a non-verbal period. They collect information about English. They may use gesture to communicate.
- Children begin to 'go public' with their new knowledge. They may use individual words and phrases in English. Their speech may be imitative: for example, repeating the names of objects after an adult says them. They may use some formulaic English: for example, naming colours or counting. They may use some multi-word formulaic English, like 'help me' or 'don't like'.
- Children begin to develop productive use of English. They move beyond using just memorised chunks, creating original phrases. For example, they may say 'I want [and add a noun, like bike]'. Children may still sound like non-native speakers and may make mistakes with their grammar and vocabulary.

(Tabors, 1997, p. 39)

An excellent, free assessment tool from the Bell Foundation can help us to check children's development in English (Bell Foundation, 2025). Most children in the early years will be in Bands A and B. We can use these assessments when children move into Year 1, to ensure continued support for their English-learning needs.

Children speaking more than one language might switch fluidly between languages, depending on context. For example, emerging evidence about how children of Bangladeshi-heritage experience language use at home shows that:

- Bengali/Sylheti use by parents was often motivated by the desire to strengthen and maintain relationships, and this was sometimes influenced by family members outside of the household (e.g. family members living abroad).
- Children were sometimes a motivating factor for parents to use English, particularly in cases where children preferred to speak English compared with Bengali/Sylheti.
- Sometimes, this was a cause of disappointment for parents as despite their planned strategy to speak Bengali/Sylheti, their child responded in English.
- Some parents felt that Bengali/Sylheti were valued in the UK through the use of interpreters at meetings and because translated literature was available from the local authority and health services.
- Ultimately, parents valued English use in the UK as it is the national language, just as many described Bengali/Sylheti as being more highly valued in Bangladesh.

(Choudhury and Hodgkiss, 2021)

Helping young children to learn english as an additional language

Tabors's (1997) research is seminal, but it is important that we do not interpret it to mean that our role is limited to passive observation of children moving automatically from one stage to the next through immersion in a 'language-rich environment'. We need to be intentional in our pedagogy and create a curriculum of well thought out activities and opportunities for children to learn and use English.

This involves carefully scaffolding young children's use of English: starting with giving the children just enough words for them to communicate what they want to say and gradually reducing our input, so they become more independent over time.

We can scaffold learning English by:

- Using symbols and other visual aids, so that children can point to what they want. If they indicate they want a turn on a bike, we can say the word 'bike' and then expand on this, 'Do you want a bike?'

- Commenting on children's play. We need to take care to give just a few key words and not flood the child with English. At the sand tray, we might comment, 'You're digging in the sand'.
- Encouraging children to play with each other, even if they do not share a language. Children are inventive. They may use gesture, hold up real objects and use some words to understand each other.
- Avoiding actions which reduce children's confidence. If a child says 'melon' instead of 'lemon', we should not correct them by saying, 'No, it's a lemon'. Correction like this might put them off speaking in English next time. 'Testing' children by asking them multiple closed questions ('What colour is that? How many have you got?') is also unhelpful. Gently rephrasing sentences when children make a mistake with the grammar or vocabulary is a better option. For example, saying 'you've got a lemon' when a child incorrectly says 'melon'. If a child says 'give bike', we might say 'you want Ashraf to give you the bike?'
- Sharing the links of books, songs and rhymes on YouTube with their families, so children can practise at home.

Running through the curriculum, we need to plan for some activities where we expect the children to join in, but without putting pressure on them to do so (this would only put them off). In the following case study, Shaghaygh Khademian explains how an early years team stepped in to support a young bilingual learning to enable her to develop her confidence to access the whole of the EYFS curriculum. It is notable that the educators considered her holistically as a learner, with a range of strengths and needs, rather than narrowly focusing on support for her to learn English.

Case Study 11.2

Supporting Confidence, by Shaghaygh Khademian

Sofia is a young, bilingual Spanish-English child aged 3 who started in our nursery class in the autumn. In her first weeks, she was reluctant to go into the Creative Area. When her friends went there, she would feel sad and left out, watching them from the Book Corner.

As EYFS lead, I noticed this and spoke with her class teacher. As we talked together, we started to build up a picture of Sofia. She was confident to play outdoors, and loved running, jumping and climbing with her friends. But she did not seem to feel confident or comfortable in a lot of the indoor areas. As a child who was just starting to speak English, it was hard for her to talk about what she wanted to do, and what she needed help with.

We decided to take some creative activities outside. We set up an activity with big paint brushes and rollers, for mark-making with water. We encouraged her to take part, and brought her friends over to join in. Playing together like that, her confidence in using brushes and making marks started to grow.

A little while later, she started to become more confident about following her friends into the Creative Area. She picked up a paintbrush and did a very small picture of herself. It seemed like she was unfamiliar with using pens and pencils. Compared to what her friends were doing, it was very simple, just a circle with some dots for her eyes and nose.

When we talked about this as a team, we decided that we would try, whenever possible, to sit with her and draw alongside her. This worked well – sensitively being part of her world seemed to be important to her, rather than us just noticing what she was doing and being generally encouraging.

We offered her some pencils which she thought she would like. We noticed that she was swapping pencils and pens between her left and right hand, so we made a note to keep a close eye on her to see when she began to have a preferred hand. Some children do not establish hand dominance until they are four or five years old, so we did not worry, but it made us understand more about why she might be reluctant to draw and paint. If she did show a preference for using her left hand, we would need to make sure she knew where to find specific equipment like the left-handed scissors. We would also encourage her to sit at the left end of the table, so she did not knock arms with right-handed children all the time, and model a correct left-handed pencil grip.

A little bit later in the term, I observed another breakthrough. Sofia went into the Creative Area, and I went to sit next to her and draw with her. She made the outline of a shape and said it was a pear. She looked thoughtful and coloured it in with one of the special pencils. She turned to me and confidently said 'I coloured it green'.

Thinking about Sofia with the team promoted several reflections. It was important to be alongside her, in her world, to help develop her confidence, and to model the use of equipment she seemed to be unfamiliar with.

We also reflected that we often notice the children who lack confidence outdoors, but do not always pick up on children who avoid particular areas indoors.

It was especially pleasing when a parent came to visit towards the end of the autumn term, and noticed Sofia making cards with her friends. The parent turned to me and said, 'look how lovely her drawing is'.

Some further examples of ways to support children's encouragement to enjoy and take part in a broad curriculum are:

- regularly singing songs or rhymes that are simple enough for children to learn some (or all) of the words
- setting up culturally relevant role play to support children to learn key words related to familiar objects and situations: for example, cultural textiles for dressing up, specific cooking utensils and floor seating
- sharing simple books like *Where's Spot?* (Hill, 2013) and encouraging all children to say key words like 'dinner' and 'door'

- sharing books like *We're Going on a Bear Hunt* (Rosen, 2000), with catchy and repeated refrains, so children can join in
- providing books in home languages so that the child is supported to make links between the two languages
- using wordless picture books as a focus for conversation, encouraging children to point to details in the pictures and talk about what they notice

High-quality, meaningful interactions between educators and children are the 'pedagogical thread' which needs to run through all aspects of the curriculum. Educators need to take time to prioritise sustained, back-and-forth conversations with every child who is learning English as an additional language. The following case study shows how an educator, Kate, develops a sustained conversation with 3-year-old Adam. Kate is intentional in her approach to planning, choice of resources and her sensitive interactional style. She chooses to use the practice of interactive reading, informed by the ShREC approach.

Case Study 11.3

Finding the Elephant

Adam is 3 years old and attends nursery part-time in the afternoon. He is learning three languages: Arabic, French and English. He chooses to spend a lot of his time at nursery outdoors. He is motivated by physical play such as climbing and riding a balance bike. He is often quiet and does not readily initiate interactions with the educators or the other children.

Adam has recently started to show some interest in the new reading den in the garden, a quiet, cosy space filled with blankets, cushions and lots of books. During the weekly planning meeting, the team of educators discuss Adam's progress. His key person, Kate, says that she has noticed that he enjoys being in the den looking at books by himself. She is keen to build on this by dedicating time to join Adam in his newfound interest.

Adam rides his balance bike around the garden several times. He slows down and stops next to the reading den in the corner of the garden. He stands up, still holding onto his bike, and reaches into a basket full of books. He pauses, looking at the front cover of the book *Have You Seen Elephant?* (Barrow, 2015). Adam gets off his bike and climbs into the den. Kate notices this and decides to join him. She smiles and greets him with a warm 'Hello'. She is sensitive in the way she approaches the interaction, carefully watching to see what Adam is looking at so she can share attention with him. Kate follows Adam's lead as he looks through the book. She responds by commenting on what he is interested in and expands his language by adding more words. The impact of this is clear: as the conversation progresses, Adam's confidence increases and he begins to use more language.

Kate:	Hello Adam.
	Adam looks at the book.
Kate:	You're looking at a book: *Have You Seen Elephant?*
	Adam points at the elephant on the front cover.
Kate:	It's the elephant, the elephant is hiding.
Adam:	(whispers) Effalent. (He giggles and opens the book.)
Adam:	Oh! Effalent, effalent…
Kate:	Yes! It's the elephant. The enormous, grey elephant.
	Adam (turns the page and exclaims loudly): It's elephant! Oh… (He looks closely at the illustration of the elephant and points at the elephant's trunk.)
Kate:	Oh, you can see the elephant again… this is the elephant's trunk. Trunk. The elephant's trunk is long.
	Adam notices some numbers on the next page. These capture his interest, and he starts to count
Adam:	1, 2, 3, 4… (he pauses and points at number 5).
Kate:	5, this is number 5. The boy is counting, the elephant is going to hide!
Adam:	Oh no, elephant gone…

EAL and SEND

It is important not to assume that a child who only speaks a little English has a special need. They are most likely to be a typically developing bilingual child, rather than a child with a learning or language difficulty. They need lots of opportunities to hear and speak English with their peers. Educators sometimes refer to 'my EAL and SEND children' in one phrase, grouping both sets of children together. This is unhelpful. The SEND Code of Practice specifically states that:

> Identifying and assessing SEN for young children whose first language is not English requires particular care. Early years practitioners should look carefully at all aspects of a child's learning and development to establish whether any delay is related to learning English as an additional language or if it arises from SEN or disability. Difficulties related solely to learning English as an additional language are not SEN.
>
> (DfE, 2024b, p. 85)

Some children learning EAL may come from backgrounds where adults do not think that they should involve children in conversations and do not view children as conversational partners. Others may be refugees, experiencing trauma because of their relocation.

Having culturally sensitive discussions with parents is an appropriate way to inform ourselves: we need to make the effort to listen to parents' own accounts of their family life and experiences, ethnicity, identity, faith and culture. We should guard against making any assumptions. After listening to the parent, we can offer support, guidance, or referral to a specialist agency.

This does not mean we should ignore the potential overlaps between EAL and SEND. It is important to look out for children learning EAL who might have a speech, language and communication delay or disorder. Again, it is important to avoid making assumptions. Instead, ask the parents about their child's use of their first language at home. We might look out to see if the child and parent chat together at the start or end of the session. If children are making little progress in both their home language and in English, they will be severely disadvantaged. They will need specialist help from a speech and language therapist. Using bilingual staff or an interpreter will help make this a rich assessment.

In the following case study, I relate the story of Afya and her family and show how detrimental it is to jump to conclusions based on initial observations, rather than getting to know the child and carrying out a proper assessment.

Case Study 11.4

Misdiagnosis and EAL

Afya is a 4-year-old girl with physical disabilities from Somalia. She arrived in the UK a year ago with her adoptive parents, who found Afya under a tree as a baby, abandoned by her birth parents because of her physical defects. She has no function in her lower body and limited movement in her hands.

The family was granted asylum status and housed in a hotel. Afya's family applied for her to join many schools, but she was often rejected, with schools stating that they could not meet her physical and complex cognitive and speech and language needs. Finally, there was a school that accepted Afya, but they said they could not have her on-site due to her complex needs. Alternative provision was provided in the home to ensure that Afya was still educated.

The initial assessment of Afya's needs said that she had cognitive and speech and language needs in addition to her physical disabilities. Due to the family context, a bilingual educator was provided to work with Afya in her home whilst she waited for an appropriate school place. This was to ensure that Afya and her family felt comfortable.

After a few sessions, the educator reported that Afya in fact spoke a great deal of Somali and appeared to have no cognitive disability. It was determined that she was an EAL learner as opposed to having speech and language difficulties. This changed the entire perspective of Afya's needs and her ability to transition into a mainstream school.

Afya was eventually placed in an appropriate single-storey school with modifications made to the environment to ensure that she had wheelchair access. Moreover, the educator carried on working with her to support her transition into school and ensured that she was able to access the curriculum alongside her peers.

This case study indicates how easy it can be for assumptions to be made about a child's needs based on their appearance. Fortunately, Afya got the right assessment and support, which made a huge difference to her future. Rather than being mistakenly placed in a school for children with profound and multiple learning difficulties, Afya is now alongside peers of her age in a mainstream school with adaptations.

Conclusion

Young children are remarkably powerful learners, but we must not make the mistake of thinking that learning a new language is easy for them. We must support them as they learn English, and watch out for those who are struggling. Children who are not progressing towards proficiency in English will find the Key Stage 1 curriculum very difficult.

Additionally, it is important to consider some of the benefits of being multilingual. People who speak just one language are not able to engage in the range of learning, travel and culture that multilingual people take for granted. There may be cognitive advantages to multilingualism, too (Bialystok et al., 2012). For example, multilingual people may have a better understanding of how language works (metalinguistic awareness). They may find it easier to learn other modern foreign languages (Chalmers and Murphy, 2021).

In our increasingly connected world, being multilingual is a great asset. As educators in the early years, we must do all we can to help children learning EAL to develop fluency in English, providing all the support they need. It cannot be left to chance.

Reflective questions

1   How do you demonstrate to parents and children that multilingualism is an asset?
2   What do you do to make sure that *all* parents are involved in supporting their children's learning at home?

Inclusion

Lindsey Foster

As professionals working in the early years, surely we have to be concerned about the poor outcomes for children with special educational needs and disabilities (SEND). For example, the Education Policy Institute's (EPI) 2024 report highlights that 'by the end of reception year, children receiving SEN support were over a year behind children with no identified SEN in 2023, highlighting that there are already sizeable gaps for pupils with additional needs' at the end of the Early Years Foundation Stage (EYFS). This gap widens to 17 months by the end of primary school and to 22 months by the end of secondary school.

While all these gaps are troubling, it is notable that the gap for older children has narrowed over time, whereas it has widened for children with SEND in the early years. This trend suggests that the youngest children have been disproportionately affected by the COVID-19 pandemic lockdowns and rising child poverty in recent years.

Settings describe a rise in the number of children with SEND, leading many to feel overstretched. A 2022 briefing from the Early Years Alliance reported that of all respondents providing care and education to children with SEND:

- 92% have had to use their own funds to support them
- 42% have never declined a place to a child with SEND; of those who have declined, not having enough staff (74%), not being able to afford to deliver appropriate care (51%) and not feeling able to keep the children safe (43%) were the most commonly cited factors

Only 6% of local authorities believe they have enough provision for all children with SEND in the early years (Coram, 2024).

There is no doubt that meeting rising levels of need is a challenge. However, research suggests that there are approaches which educators can use to improve the learning and overall experience of young children with SEND in the EYFS. In this chapter, I will be considering six key approaches:

- an inclusive mindset
- strong relationships with parents and carers
- links with wider services
- bespoke assessment and planning
- access to a broad curriculum: scaffolding
- self-evaluation

We must act with urgency to ensure that children with SEND have a better experience and achieve improved outcomes during the crucial early years of their education. However, this should not lead us to hasty decisions or despairing attitudes: instead, we need to draw on our professional expertise and on robust research evidence to make wise decisions in the best interests of the children.

An inclusive mindset

The Education Endowment Foundation's (EEF) guidance report *Special Educational Needs in Mainstream Schools* states that 'an inclusive school removes barriers to learning and participation, provides an education that is appropriate to pupils' needs, and promotes high standards and the fulfilment of potential for all pupils' (EEF, 2020b, p. 8).

A key factor here is actively helping every child to access an ambitious curriculum. For example, some children have temporary needs. They may have experienced fewer sustained and supportive interactions before they start in a setting and find it difficult to communicate confidently and focus on their play and learning. Rather than jumping to conclude that they have special needs, educators may need to keep a watchful eye on their development as they settle in. They may need to spend more time with some of the children, to develop warm and supportive relationships with them and to encourage their play, independence and communication. As they access a high-quality early education, making strong progress from their starting points, the concern about possible SEND will diminish.

It is also important to remember that child development is not linear. An early developmental delay might not have long-term consequences. For example, some children have late language emergence, and are not able to say many words at age 2; but with the right support, 80% of them will develop age-appropriate communication skills by age 7 (Rice et al., 2008). For that reason, it is important to monitor children's language development throughout the early years and offer extra support when it is needed. Flexible and responsive approaches can have a life-changing, positive impact on children.

When children are not progressing well, despite being given extra support and attention, research evidence suggests that early identification of SEND is at the heart of an inclusive approach. The Institute for Fiscal Studies (IFS) found that children growing up near Sure Start Children's Centres were more likely to be described as having SEND at age 5, but were significantly less likely to be described as having SEND at ages 11 and 16 (Carneiro et al., 2024, p. 5). Identifying and responding to needs early can lead to a reduction in children's needs when they are older.

Communication is central to every child's learning. Where children are not using verbal communication, it is essential to use an augmentative approach like signing (e.g. Makaton) or visual symbols (e.g. on a core board) and to ensure that all children learn to use the augmentative approach. Without communication between children and adults, and children with their peers, the opportunities for learning are severely restricted.

Having an 'inclusive mindset' is crucial. Research evidence suggests that this positive mindset leads, in turn, to more positive interactions between educators and children (EEF, 2020b, p. 11), as the following case study shows.

Case Study 12.1

Overcoming Barriers: The Importance of Adaptations

Chris is 3 years old and has Down syndrome. He uses a frame to walk, and Makaton signs to communicate.

The special educational needs co-ordinator (SENCO) and Chris's key person discuss his needs, arranging provision that is accessible. The key person speaks to Chris's parents to learn about his interests and plans activities that she thinks will absorb Chris on his first day.

One of Chris's identified barriers to accessing the nursery curriculum is his mobility. His key person modifies key activities so that he can reach them whilst using a walking frame. She also makes sure that there is space in the nursery room for Chris to crawl when he wants to.

Consequently, Chris is able to play and learn alongside the other children from his first day. His strong relationships with staff help him to settle in well. Chris feels safe and is happy to say goodbye to his parents in time.

Educators support Chris with making friends by modelling turn-taking and different ways of interacting. They support his communication by commenting on his play, using signs, gestures, objects and sharing stories and songs.

Over time, Chris becomes a confident learner.

This is an example of providing inclusive practice. Chris did not have a programme that separated him from the other children or excluded him from activities. Rather, the setting made adaptations which enabled him to access a rich curriculum.

Strong relationships with parents and carers

Early years practitioners are important people in the lives of parents and carers. We are often the first people to suggest that their child might have delayed development, or a special educational need. It is crucial that such discussions are handled with sensitivity and that we think ahead about the words we will use, ensuring they are accurate, clear and focused on the child's strengths as well as their needs. The Progress Check at Age 2 advises:

> Discussions of a sensitive nature with parents should always be conducted somewhere private. Try to make the discussion as comfortable as possible in a space where there will not be any interruptions. Make sure that there is water and a box of tissues to hand. Try to schedule a time when parents are most available. Suggest that the parents come together or have a friend or family member accompany them.
>
> (DfE, 2022a, p. 28)

The SEND Code of Practice (DfE, 2024b) states that children, parents and carers must be actively involved in assessment and decision-making processes at all stages. It is crucial to listen to parents' concerns and include their views in any plans: they have invaluable insights into how well the child is doing outside the setting.

Parents of children with SEND are also on a learning journey. It might be difficult for them to accept that their child has SEND or understand what this may mean. Very often, early years settings are the first place where there is sustained professional engagement with a child and their family, so it is important that we do this well and establish a respectful, open and honest partnership.

The following case study from Honey Kaur, a childminder from Newham, illustrates the importance of working closely with the child's family. It showcases the importance of building a secure and trusting relationship.

─Case Study 12.2─

The Importance of Working With Parents, by Honey Kaur

When Leo arrived, aged 18 months, I soon felt concerned about aspects of his development. My concerns included his limited speech, difficulties with social interactions, and the way he would only eat a very small range of foods.

Leo manifested behaviours often associated with sensory processing challenges. He showed a preference for dry foods and struggled with textures and food types that were new to him. This was not only impacting his nutrition and energy levels, but his social interactions. He tired quickly and fell into a deep sleep at nap time. He would become frustrated with peers and adults and highly emotional.

Leo's initial assessment showed clear signs of delayed speech and language development. He was not able to imitate sounds, and his gestures were limited to pointing. Leo's parents knew there were concerns, but not the extent of them. I was sensitive to this, taking things one step at a time.

My priority was to build a trusting relationship with Leo's parents. This would be key to him settling and making progress.

Leo's home language is Portuguese. I sought out a Portuguese-speaking colleague who was able to get communication going with his parents and explain my concerns in a way that was culturally sensitive. Leo's parents came from a background where families are close-knit, with children typically staying at home with extended family until going to school aged 6. Having migrated to a new country, they didn't have this network of relatives to rely on. Childcare outside of the family was unheard of to them, but they needed it while they worked to make ends meet. I bore this huge challenge in mind during all my encounters with them, discussing Leo's behaviours with sensitivity and confidence, so as not to alarm them. I noticed that this helped Leo's parents to feel more comfortable and less alienated.

Leo's parents were concerned that speaking Portuguese would hold back his language development. I reassured them of the benefits of bilingual development, not least that Leo would be able to express himself more easily and connect with his cultural identity.

I shared strategies with Leo's parents that they could use at home such as helping him make healthy food choices. For example, I showed him an apple on one plate and orange on another – he could then make an independent choice of a healthy snack.

Leo's parents reciprocated by sharing their strategies with me. They brought Leo's favourite toys to help him to settle and shared a song from home that helped calm him when feeling upset or frustrated. Over time, we all began to see improvements in Leo's development. I think a lot of this was down to our consistent approach.

Though Leo's parents could follow most things I said, they found it difficult to reply. I could see and understand how this was frustrating for them. In response, I used visual aids and gestures to communicate with them about Leo's development. This was useful and helped us to relate to each other in a relaxed way. I expressed my regret at not speaking Portuguese: it was important for me to make it clear that our communication difficulty did not come from them, but from both parties.

With my encouragement, Leo's parents came to Stay and Play sessions and coffee mornings. This helped them as they saw Leo playing with other children, and it enabled them to spend time with other parents who spoke about their children's experiences, including difficulties. Leo's parents began to see how children can be so different yet share similarities. They felt reassured by hearing other parents speak about overcoming challenges and the strategies they used.

I made it a priority to try to reduce the anxiety around food and eating, seeking support from our local health and nutrition team. Working as a team with Leo's parents, we introduced sensory-friendly foods. Leo gradually began to eat more of a range of foods. We let him do this at his own pace, never putting too much emphasis on it – this would only make it more of an issue and our intention was to reduce emotions around food and eating.

In collaboration with Leo's parents, I worked with the local authority's SEND team and got additional support for Leo and his family. We put an Early Help Plan in place with clear, realistic targets to work towards.

Links with external services

As the case study above shows, when early years educators work collaboratively with external services, they can improve the outcomes of children with SEND and empower parents.

Some examples of those external services are:

- health visitors
- Family Hubs
- occupational therapists
- physiotherapists
- speech and language therapists
- local authority SEND teams

The best partnership models keep the child at the heart and promote strengths-based, child-centred practice. For example, a speech and language therapist will have specific expertise in assessing a child and suggesting a programme of activities to support their progress. However, the therapist is only likely to see the child rarely, perhaps every few months, so it will be down to the parents and educators to put that programme into action every day to maximise its impact. The programme will need to be practical and feasible, considering the realities of family life and the many responsibilities of the educator. Furthermore, the programme will need to consider the child's overall wellbeing and the importance of their wider engagement in play, learning and making friends. All of this points to the importance of specialists working collaboratively with parents and educators to develop a specific programme for a child.

External professionals can also play a vital role in supplying specialist equipment and modelling effective practice. For example, a physiotherapist may provide a standing frame to help a child who is not yet stable on their feet, and show parents and educators how to help the child use their frame. A speech and language therapist might demonstrate practical tips for promoting language development through play. Ideally, external specialists will be readily contactable online or by phone to troubleshoot any issues, so that programmes and techniques can be adapted quickly, without waiting several months until the planned review.

Family Hubs and Children's Centres can provide vital additional support to supplement the work of the early years setting. Parenting a child with SEND can be stressful, tiring and isolating: outreach services can help parents and carers to meet others facing similar issues, for social support, and can help with housing, financial and other challenges. Some families may be eligible for Disability Living Allowance (DLA), which can be complex to apply for. DLA helps families with the extra money they need to care for their child, and when their child is aged 3 or 4 years old they will also be eligible for the Disability Access Fund (DAF). DAF brings in over £900 of extra funding to their setting.

Early identification and specialist support for children with SEND can have positive, long-term benefits as Carneiro et al. (2024) demonstrate in their evaluation of Sure Start local programmes. Just as important, early intervention can boost children's wellbeing and enjoyment. For example, a child with communication delay might not always be able to communicate what they want and need with family members, or in their setting, and this can lead to angry, frustrated behaviour. With specialist help, the child might make strong progress in their speech to overcome that barrier or learn to use signs or symbols to communicate. As a result, they may feel less frustration, improving their wellbeing.

Bespoke assessment and planning

A culture of excessive assessment and paperwork is unhelpful, taking educators away from spending time interacting with the children. As the SEND assessment guidance and resources created by Dingley's Promise for the DfE (Dingley's Promise, 2024) states, 'for children with SEND, a simple and clear method of assessment to capture where children are, so that you can give them the right support at the right time, is essential'.

The overall monitoring of children's progress in a setting will highlight children who are not progressing well, so that educators can meet with parents, explore any possible background issues, and adapt their approach to offer extra support. A child who has delayed communication may benefit from more time in small groups and with 1:1 support from their key person, playing and sharing books together. If you learn from a discussion with parents that their child was born prematurely, it will be appropriate to adjust expectations in line with their prematurity. Other children may be 'looked after' and may have experienced several transitions from one foster carer to another. They will need more time and support to settle in and feel secure.

Where such adaptations are not effective, settings will need to undertake more detailed assessment and link with external professionals. A robust assessment tool can be especially helpful. For example, the Early Talk for York programme found that where settings were trained in using the Wellcomm speech and language toolkit, they made more accurate referrals to speech and language therapy.

Assessment on its own will not make a difference: it is vital to turn the insights from assessment into positive actions in the child's interests, using the 'Assess-Plan-Do-Review' cycle (see Figure 12.1). This is explained in the Progress Check at Age 2 (DfE, 2022b, p. 27).

It is important for each step of this to focus on the whole child – not just areas of concern – and to celebrate their progress as well as setting further targets. The more parents and carers are involved in co-creating plans, the more impact they will have: consistency across the home and setting will maximise the support for the child.

The 'Early Years SEND Assessment Guidance' (Dingley's Promise, 2024) helpfully includes specific examples of how to observe the learning of children with SEND, set goals, and create 'One Page Profiles' and 'Support and achievement play plans (SAPPs)'.

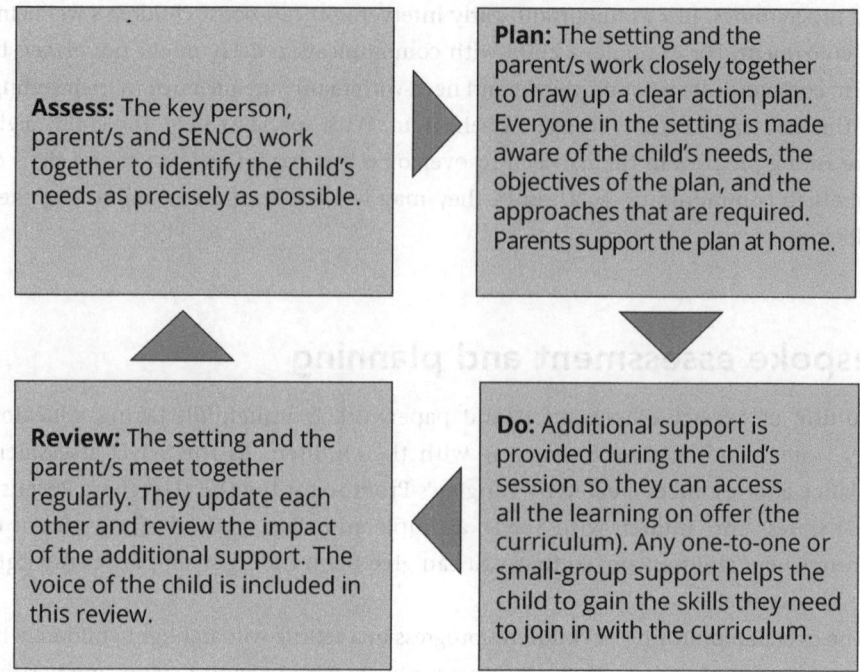

Assess: The key person, parent/s and SENCO work together to identify the child's needs as precisely as possible.

Plan: The setting and the parent/s work closely together to draw up a clear action plan. Everyone in the setting is made aware of the child's needs, the objectives of the plan, and the approaches that are required. Parents support the plan at home.

Review: The setting and the parent/s meet together regularly. They update each other and review the impact of the additional support. The voice of the child is included in this review.

Do: Additional support is provided during the child's session so they can access all the learning on offer (the curriculum). Any one-to-one or small-group support helps the child to gain the skills they need to join in with the curriculum.

Figure 12.1 The 'Assess-Plan-Do-Review' cycle

Access to a broad curriculum: Scaffolding

Children with SEND are at risk of experiencing a narrower curriculum and more negative interactions with adults. The Researching Effective Pedagogy in the Early Years (REPEY) study found that children who were described by practitioners as 'struggling' to learn did not experience the same broad curriculum as the other children. For example, they 'experienced double the amount of Personal and Social Education' (Siraj-Blatchford et al., 2002, p. 62). Whilst that focus may have been helpful, there will also have been a trade-off: the children will have experienced less time on other areas of learning. The 'struggling' children also received 'the most behaviour management interactions from adults', whilst those children whose learning was described 'as expected' received 'more social talk and caring interactions from the adults in their settings' (Siraj-Blatchford et al., 2002, p. 64).

It is important to consider how we might ensure that children with barriers to their learning receive the same level of social talk and caring interactions with adults. When children become frustrated and angry because they cannot do something, or cannot communicate their needs, it is important for educators to respond calmly (however frustrated we might feel ourselves!) and maintain a low-stress, caring environment. Research evidence also points to the importance of explicit teaching to help children recognise and name their emotions, and to help them learn to manage strong emotions.

A powerful technique to ensure that children with SEND can access the same broad curriculum as others is 'scaffolding'. The EEF explains that:

> Scaffolding involves providing temporary support for a child during a task, to adjust the level of challenge. This can include educators helping with elements of the task that are too difficult for the child to accomplish on their own. That means the child can concentrate on what they can do and gradually complete a challenging task.
>
> (EEF, 2024c)

For example, to help a child learn to use a knife, you might:

- put your hand over theirs, holding the knife together as you move it to cut food
- model: show the child how you cut with a knife, and then let them try
- prompt: remind the child to press down and move the knife backwards and forwards to cut

With regular encouragement and repetition, the child will gradually learn to cut. You could use similar techniques to help a child play with blocks, make models with Duplo, or mix flour and water to make playdough.

It used to be common to use the technique of 'differentiation' as the main way of supporting children with SEND. A 'differentiated curriculum' meant that children with SEND were given different, usually easier, activities to take part in. Whilst children with the most complex needs might need an individualised curriculum, for many other children with SEND the approach of 'differentiating down' can be accompanied by low expectations. As a result, they might miss out on lots of important learning. On the other hand, scaffolding can enable children with SEND to access a broad curriculum, so they have an equal chance to learn and thrive in the early years. You can see a practical example of this approach in the case study below.

Case Study 12.3

Inclusive Practice

Justin is autistic. He has limited language and communication, using sounds and gestures. He is very interested in cause-and-effect toys and the outdoors. Justin is self-directed, flitting from one activity to the next. His key person wants him to achieve one of the goals in the curriculum: to bake a bread roll.

This is not something that Justin is initially interested in, but his key person is ambitious about his potential. She starts by encouraging Justin over to the cooking area and helping him to mix two ingredients in a bowl. He does this with adult support,

(Continued)

following a visual timetable. Supported by his visual timetables, Justin spends time every day having a go at this first step towards the goal of baking a bread roll. With lots of repetition, hand over hand support, modelling and prompting, Justin completes this step independently. He is very proud of his new skill and moves confidently on to the next step.

This is an example of inclusive practice where careful sequencing is used to build the child's learning over time.

If the 'differentiating down' model had been used, Justin would have missed the opportunity to learn about baking a bread roll. It would have been seen as too difficult. Instead, Justin might only have followed his own lead and got involved in a narrower range of activities. He might have missed important early learning in physical development and understanding how substances change when you mix them together. This would *not* have been inclusive practice.

Self-evaluation

Becoming an inclusive setting is a process, not a one-off event, and it requires continuous attention. With each new cohort of children, there will be new challenges and different needs. Educators will need to keep practice under review and work collaboratively to find solutions to any problems which arise. As a leader or manager, it is important continuously to reflect on:

- How inclusive is your setting?
- Are you continuously working towards further improvement?

One way of doing this is by using a structured observation rating scale: 'The Inclusive Classroom Profile' or ICP (Soukakou, 2012). This is designed to assess the quality of the provision for children with identified special educational needs and disabilities. There are 12 items in the profile. Most of them are assessed through making direct observations, taking approximately three hours. These can be repeated throughout the year, enabling the setting to evaluate where they are doing well and where they can improve.

In addition, many local authorities offer professional development programmes to help settings develop their inclusive practice, often with an award once the programme is completed. If you are a school, you might consider applying for an Inclusive School Award, which uses a nationally recognised framework to celebrate the work you are doing to be inclusive.

Conclusion

Working towards true inclusion means embracing and celebrating differences, not seeing them as problems. Many of the approaches which are effective for children with

SEND, like scaffolding, are also positive for every child: inclusive practices benefit everyone.

Children grow and learn in different ways and at different speeds, so each child should be valued and supported to reach their potential. Strong relationships between children, parents and practitioners create the culture of respect and support in which every child can thrive.

However, it is also important to note the additional elements, beyond everyday high-quality practice, which can help children with SEND enjoy their time in the early years and make good progress. Examples include working closely with external professionals, and using careful, detailed assessment and planning that follows the 'Assess-Plan-Do-Review' model. A well-designed environment, together with effective use of specialist equipment, can help to remove barriers to participation.

The best inclusive practice puts the child at the heart of everyone's thinking and actions. Parents and carers, educators and other professionals work together in a spirit of learning and collaboration and attend to the child's 'voice' (however they tell us about their experiences, what they like and dislike). When inclusion breaks down, the child is not at the centre, but stuck in the middle. The professionals around them might blame each other when things go wrong, or try to offload their responsibilities to another agency or setting.

In this chapter, I am arguing that every child has the right to access and participate in a high-quality setting. Developing inclusive practice means being on a continuing journey to make that the reality for every child.

Reflective questions

1   Is your curriculum ambitious for all children with SEND?
2   How do you ensure that your provision is inclusive?
3   What do you do to include parents and carers when assessing children's learning?

13

Helping Children From Socio-Economically Disadvantaged Backgrounds to Access the Curriculum

Ed Vainker and Matilda Browne

Ensuring that the curriculum works for all is the priority for any school or setting. The success of a curriculum is determined by how well it serves the children who start the year furthest away from the intended destination. Over the last 10 years, we have sought to enable our children to flourish by working with their families and the wider community. Alongside this, we work on refining the experience they have when they come to our school. We are convinced that a curriculum that serves our children experiencing disadvantage will also be a curriculum that helps every child to blossom.

We believe that parents play a critical role in ensuring that all children can access the curriculum.

This chapter explores:

- the importance of the first 1,001 days
- the value of an effective induction
- approaches to supporting disadvantaged children in the early years

Getting to the starting line – The first 1,001 days

The opportunity to help children who experience disadvantage to access the curriculum and thrive in school (and beyond) begins at conception. At Reach in Feltham, we have developed a 'cradle to career' model, which seeks to support babies and parents right from the start. We have worked with hundreds of babies and their families in the first 1,001 days over the past five years, and our model is now being commissioned as part of the Hounslow Family Hub Start for Life offer.

Educators in the early years understand that public policy is far behind what we now know from science. The first thousand days are critical in ensuring that children flourish. However, that period is under-resourced, and parents face a postcode lottery in terms of their local offer.

Initially, our focus was on providing ante-natal education, based on the absence of this sort of support in Feltham. Over time, we have realised that positive, trusting relationships and fostering a sense of community are critical in supporting parents and their children. It is also crucial to hold parents in mind and notice what is going well in their parent–infant interactions. This helps parents to see their strengths and builds their confidence.

Informed by the inspiring work of sector-leaders such as the Association for Infant Mental Health UK and the Parent–Infant Foundation, we developed an offer focused on the first 1,001 days, which we have run in Feltham over the last five years.

Case Study 13.1

Invaluable Support for a Parent

Sweta and her husband moved to Feltham in 2019. They have two children: a 2-year-old boy, Shreyash, and a 3-month-old daughter, Saanvi. Sweta has not been able to go back to her work as a carer since the birth of their first child. She decided to stay home and take care of him due to his challenges and medical complications. Born prematurely, Shreyash used to cry all the time, frequently vomiting and sleeping poorly. As a first-time mother, with no local support network and no knowledge of how to deal with these challenges, Sweta found herself emotionally and physically exhausted, often on the brink of tears.

Health visitors referred her to Reach because of its diverse perinatal offer. Following an in-depth induction, the Hub's Perinatal Lead and Sweta opted to access some one-to-one sessions from the parent–infant team. Sweta commented how, at first, she was uncertain about what to expect from the sessions. She was also concerned about how she would be perceived, especially because her efforts to get Shreyash to play with her and enjoy time together were giving no results. However, slowly and gradually, with some one-to-one guidance, Sweta reported significant positive change. She noted that she began to feel more relaxed and that Shreyash seemed more connected to her. She described how she found the sessions a 'huge source of support'.

Sweta comments, 'He never used to come and kiss and hug me, well, maybe once in a blue moon. I used to kiss him and he used to get irritated but now he is coming to me more often and he wants me to play with him. ... I have gained a much better understanding of how to communicate with my children and learnt to see what entertains them the most.'

Sweta says that, right from the start, she implemented the suggestions and ideas from the sessions and 'from the very next day things started to change'. Sweta's determination saw an increase in playing together time from 1 minute to 20 minutes per session and significant positive change in their relationship together. Sweta has continued to access support from Reach in Feltham.

In our experience, it is this sort of support that enables parents to help their children, regardless of their starting points. We celebrate 'serve and return' interactions: a term that refers to carers being sensitive and responsive to their young child's signals and needs. Such positive interactions help build the healthy infant brain. Equally, they reduce stress levels that have the potential to be toxic and impact negatively on the baby.

Starting to support parents at this very early stage is unusual. We are now working with schools around the country who are building their own 'cradle to career' models, including a more strategic role in supporting in the first 1,001 days. Schools and early years settings are anchor institutions in communities. We are trusted, embedded and universal, and can play an important role in this critical period of a child's development.

Inducting a new cohort into our settings

This focus on strong relationships with families remains a critical element of our work as we move into the EYFS. Supporting our students who experience disadvantage to access the curriculum begins with fostering a relationship of trust with parents and carers. This section explores how we build that trust, seek to develop a shared understanding and, ultimately, aim to build capacity in parents.

We take the induction of families seriously. Whether moving into nursery or Reception, we visit every child in their home where we aim to build the relationship, share elements of our approach and take a detailed biography of the child. Home visits are key for learning from the parent or carer about their child. If we understand a child's context, we are more able to develop a curriculum to support them. Our induction ensures that we are reflecting their reality as well as pursuing a breadth of knowledge. This happens through a range of settling-in activities in the classroom, and opportunities throughout the summer to build confidence and familiarity with the staff and setting.

From there, we invest in ensuring that parents have a clear understanding of the purpose of the EYFS – including the Prime Areas and the Characteristics of Effective Learning. We have found that parents sometimes have a narrow understanding of school readiness, so this is useful and important.

—Case Study 13.2—

Supporting a Parent to Understand Play

Sylvia joined our 2-year-old cohort in September 2021. When she joined, Anna, her mum, explained that she was very advanced for her age. Sylvia is the youngest in a family of six siblings. Her attendance was poor, so we met Anna to discuss Sylvia. Anna explained that she did not see the need for nursery as Sylvia was a fluent speaker, knew all her numbers and was confident in talking about the world around her. All this was true. However, Sylvia had difficulty playing with other children, consistently leaning on adult support. She also struggled to tolerate delay. We thought it would be beneficial for Anna to gain a clearer understanding of the value of the early years. We spent time jointly observing Sylvia in play and talking about her strengths and areas of weakness. Through doing this, Anna felt more involved in the nursery, had a greater understanding of our curriculum and was ready to work in partnership to support Sylvia's outcomes across the EYFS.

Our final priority is building parental capacity. We have seen a strong positive impact on children's outcomes from our work with parents. At Reach, this includes delivering the Family Links parenting programme which supports families with two areas that are priorities in our classrooms: clear communication and strong routines. The programme builds parental capacity and fosters further alignment between home and school.

In the classroom

We have the difficult job, as educators, to create a parity of experience in our classrooms, in turn supporting strong outcomes for all. This requires a balance between fostering children's interests and identifying the key skills and knowledge they need to engage in higher-quality play and more meaningful experiences.

Both children presented in Table 13.1 are classic examples of those joining EYFS classrooms all over the country. The assessment information does not tell you a huge amount about each of them as a person. The information does, however, give you an idea of the language that they may arrive in the setting with; the skills that they may have honed; the experiences that they have had. We need a curriculum to challenge both these children. In the case of Child A, we need to provide access to the knowledge that Child B has collated through their lived experience.

Table 13.1   Information about two children at Reach in Feltham from their home visit forms

Child	At home I enjoy	I have visited	I have been on a	I can/am learning to
Child A	watching TV, playing video games	park	train	ride a bike
Child B	cooking/baking, drawing/painting, building things, reading stories, listening to music, watching television, dancing, feeding birds & animals	zoo, farm, aquarium, beach, central London (or another big city), museum, park	train, bus, boat, aeroplane	ride a bike, swim, use a climbing frame, catch a ball

In this section, we will break down one of those experiences.

Visiting a zoo involves:

- the journey there
- the entrance process
- seeing the animals
- noticing the habitats of the animals
- hearing the noises the animals make
- having lunch
- going on the climbing frame
- the journey back
- recounting their experiences, the following day

As educators of children who experience disadvantage, we need to break down an event like visiting the zoo and consider how we can ensure that all children can access this bank of knowledge and skills. In some cases, we might reproduce the experience. In other cases, our teaching and input will need to suffice.

Why? Because, for example, imagine these same two children listening to the story *Dear Zoo* (Campbell, 2010), an EYFS classic. Unless the educator understands the curriculum and has proactively planned to close these gaps, Child B will get a lot more out of it than Child A. The gap, consequently, widens. It is for this reason that educator interactions in play are so important.

In our setting, we discuss children's learning as a diet tailored to the needs of the specific child. Some children may need further:

- instruction in play
- interaction with educators
- focus on key vocabulary
- introduction to the new elements of the experience
- teaching of important knowledge

What we are not saying is that Child A will not learn from Child B and vice versa; of course they will. But because we have a responsibility for ensuring the progress of *all* children, we cannot rely on happenstance. We must be intentional in everything we do to ensure that no child is left behind.

Through this intentionality in the classroom, along with creative, proactive work to support parents and the wider community, we can ensure that all children are able to access the curriculum and flourish. All regardless of their background.

Reflective questions

1   Why is getting to know the children we work with so important when it comes to curriculum?
2   How can we ensure that the curriculum is not based on what most children already know or have experienced?

14

Valuing Outdoor Learning

Sarah Porter

I grew up in a town and then a village. I was lucky to be able to roam through woods and fields and walk to the village on my own. I remember crossing streams, building dams, making dens and arriving home to tell my parents all about it. My memories of exploring the world around me are vivid. They make me who I am and have helped to form my values as an educator.

Most of my teaching career has been in towns and cities. One of the most exciting parts of this has been learning with children and families outdoors. Whether in a built-up urban environment or a rural one, children can get outside to explore their natural surroundings.

Early in my career, I worked in a setting with an amazing baby room where the babies could explore freely, crawling outside into the garden. If babies and young children are to learn the difference between earth and grass, they need to see and touch it. It is never too early for direct interaction with the physical world.

My recent experience includes working with families who have been housed temporarily in hotels and B&Bs, in collaboration with the Magpie Project. The Magpie Project is a charity in the London Borough of Newham that supports mothers and children under 5 who are in poverty and at risk of homelessness. These experiences have made me realise that although we encourage all parents to go outside with their children, we must consider each family individually. For some families it is easier than for others.

Exploring nature and physical development

Friedrich Froebel, the 19th century German educator, developed a set of underlying principles for his kindergartens. One of these was *engaging with nature*, placing strong emphasis on the importance of outdoor play. This has inspired the tradition of the nursery garden. Froebel states that nothing unites educators and children more than gaining an intimate knowledge of nature together, which he calls the 'conjoint study of nature' (Froebel, 1912, p. 101).

It is also important to note the key difference between learning outdoors and taking learning outside. Learning outdoors means engaging with the environment and developing a deep and unhurried relationship with nature. Taking learning outside is just going outdoors to do what is usually done inside – for instance, sitting at a table and mark-making.

There are many ways for children to relate to their outdoor environment. Adults and children can go for a walk, observing and talking about nature. Babies may point at something that catches their eye, like a bird or a dog. Froebel urges educators not to 'drive children like sheep' when they are outdoors, nor 'lead them like soldiers'. Instead, he argues for a slower and more appreciative approach, 'pointing out to them whatever nature or the season offers' (Froebel, 1912, p. 101).

Taking risks

Toddlers begin to test their physical abilities outdoors. They try out different surfaces, noticing how they have specific properties that require particular skills. They work out how to keep their balance on grass, paving slabs and slopes.

Recently, I rang a parent to say their child, Lily, had got a minor bump on her head when playing on the monkey bars. The parent said that every day Lily came home talking about 'trying to be as good as her friend'. Lily was doing her best to achieve this. The parent understood how important this was to Lily and how it meant challenging herself and taking risks. Her main concern was that her little bump didn't stop Lily from trying.

The high levels of motivation young children can show when trying to master a skill outside is fascinating and will support their learning in other areas of the curriculum.

In the case study below, Honey Kaur, a childminder in Newham, describes how giving her key child opportunities to explore outside supported his learning.

──Case Study 14.1──

The Great Outdoors, by Honey Kaur

Jamal, aged 18 months, returned from a summer break having taken his first steps. He showed no fear, quite the opposite. He wanted to delve into everything and anything outdoors. This was new for Jamal – and wonderful to see. It highlighted to us the importance of having an inviting outdoor space.

Before the summer, Jamal had been irritable and frustrated during most of his interactions and play. He struggled to sit in the highchair and despised being in the pushchair. Now, able to be more independent, Jamal's curiosity came into its own: he was enjoying outdoor adventures. As soon as Jamal went outdoors his eyes lit up. He was excited to see the tuff tray filled with sand, the mud kitchen topped with soil, buckets and spades and an array of kitchen utensils. Jamal's favourite was the water area. He wanted to splash in it, bath in it, drink it and fill anything he could find.

For Jamal, the outdoors was a place where he felt able to explore, avidly using a range of resources from plants to huge tyres. He touched, smelt, climbed, crawled, tested out and created.

As the weeks went by, Jamal's walking became stronger and his gross motor skills progressed – he was climbing large tree stumps, lifting his legs and heaving his body up. Throughout this time, we showed our interest in Jamal's play by following his lead and gently commenting on what he was doing. He responded well, smiling and making eye contact.

We shared Jamal's newfound curiosities and interactions with his family. His mum was happy to see that the outdoors enabled him to be calm and free. She explained that he needed this for his wellbeing as they live in a busy household with extended family. It is so important to have an outdoor area that has been well thought out – many of our children have similar home experiences to Jamal's.

It was a warm summer and Jamal was spending most of the day outdoors, so we needed to keep him safe. Water play was ideal for helping him to stay cool.

We also made sure that:

- there were shaded areas
- he drank enough water
- we applied sunscreen
- he wore a sun hat – though Jamal often chose to wear the firefighter helmet!

Over time, Jamal's parents shared their concerns that he was not developing as quickly as other children: not talking as much or able to sit still for long. I felt it was important to acknowledge these whilst also sharing with them all the learning that Jamal was engaging in and the progress he was making. I spoke about how Jamal was:

- investigating his curiosities
- focusing and sustaining his attention
- developing his gross motor skills
- problem-solving: when Jamal found a wheelbarrow in the way of his play, he persisted until he found a way to manoeuvre around it

I explained how we were working with Jamal on further developing each of these aspects of learning, as well as supporting his communication.

In our setting there are no time constraints on how long the children spend outdoors. Come rain or shine, Jamal knows that he can take his time to explore, absorb and further his learning.

It's a joyous experience for us all.

The interconnected curriculum

The Early Years Foundation Stage (EYFS) states that 'all areas of learning and development are important and inter-connected' (DfE, 2025, p. 8). This seems particularly true of learning outside.

A child stirring a pot of soil and water in the mud kitchen may add some leaves as they fall off the trees. The pebbles and sticks they collect for the pot will be different sizes and shapes. They may look up at the trees and notice the wind blowing the branches. It will be more meaningful if an interested educator joins in, talking about how we notice and experience the seasons and the wind.

Children also begin to focus on tiny objects when spending time outdoors. They find small pebbles, daisies and blades of grass. Reaching for these and picking them up supports their fine motor skills.

Outdoor activities often enable children to become deeply involved in their learning.

Case Study 14.2

A Persistent Learner

I watched a curious 3-year-old spend an entire morning devising a system of gutters and pipes. Fully absorbed, he was attempting to link them together to run water into the sandpit. Although the system fell apart several times, he persisted. In the end, he was able to pour water down the pipes and watch it travel along the gutter into the sandpit.

· This child was an active learner, following his interests with a project in mind. He persisted in his aim, not deterred by setbacks. He was learning about the natural materials which make the world around him. He was discovering how they behave and can change.

The way that an educator responds to children exploring outside can often impact on the quality of the learning experience. The educator needs to understand what is happening by carefully observing the children and tuning in to what they are doing. Through doing this, the educator can scaffold the child's learning through conversation and interaction.

Case Study 14.3

New Vocabulary for New Ideas

Recently, in the nursery garden, I observed an educator watching a group of two children working together to lift a large heavy plank off an A frame and reposition it at a steeper angle. I was interested to see how she would respond to the children.

She approached them and watched for a minute or two as they tried out the slide at a steeper angle. She then went over to talk about why they had moved the slide. The children were excited to tell her, 'it makes us go faster'. The educator sensitively responded, agreeing they had placed the plank at a steeper angle and that meant they would slide faster down it.

The children and educator discussed how the plank at a less steep angle had not been so much fun because they had gone down slowly. The educator's response was sensitive. She moved close to check the children were safe and tuned into their thinking to appreciate that they were testing out an idea. As a result, she was able to extend the children's learning by discussing the angles the plank was placed at and how that influenced objects and people travelling down it! She offered new vocabulary to the children to help them articulate their ideas.

Gardening

> Through gardening children experience the cycles of life and death, growth and decay.
>
> (Tovey, 2016, p. 65)

Gardening outside is a very different prospect to growing seeds inside. Though inside gardening is valuable, it is not as rich. When digging over a raised bed outside, children come across worms, spiders and beetles. They get to know the names of the creatures they find and talk about them. Conversations are endless.

Planting seeds, bulbs and vegetables is a sustained activity. The children need to water and check on their plants several days a week. Some may predict what might happen and test it out. The links between time and nature become apparent. Children recognise that growing is a process with its own timeline: it cannot be rushed.

Gardening can also provide a connection between home and school. I was planting seeds with some 2-year-olds in the spring. Amina was keen and planted several pots of seeds. She whispered something to me. My Bengali-speaking colleague translated this as 'Grandma'. Later, when I asked her mum, she said Amina regularly helped her grandma in the garden – she was clearly keen to tell me that gardening was an important part of her home life.

Observing cycles of growth in the garden can lead to an understanding of where food comes from. Children can eat the lettuce, tomatoes and potatoes they planted: they see that food has origins. They can learn that the yams and okra they see at the market are the end products of a long process.

Managing a small outdoor space

Learning outside can be challenging in a setting with little outside space, or none. However, nurseries and childminders can be creative, even on a tight budget. A childminder linked to our nursery school has a friend with an allotment, so she takes the children there to observe the seasonal changes. Even a tiny nursery garden or a childminder's patio can have a small mud kitchen.

Life and death

Tovey describes how being outside can lead to children observing 'life and death' (Tovey, 2016, p. 65).

One summer a few years ago, a beautiful starling flew into a glass door in the nursery and died instantly. The site supervisor picked it up and asked us if the children would like to see it. The children were engrossed by this beautiful bird, asking lots of questions.

Children are often reflective about death, wanting to understand what has happened. For example, they asked if the bird could still see and fly. Death is integral to learning about the cycle of life.

One of the ways that the children learn about the lifecycle is by observing our nursery pond and a second pond in the neighbourhood. Frogs typically lay their spawn on mild, sunny days in early spring, and the children often witness this event. The pond becomes lively with the sounds of croaking frogs, followed by clusters of gelatinous spawn. Over the following weeks, the children observe the remarkable metamorphosis as the embryos develop into wriggling tadpoles, then grow legs to become froglets, before finally maturing into adult frogs.

We always let families know if we have discussions involving death in case the children have questions they want to pursue at home.

Sensory learning

Being outside provides a wealth of sensory experiences. Splashing in puddles is fun and also enables children to learn about how water behaves. They see how it feels and what effects they have on it.

Simply planting a few pots of herbs can provide a range of smells. Coming up with words to describe these smells, supported by the educator's input, extends children's language skills.

Feeling the smoothness of pebbles and the prickles of plants attunes children to natural textures. Finding words for what they feel like and comparing them to other objects helps children to use more elaborate forms of language.

Even in urban environments, there are moments of wonder that adults and children can enjoy. For example, they can smell an East London bluebell wood and see the colours of a red admiral butterfly.

Connecting with the local environment

Using the area around you as an outdoor learning resource is important. Babies and toddlers can find a walk around the block interesting, especially on a rainy day. They watch rainwater run down a drain, stamp through puddles and listen to sounds.

One small setting near us made connections with a community garden. The children went there to do some planting and then care for their plants. The daily walk also gave them a chance to notice their local environment. It is important for young children to feel that they are part of the area they live in and have a voice there.

During a woodwork project we made weekly visits to a local hardware shop where the staff greeted us in a friendly manner, recognising that we had visited before. We often visit a local shop specialising in Caribbean fruit and vegetables. The people serving in the shop chat to the children and show them fruit and vegetables they may not have seen before. This is part of understanding what it is to live in a community – the children can contribute their own family and cultural experiences as an important part of the conversation.

If you let parents know that the children have visited shops or different areas in the community, they will be more likely to have conversations with their children about it, perhaps revisiting them.

Working with parents

Many parents will be happy that their child is learning about the outdoors. Some may struggle, worrying they will get dirty, cold or sick or hurt themselves and get lost. It is important to listen to parents' concerns and try to reassure them.

Explaining the learning that goes on outside can be encouraging, as can sharing how you plan and assess risks. Parents often feel more confident if they join in one day and see what goes on for themselves. Sharing photos and videos and talking to parents about their own memories of outdoor learning can also help gain their trust.

It is important to consider each family's unique situation. Jane Williams, CEO of the Magpie Project, highlighted the challenges faced by families living in temporary accommodation to me (Williams, 2023). For example, families in hotels/B&Bs might not have access to washing and drying facilities. This made me consider families in my setting who are in a similar position and how difficult it must be for them to be presented with a bag of wet muddy clothing by the nursery and told that the child had a wonderful time in the mud kitchen.

Some families of children who have special educational needs and disabilities (SEND) may also find outdoor learning challenging. Many don't feel confident taking their children to playgrounds at the weekend.

We need to be sensitive to such families and always consider the unique circumstances of each child.

Trying to respond to families living with challenging circumstances, we used a research grant from the Froebel Trust to run Saturday Forest School sessions. The project started in autumn 2022 and is still going. We planned the project to minimise stress for families, so it was in the afternoon, and it did not matter if you arrived late. Siblings were welcome. We gave high-quality wet weather clothing to all families. We cooked together around a fire and if we went out, we provided snacks. We kept the door open to one of the nursery rooms, so that if children felt uncomfortable being outside, they could go in.

It was so wonderful to see families being able to enjoy a supportive space where we could welcome and value them. Cooking and eating together became a way of sharing and connecting.

The Froebel Trust made a short film about this project, *Family Time in Nature*, which you can see on their website (Froebel Trust, 2024).

One of the children attending the project was 3-year-old Saad, a child with autism. You can read about his experiences in the case study below.

—Case Study 14.4—

Saturday Forest School

Saad participated in the Saturday Forest School project along with his mum and sister. His sister initially came along to help with translation, but she really enjoyed it so she continued to come. Saad's mum and sister said they didn't take him outside much at weekends as they were worried he would get dysregulated. They came regularly and Saad's mum helped with the fire on days when we cooked outside.

After a few weeks, Saad's mum and sister told Nadia, the Forest School lead, that they noticed Saad was calmer and happier when he was outside. Nadia suggested some activities they could do when the project was not running. The family reported back that, having seen Saad playing with leaves on one of the project days, they took him to the park at the weekend where he explored various leaves. They shared pictures.

Towards the end of the project, Saad's mum and sister took him out regularly at weekends and felt more confident about it. Staff in nursery also noticed that Saad was happier to play with mud and other messy sensory experiences after attending the project.

The locality and further afield: Forest and Beach Schools

Babies are aware of their immediate family and their home. As they develop, they become more aware of the wider world. They get to know nursery staff, familiar shops and routes in their community.

Early years settings can give *all* children opportunities to explore their local community. We can visit parks and community gardens, inviting families along too.

Forest School is a powerful way for children to access local wooded areas. They climb trees, gather conkers, make dens and sit around a fire. All these, and more, contribute to their understanding of the world around them. Forest School can help develop their confidence and social, physical and communication skills.

For some children, it is totally new, so they may feel wary. The clear structure of Forest School, the expertise of trained leaders and regular visits help them feel safe. It is important that Forest School is inclusive: *all* children must be part of it.

In my setting, Forest School has piqued the interest of several educators so much that many have trained as Forest School leaders. In the following case study, Adam Mohamed from Sheringham Nursery School picks up on a valuable aspect of Forest School.

Case Study 14.5

Walking and Talking, by Adam Mohamed

At Sheringham Nursery School and Children's Centre in Newham, children take part in Forest School sessions in the local park. Rich communication and language opportunities are integral to all aspects of this, from the moment we leave the nursery gate.

Our journeys to and from Forest School provide wonderful chances to talk with the children. We let the children initiate conversation wherever possible, though sometimes we start a conversation if the child is not confident or able to. We then try to follow their lead as much as possible as we talk and walk.

Rather than thinking of our walks as a means to an end, we prioritise them as times when important learning happens. We have discussions prompted by the number of bicycles we see, interesting buildings, builders at work, the weather, the directions we take and the sounds we hear.

One day, a child noticed a shoe on the ground. We encouraged the children to think about where it might have come from.

Samira: Look, a shoe!

Adam: Oh yes, it's a shoe. It's not mine because I have both of my shoes. I wonder how it got here?

Samira: Maybe someone lost it?

Adam: Everyone, check if you lost your shoe!

Abdul: It's big.

Adam: Yes, it is a big shoe. Too big for you.

Laila: Maybe a giant lost his shoe.

Adam: Oh no, poor giant. The giant has only one shoe. I wonder if the other shoe is here?

(Continued)

Laila: He is angry because he lost his shoe.

Samira: No, he lost shoe. Other shoe not here.

Adam: Everyone, Laila thinks the giant is angry because he lost his shoe. How could we help? Where could the other shoe be?

Abdul: He has shoe. He lost one shoes. Oh no.

Adam: We could leave the shoe next to the gate.

Laila: Yeah, he can find it.

Adam: We can see if the shoe is still there next week.

During our next trip to the park the children kept an eye out for the shoe. When they spotted it in a slightly different location, they recalled their story and developed it. 'Maybe the giant has got new shoes now?'

Not every walk to Forest School will involve a lost shoe or upset giant, but each and every one can involve rich conversation. The destination is important and exciting, but educators must be sure not to miss out on the huge gains of talking whilst we walk.

Beach School is less familiar than Forest School, and especially valuable because the beach presents a unique landscape and skyline. This may be entirely new to many children; others may only have visited a crowded beach in the summer. A beach in winter has a different feel. You hear birds and have a clear view out to sea. You have more space to find seaweed, shells and sea creatures. You can make large patterns in the sand.

During our beach visits, I have watched children fully absorbed in the environment. They develop their own games, dig, throw stones into the sea and collect objects. One day we were taken aback by the high tide, so had to stay on the promenade. The children were completely enthralled by the power of the waves crashing on the wall.

To sum up, all children must be given the chance to engage with the excitement and pleasure of the outdoors. This will open up a whole new world to them: one of joy and abundant learning. No one should miss out on this.

Reflective questions

1   Can you think of three specific ways in which you support children and families with learning about the natural world?

2   How would you support a child in insecure housing and with limited washing facilities to take part in outdoor play?

15

Professional Development

Developing Quality and Improving Outcomes for Every Child

Siobhan Campbell and Melissa Prendergast

Introduction

Investing in early education and care is one of the most powerful levers we have to improve equity: high-quality provision is positive for every child, but the benefits for disadvantaged children are greater (Melhuish and Gardiner, 2021). However, as Kathy Sylva and Naomi Eisenstadt (2024) argue, achieving the sort of quality that can change children's life chances for the better requires a sophisticated understanding of early education:

> The early years are no longer viewed as a time only for play and socialising but as a unique phase of learning which demands skilled educators who understand child development as well as developmentally appropriate practice.

> (Sylva and Eisenstadt, 2024, pp. 6–7)

In this chapter, we will be explaining how settings and schools can design sustained, high-quality professional development and put it into action. That way, they can ensure that educators will develop both their understanding of child development and the practices and pedagogical skills which help all children to thrive, especially those experiencing disadvantage. Professional development is only worthwhile if it leads to positive changes in everyday practice. As Sylva and Eisenstadt explain, 'it is this increasing emphasis on what practitioners "do" (pedagogy) and not only "what they have" (resources and the environment) that should be the driving force in future provision' (Sylva and Eisenstadt, 2024, p. 16).

Throughout this chapter, we are drawing a distinction between the type of professional development that enables settings and schools to keep developing quality, and other approaches which are much less likely to have any impact.

Lots of us spend time reading and researching, both in books and online, and trying new practices. Whilst this can create a strong culture of thoughtful and reflective practice, the effect of our actions as individual educators will be limited.

We might also feel comfortable with the 'easy to action' tips we gather from colleagues and the publications we read. But where is the evidence for these tips and tricks we pick up along the way? What is the point of them unless they lead to improvement in our practice and to better outcomes?

We might also enjoy a conference or a training day and then come back to our setting and 'cascade' what we have learnt. Whatever the quality of the day we attended, it is highly unlikely that our compressed account will give our colleagues the full range of information and insights they need.

The activities in which we invest time, energy and financial resources should have a positive impact on our children. They should help us to provide high-quality provision, improve outcomes and narrow the disadvantage gap. For that reason, we need to place research evidence at the heart of professional development by:

1 Ensuring that the content of training is evidence-informed and, where possible, has been trialled in many different types of setting. We want to focus our efforts on the approaches which are most likely to work and make a positive difference.

2 Designing and delivering training which is engaging, encourages participants to reflect on their practice, and sets out a pathway for everyone to make sustained changes in their practice.

This chapter will support you to make informed decisions about the professional development you invest in. It will help you identify the features of professional development that make it effective and 'lasting'. No single programme or form of professional development works in the same way in all contexts. We will highlight resources that will support you to adapt professional development to optimally suit your context and respond to the unique needs of your setting.

Effective professional development

It is important to be clear about what we mean by professional development. We can draw on the evidence review for the Fostering Effective Early Learning (FEEL) study, which offers the following definition:

> Professional development applies to a range of activities which attempt to increase the knowledge, skills, and/or attitudes of ECEC [Early Childhood Education and Care] educators working with young children and their families/ carers. Ultimately, through supporting educators and their practice, the long-term aim of professional development is to enhance the children's personal, social, behavioural and cognitive outcomes.
>
> (Siraj et al., 2016, p. 21)

By improving our knowledge, skills and practice, we can develop the quality of our pro-vision, leading in turn to better outcomes for children.

It is also worth defining what we *don't* mean by professional development. There are many activities in a school or setting which are useful but are not examples of profes-sional development: for example, briefing meetings, sharing an updated policy on late collection, or handing out planning for the week. Similarly, a training day or a confer-ence keynote might be engaging, entertaining and an all-round positive experience for everyone attending. But if, at the end of all the activities, participants have not increased their knowledge or improved their pedagogical skills, no real 'professional development' has occurred. If the information behind the activities is unsound, the impact may even be negative. For example, the training programme for 'Brain Gym' was excellent, leading many schools to adopt the approach. However, there is no evi-dence that Brain Gym improves children's learning, leading Ofsted to describe it in 2018 as a 'gimmick' (Weale, 2018). The time spent on gimmicky programmes takes time away from approaches that might benefit children, leading to a negative impact if we are not careful.

To help us to avoid these pitfalls, the Education Endowment Foundation's guidance report *Effective Professional Development* (EEF, 2021) argues for a 'balanced design' which includes 14 mechanisms grouped into four categories:

a   Building Knowledge
   i   Managing cognitive load
   ii   Revisiting prior learning
b   Motivating Teachers
   i   Setting and agreeing on goals
   ii   Presenting information from a credible source
   iii   Providing affirmation and reinforcement after progress

    c   Developing Teaching Techniques
        i   Instructing teachers on how to perform a technique
        ii   Arranging social support
        iii Modelling the technique
        iv Monitoring and providing feedback
        v   Rehearsing the technique

    d   Embedding Practice
        i   Providing prompts and cues
        ii   Prompting action planning
        iii Encouraging monitoring
        iv Prompting context-specific repetition

(EEF, 2021)

The EEF's *Guide to Effective Professional Development in the Early Years* (2023b, p. 6) shines a spotlight on five of the key mechanisms and recommends that 'when early years settings consider attending, designing, or providing professional development they ensure it encompasses the four areas and at least one mechanism in each area. The more mechanisms included, the more likely the professional development will lead to improved outcomes for children.'

    The five spotlights are:

1   *Building knowledge: managing cognitive load.* Professional development should include information that is clearly presented, with time for discussion and reflection. Participants should not be bombarded and subjected to 'information overload'.

2   *Motivating educators: presenting information from a credible source.* The information at the heart of professional development should be rooted in research evidence and therefore most likely to support practice development. Knowing that what you are learning will help to develop the quality of your setting is highly motivating: you are not wasting your time on gimmicks.

3   *Developing teaching techniques: arranging social support.* It is hard to change practice, especially when you have been doing things in a particular way for a long time. So the opportunity for educators to observe each other, provide sensitive feedback and reflect on making changes together is invaluable. It can ensure that changes in practice stick, rather than being forgotten about a few months after the training sessions.

4   *Embedding practice: providing prompts and cues.* Educators are always busy, so a brief memory-aid or prompt can be very helpful. For example, the four-step ShREC approach helps educators to become more specific and intentional in their practice when developing conversations with children. It encourages educators to pause, be thoughtful and follow each of the four evidence-informed steps to

improve children's communication. In time, following these steps becomes automatic, but the prompts are helpful at the start of the journey to change practice.

5   *Embedding practice: prompting action planning.* Learning about the impact of interactive reading and how to put effective practices into action ensures that educators have the key knowledge they need. However, making sure that happens may require a brief action plan: for example, which books to share in the two weeks ahead, when to read them, and which children to include.

Case Study 15.1

Early Years Conversation Project (EYCP)

You can see the 'arranging social support' mechanism in action in the Early Years Conversation Project (EYCP). The EYCP is a programme of professional development to develop the practice of educators working with 2-year-olds in order to improve their communication and language development

Video reflection is a key element of the EYCP. The programme aims to develop educators' knowledge and pedagogical practices and in particular the use of the ShREC approach (James, 2022) so that it becomes so natural that it is the educators' 'way of being'. During support visits from a mentor, the educator is filmed using the ShREC strategies whilst sharing a picture book with a child or small group. The mentor is then filmed modelling the strategies whilst engaging in interactive reading. This is followed by a structured reflection on the videos and a professional conversation. The mentor supports the educator to develop their skills in noticing the strategies they were using, naming them and then analysing the effect they had on the child/ren. Next steps are then identified for the adults and the child/ren. Using the strategies over and over again in the same context of interactive reading allows the educator to hone their skills. Watching themselves using the strategies and analysing the impact helps them connect the theoretical knowledge they learnt on the programme with the behaviour they need to enact to make an impact on children's outcomes.

Supporting intentional and relational pedagogy as the route to quality

Iram Siraj and colleagues argue that 'PD programmes seeking to enhance effective teaching and learning should combine relational and intentional pedagogies to improve teacher–child interactions and child development outcomes' (Siraj et al., 2023, p. 2). This is highly skilled work that requires ongoing, high-quality professional development.

Intentional pedagogy is a deliberate and purposeful approach to teaching in which educators actively design and support learning experiences that foster children's development across cognitive, emotional and social domains. This approach helps the children to acquire the skills, dispositions and knowledge they need to succeed in education and later life (Kingston and Siraj, 2017). Intentional educators do not leave learning to chance. They plan for all aspects of learning across the pedagogical continuum (EEF, 2023c, p. 1), both inside and outside, and during every moment in the day. This includes ensuring that routines and transitions are purposeful opportunities for learning and not dominated by procedural talk from adults and quiet compliance from children. As Epstein (2007, p. 3) says, 'each type of experience takes advantage of planned as well as spontaneous, unexpected learning opportunities'.

Relational pedagogy involves building strong, trusting relationships with all children within a class or room and supporting positive relationships between them (Siraj et al., 2023). As Baker (2024) suggests, 'skills to support children's positive relationships with adults should be prioritized, because relationships matter for children's general development, their engagement in learning and for their academic outcomes'.

This highlights the need to equally value and support both the care *and* education elements of our work. Further to this, it is important to integrate the development of intentional and relational pedagogy, with the educator's knowledge of how children develop and learn in different areas, such as communication and language, mathematical concept development and self-regulation. When intentional and relational pedagogy are combined with knowledge of child development and the content of the curriculum, educators' practice improves (Siraj et al., 2023). This allows educators to apply powerful pedagogical strategies to support any type of learning in any context throughout the day – indoors or outdoors, when changing a nappy or sharing a book. It ensures educators scaffold children's learning at just the right level and in just the right way to extend it.

However, despite this evidence of the importance of integrating different aspects of understanding and practice, Huang et al. (2024) found that professional development for early years educators tends to focus on aspects of teaching or child development in isolation. The authors suggest:

> ... this segmentation can compromise their practice sustainability, given that early childhood teachers manage diverse curricula and oversee holistic child development. It is essential to recognize that teaching is multifaceted, characterized by the continuous interplay of various domains of knowledge. As such, a more integrative PD approach, combining domain-specific instruction and broader interaction techniques, is crucial for advancing quality teaching.
>
> (Huang et al., 2024, p. 1353)

In brief, we have clear evidence about the holistic and integrated nature of quality. But, it is challenging to pull it all together to inform decisions about the specific professional development our teams need. Fortunately, there is a set of tools that can help.

The Curriculum, Leadership and Interaction Quality Rating Scales (CLIQRS) are a family of assessment tools designed to evaluate and enhance the quality of early childhood education provision for children aged from 2 to 6 years. Developed by experts in the field, including Professors Iram Siraj, Edward Melhuish and Kathy Sylva, these scales focus on various aspects of early education and care including the quality of environment, curriculum and pedagogy. They include consideration of relational and intentional quality and the quality of interactions. These tools allow leaders and educators to self-evaluate, providing results that will identify where improvements need to be made. The CLIQRS are evidence-informed tools that reduce the subjectivity and potentially personal nature of educator improvement. Not only that, the CLIQRS tools have predictive validity because they assess key elements of early childhood education that research has shown to directly influence children's cognitive, social and emotional development. Using CLIQRS to inform your professional development programmes will lead to positive outcomes for the children in your care.

Video reflection as a tool for bridging the 'knowing–doing' gap

Professional development needs to focus beyond just building knowledge. Educators need to be supported to put their knowledge into action by developing 'procedural knowledge' (Mathers, 2021).

Effective teaching requires educators to know what they intend children to learn (curriculum) and how they intend to explain that content to the children (pedagogy). Educators' knowledge of pedagogy can then be divided further into declarative (knowing that) and procedural (knowing how). For example, in the teaching of early maths, an educator will know how to count (declarative knowledge): remembering the sequence of numbers, using one count word for each object, and knowing that the last number they say tells them the number in the set. If you don't know how to count, you cannot teach children how to count. However, this declarative knowledge only takes the educator part of the way to success. They also need to know the pedagogical practices which will help children to learn how to count (procedural knowledge). If you imagine an educator counting five ducks with a child, they might use the practices of emphasis (explicitly pointing to each duck in turn as they count up) and gestures (making a circular gesture encompassing the whole set of ducks when saying 'so we've got five ducks'). Both declarative and procedural knowledge are required for expert practice.

In her research, Mathers found that educators' knowledge of language-supporting strategies predicted the quality of their practice. However, simply knowing the strategies and identifying them in video clips of interactions between adults and children was not enough. It was crucial that educators knew *why* they might be effective. Her study found that the children who made the most progress had educators who connected their knowledge of pedagogy with their knowledge of child development and could explain why a strategy might be used or what effect it might have. This explicit knowledge is important if educators are going to be intentional in their teaching, equipped with the skills to make minute by minute decisions during interactions with children. This has important implications for professional development to develop expert-level skills in early years pedagogy:

> Professional development must explicitly support teachers in developing procedural as well as theoretical knowledge to support their live decision-making during classroom interactions.

> (Mathers and Siraj, 2021, p. 12)

Watching video clips of real-life interactions and then reflecting on them is a powerful medium in which educators can develop their procedural knowledge. It is concrete and real, as well as theoretical. The uncomfortable feeling of watching oneself on screen is quickly diminished when the benefits of interpreting the effect of our practice or noticing children's responses becomes apparent.

Having structured opportunities to reflect on and analyse practice can make the relationship between pedagogy and child outcomes explicit. This goes beyond the simplistic approach of modelling a pedagogical practice for an educator to copy, or providing a script for them to follow. Reflection, discussion and developing procedural knowledge are important elements of professional development in the early years. Furthermore, Mathers (2021) found that taking part in this type of professional development was a stronger predictor of procedural knowledge than educator experience. Sylva and Eisenstadt (2024) summarise the point well:

> While knowledge of the curriculum is essential for effective practice, so too is knowing how to transform that knowledge into pedagogical interactions suited to the talents and interests of individual children. Reflecting on their own practice in a critical way is key to continuous improvement.

> (Sylva and Eisenstadt, 2024, p. 19)

Adult learning and the challenge of behaviour change

The professional culture of our settings matters, so it is no surprise to learn that our working environment affects how well we do our work. Kraft and Papay describe this as follows:

> Teachers working in more supportive professional environments improve their effectiveness more over time than teachers working in less supportive contexts. On average, teachers working in schools at the 75th percentile of professional environment ratings improved 38% more than teachers in schools at the 25th percentile after ten years.

> (Kraft and Papay, 2014, p. 476)

Kraft and Papay (2014, p. 479) outline how we can promote improvement at a faster rate through:

- collaboration with colleagues
- receiving meaningful feedback on our practice
- recognition of our efforts

When these ingredients are present, staff are more likely to thrive.

It can, however, be hard for us to change small habits, let alone make big shifts in our practice or introduce a continuous trickle of changes. The importance of handwashing in hospitals is a commonly used example of the difficulty of making changes. It is worth thinking about why this is the case. Handwashing is a straightforward action and there is widespread consensus that it is beneficial. It can even save lives. Yet its implementation in hospitals is inconsistent.

We need to think more carefully about what support is required to achieve widespread and consistent changes in behaviour. Staff training alone has evidently not led to sustained change in hospitals.

A combination of the following can help to achieve long-term change (Wilson et al., 2011):

- eliciting peer pressure
- the importance of role models
- incorporating 'opinion leaders'
- culture-changing interventions

Wilson et al. point out other factors that may undermine planned changes, including:

- staff turnover
- gaps in our knowledge
- insufficient training
- unclear communications
- changing priorities
- competing demands
- competing educator and leader beliefs

These points show how much the culture of a professional environment and focusing on fewer priorities really matter. If we recognise the weak spots in our settings, we can work on them. We will then have a much firmer foundation for any professional development we pursue.

The EAST framework from the Behavioural Insights Team (Service et al., 2015) offers an understanding of how to encourage the desired behaviours. They suggest making them easy, attractive, social and timely:

- *Easy* is all about simplifying the message. By making something come across straightforwardly, we make it more likely to be adopted.
- *Attractive* is about attracting attention to what we are aiming for. This could be in how we present what we are doing. It could also include designing reward systems for maximum effect.
- *Social* is about using the power of networks, encouraging commitment to others and setting up a group to lead by example.
- *Timely* is about encouraging behaviour changes people are most likely to be receptive to.

You will notice that these align with several of the mechanisms identified by the Education Endowment Foundation.

Challenges and opportunities in professional development for early years educators

Early years teams consist of a range of educators with different qualifications and backgrounds working collaboratively in a shared space. This makes them different to most other teams in educational organisations. The evidence review for the Fostering Effective Early Learning (FEEL) study notes:

> Educators often have different understandings and experiences, and different qualifications and roles within their schools and settings. Given these differences, they may benefit from different approaches to professional development and different content in the professional development.

> (Siraj et al., 2016, p. 22)

This variation in starting points matters less in forms of professional development such as coaching. Here we can make individual adjustments according to content. However, this variation makes a real difference when we look at larger scale professional development programmes, which may need elements which are bespoke to different members of the team (e.g. newer or less-qualified educators). Iram Siraj and colleagues report that:

> The FEEL study advocates team working and collaboration, and includes different styles and processes for learning as one way of supporting learner diversity and allowing educators to develop and change at their own pace.

> (Siraj et al., 2016, p. 22)

A further, significant constraint affecting quality professional development in the EYFS is extended opening hours and shift work. Once again, team working and collaboration as a form of professional development is a fruitful way around this. In many early years settings, leaders and managers are present on the ground, modelling good practice and offering feedback to colleagues as they work alongside them. Even a large early years setting can often be 'walked through' in a short period of time. This is very different to Key Stages 1 and 2 in schools, where a leader might need to make a complex arrangement to visit many separate classes, depending on timetables.

The nature of most early years settings also means that good practice can be developed 'live' when shifts overlap. In other words, it can go on with educators on the nursery floor through modelling and peer feedback. In phases other than early years, professional development often takes place outside the classroom, making it potentially more difficult to translate into practice.

Case Study 15.2

The Need for Flexibility

The nature of shift work in the early years means that getting people together can be tricky. Here are some examples of creative solutions to this.

In the London South Teaching School Hub, a project with educators in the early years uses a model of 'learn it, see it, try it'. Settings work together to pool their experience and expertise. Educators attend short, evidence-based initial training, around one and a half hours long.

Examples of things the group looks at:

- the balance between interacting and interfering
- how to individualise planning

Initial input is followed up with the opportunity to observe it in practice. Educators make an action plan of the aspects they want to develop, then they repeat the cycle.

This model allows settings to share expertise at no extra cost. It avoids paying for consultants to visit, or sending people out to attend courses. It also enables educators to put new practices into action in the setting, making it more likely that changes will be sustained.

Scheduling such sessions is specific to each setting. It is important to consult educators on the best times for them and their team. In some places, to get people together, educators agree to stay after work and have a later start on another day. Sometimes educators take 'time back' at quieter times of the week/term/year. Bringing a group of educators together requires flexibility.

Implementation

It can be tempting to think that 'the more training input, the better'. However, there is no evidence that shows 'more is better', and robust evidence to support the importance of ensuring that professional development includes high-quality content and is planned using a balanced design (EEF, 2021). Instead of focusing on the amount of professional develop-ment, we should focus on the mechanisms and their effective *implementation*. The EEF's guidance report offers a helpful analogy which explains the importance of mechanisms:

> A useful way to think about mechanisms is to think about toothpaste. You're able to purchase a range of different toothpastes. There are different types, such as toothpaste targeted at whitening, or toothpaste targeted at reducing sensitivity (i.e. forms); and there are different brands (i.e. programmes) with very specific ingredients from specific companies. However, the key mechanism that you will want in any toothpaste you use is fluoride, the specific, replicable, observable ingredient that prevents cavities. A toothpaste is more likely to be effective in reducing cavities if it includes fluoride. When designing and selecting PD [professional development], we're looking to identify and incorporate the 'fluoride', the mechanisms that are likely to alter teacher practice and improve pupil outcomes.

(EEF, 2021, p. 12)

Implementation is a process, not a one-off event, requiring sustained support for a sig-nificant period. For example, Sheringham Nursery School worked for more than three years to implement the ShREC approach, and this process still needs continued atten-tion as new members join the team, or students come on placement. This contrasts strongly with the 'train and pray' approach, in which a setting or school arranges for training and then assumes the new practices will naturally be put into action.

Good implementation is about how people think, behave and interact: it is funda-mentally a collaborative and social process. Whilst we need to ensure we have the right systems and structures in place for effective implementation, we also need to recognise that the process is dynamic, unpredictable and evolving. We need to be effective in how we work with educators to evaluate what is and is not working, and how we develop educators' professional skills and autonomy. Sometimes we may have to go backwards in our process as well as forwards.

The case study below illustrates how the mechanisms in the EEF's *Effective Professional Development* guidance report can support ongoing implementation.

---Case Study 15.3---

Early Years Conversation Project (EYCP): Mentors and Champions

The Early Years Conversation Project (EYCP), which has been running across London since September 2023, is an example of a sustained piece of professional development which demonstrates a 'balanced design' and incorporates several mechanisms outlined in the EEF's *Effective Professional Development* report (2021).

EYCP uses mentors to:

- revisit prior learning (Mechanism 2)
- set and agree goals (Mechanism 3)
- provide affirmation and reinforcement after progress (Mechanism 5)
- arrange social support (Mechanism 7)
- modelling the technique (Mechanism 8)
- rehearsing the technique (Mechanism 10)
- prompting action planning (Mechanism 12)
- prompting context specific repetition (Mechanism 14)

Mandy Young is an EYCP mentor and deputy headteacher of a maintained nursery school in Stratford, Newham. Mandy describes some of the ways that mentors put the mechanisms into action in the EYCP:

> I feel my role as a mentor is to clarify and model the strategies and to praise colleagues when they use them. Using videos of our practice is a wonderful tool to support this. Although it can be unnerving at first, practitioners often comment that it enables them to see where they are doing well and where they need targeted support. Their willingness and ability to recognise the need to change is brave and integral to the success of the programme. For an initiative to be successful, it is important that everyone is on board and understands why change is needed. EYCP Leads are vital here as they evaluate what is working and not working in their settings and explain this to their teams. They also ensure that resources, support and time are available so that practitioners feel they can make changes. EYCP leads also make decisions around prioritising what their settings will focus on – too many initiatives will overwhelm staff and dilute impact.

One of the Champions from the EYCP in 2023/2024, Iman Al-Saiq, has been working in early years education for over 10 years. Reflecting on the qualities needed for a Champion, she says:

> It takes time for practitioners to learn about new ways of working and they need to feel that they will get the encouragement and help they need. It can be hard to change and adjust our ways sometimes.

This really speaks to several of the mechanisms for effective professional development, but especially to the need for rehearsal, context-specific practice and receiving affirmation and reinforcement after progress.

Conclusion

A continual focus on developing quality in the early years is crucial, if we want to give every child the best start to life. That requires high-quality, ongoing professional development, as Sylva and Eisenstadt (2024, n.p.) argue:

> ... high-quality nursery education has resulted in children achieving against the odds of their social class and family income. But quality comes at a cost. Staff delivering intentional pedagogy need high-level training and a deep understanding of child development.

As well achieving the primary aim of benefitting the children, well-considered professional development can also promote educators' wellbeing and job satisfaction. It emphasises the professional nature of the role, and its critical importance for children's life chances, in a society which still undervalues the importance of early education and care. As the Teacher Development Trust (2016) states, 'effective professional development should be seen as a key driver not only of staff development, but also of recruitment, retention, wellbeing, and school improvement'.

Effective implementation also relies on our sensitivity to the 'bandwidth' of our colleagues. If we are asking them to give energy to something new or to explore something more deeply, we need to think about how they can fit this in. What can we stop doing, do less of, or streamline? Is what we are implementing at the heart of our strategy to develop quality? Or is it an 'extra' thing that risks diluting our work overall? If it is not at the heart of our strategy, we may need to ask whether we are working on the right thing.

The EYFS Statutory Framework states that 'all children deserve high quality early education and care. This requires a quality workforce. A well-trained, skilled team of practitioners can help every child achieve the best possible educational outcomes' (DfE, 2025, p. 17). As we have argued throughout this chapter, achieving this aim is far from simple. Effective professional development requires careful planning, ongoing support and ambition. It is not simply about faithfully putting pre-specified practices into action, important though they can be. We need to be ambitious and promote the kinds of relational approaches and intentional pedagogies which require educators to have a deep understanding of the practices they use, through critical thinking and reflection.

Using research evidence to improve professional development is not straightforward, but we are convinced it is worthwhile. As Professor Becky Francis, CEO of the Education Endowment Foundation, argues: 'evidence does not provide easy solutions, but evidence-informed improvement is a process that has integrity and holds greater promise than any alternative' (Francis, 2020).

Reflective questions

1 Where do you look for advice or information for improving teaching and learning in your setting?

2 What are the barriers to the use of evidence in early years settings?

3 Think of some professional development that had a strong, long-term impact on your practice. What made it stand out from other professional development?

4 When educators attend external professional development, who ensures they put learning into practice once back at your setting or school? From where do they get support to embed and sustain their learning?

5 What are the top three barriers in your context for changing behaviour? How might you overcome these?

Afterword

Alison Peacock

Following the global pandemic, there has been recognition that children's learning 0–5 years is of vital importance. Working with our youngest children is both a joy and a huge responsibility. As adults, whether parents, carers or educators, it is our role to provide a safe, nurturing environment that is nonetheless challenging, that inspires curiosity, provokes questions and encourages recall and reflection. We want our children to experience open-ended opportunities for play, enquiry, to build and express their imagination and to fully develop physically. Early years settings in the world-renowned Reggio Emilia, Italy, recognise the importance of providing a beautiful environment both indoors and outdoors. An environment designed for optimal children's learning rather than for adult convenience is crucial. The joy of outdoor learning, for example, is clearly illustrated in Chapter 14.

There are so many aspects to early childhood education discussed within this book, but one of the most important areas is that of communication and language development. Children need language to think. They need language to express needs, wants and opinions. From their very earliest days, the desire to communicate is strong and with this the need to be heard, to be offered patient listening with intent. Dialogue is key. Back-and-forth interactions between infant and adult build the beginnings of powerful meaning-making which is at the heart of conversation. Early literacy must always be understood through the power of talk and through physical gesture. Expression of ideas embodied through movement is fundamental and is one of the reasons that extended carpet time for young children can be counterproductive. We need to consider how flexible our early years provision is and whether routines are in place for the convenience of adults or truly to support the learning of children.

This book is full of rich case studies and evidence-informed advice about how to support early childhood education, offering a fulfilling curriculum that is fully inclusive and embraces the needs of each individual child. The world should be a wonderful, endlessly fascinating place for children. Working alongside children to help them make sense of new experiences, and to draw connections between those experiences, is to introduce and then consolidate learning. However, children will learn more when guided and supported by an educator who is knowledgeable, who can ask and answer questions and extend the child's thinking. Self-styled discovery is not enough alone but, as with most things in life, there is a balance to be found. Motivation to explore, to wonder, to play and discover are all important starting points for learning. In this book, we consider knowledge and understanding of the world, with many prompts for how to embed this within the everyday experience of an early years setting.

Within our day care, nurseries and Foundation Stage classes, the role and expertise of educators is of fundamental importance. Intuitive, caring, emotionally supportive teaching is vital but the development of intellectual cognitive skills alongside social and emotional development is key. Our children need to work with adults who are themselves life-long learners, committed to finding out all they can about how best to support children's development. The skills of early years educators should never be underestimated. Nurture alongside intellectual challenge is essential for flourishing. One without the other is not conducive to the learner's wellbeing. This is why I agree with Siobhan Campbell about the vital need for professional learning across the entire early years workforce. Colleagues need to move beyond intuition towards professional dialogue and reflection. In many settings, this is best achieved through key workers regularly talking together not only about what children are observed to be doing but ways in which their learning can be scaffolded to achieve further challenge and success. There can be no substitute for adult subject knowledge and rich language skill. Additionally, engaging with books like this one, attending conferences and webinars, becoming a member of the Chartered College of Teaching, all provide the means to extend and develop professional skills.

The future world for our children is in peril. Engagement from the earliest days with the United Nations Sustainable Development Goals should be a priority. As we saw in Chapter 8, children are often highly motivated by social action initiatives within their community and should not be underestimated in terms of what might be achieved as a collective. We have only to think of the leadership roles and activities taken on with skill by many Year 2 children who have reached the 'top' of their infant school setting. High expectations within a supportive 'can-do' environment lead to impressive achievement.

Finally, it is so important that our early years settings offer a rich, welcoming environment for all where every child sees a reflection of themselves and of their home circumstances. We need to ensure that all staff learn to see diversity and difference as strengths. Children constantly take their cues from the comments and behaviours of trusted adults, which is why equalities training and awareness-raising should be warmly embraced. Similarly, actions that may lead to the labelling of children should be resisted. We must avoid a deficit model of education at all costs. The last thing any child needs is to be stifled or restricted in their development by well-meaning adults who wish to avoid risk-taking. Our children need to understand that learning has no limits, that everyone is special and that their future is full of possibility.

Dame Alison Peacock

Chief Executive Officer of the Chartered College of Teaching

References

Abrams, D., Swift, H. and Houston, D. (2018) *Research Report 119: Developing a National Barometer of Prejudice and Discrimination in Britain*. Available at: www.equalityhuman rights.com/sites/default/files/national-barometer-of-prejudice-and-discrimination-in-britain.pdf (Accessed 27 March 2025).

Anning, A. and Ring, K. (2004) *Making Sense of Children's Drawings*. Maidenhead: Open University Press.

Archer, C. and Siraj, I. (2017) *Movement Environment Rating Scale (MOVERS) for 2-6-year-olds provision: Improving physical development through movement and physical activity*. London: UCL IOE Press.

Athey, C. (1991) *Extending Thought in Young Children: A Parent–Teacher Partnership*. London: Sage.

Bain, A. and Barnett, L. (1980) *The Design of a Day Care System in a Nursery Setting for Children Under Five: Final Report*. London: Tavistock Institute of Human Relations.

Baker, S. (2024) 'Positive relationships build a foundation for children's learning'. Available at: https://solportal.ibe-unesco.org/articles/positive-relationships-build-a-foundation-for-childrens-learning/ (Accessed 27 March 2025).

Baroody, A. (1987) 'The development of counting strategies for single-digit addition', *Journal for Research in Mathematics Education*, 18(2), 141–157.

Baroody, A., Li, X. and Lai, M. (2008) 'Toddlers' spontaneous attention to number', *Mathematical Thinking and Learning*, 10(3), 240–270.

Barrett, M., Lyons, E. and Bourchier-Sutton, A. (2006) 'Children's knowledge of countries', in Spencer, C. and Blades, M. (eds) *Children and Their Environments*. Cambridge: Cambridge University Press, pp. 57–72.

Barrow, D. (2015) *Have You Seen Elephant?* Wellington: Gecko Press.

Beck, I.L., McKeown, M.G. and Kucan, L. (2013) *Bringing Words to Life: Robust Vocabulary Instruction*. London: The Guilford Press.

Bell, A. (2024) *Beyond Buzzwords: Embedding a Systemic Approach to EDI across the UK's Professions. Full Report*. Available at: https://youngfoundation.b-cdn.net/wp-content/uploads/2024/03/Beyond-buzzwords-Embedding-a-systemic-approach-to-EDI-across-the-UKs-professions-full-report-1.pdf?x48225 (Accessed 27 March 2025).

Bell Foundation (2025) 'EAL Assessment Framework – EYFS'. Available at: www.bell-foundation.org.uk/resources/detail/assessment-framework-eyfs/ (Accessed 27 March 2025).

Benson, C. (2012) 'Conformity or diversity: Developing creativity in design and technology in the early years', in *Explorations of Best Practice in Technology, Design & Engineering Education: Proceedings of the 7th Biennial International Conference on Technology Education Research*, Volume One (TERC 2012). Surfers Paradise, QLD: Griffith Institute for Educational Research, pp. 42–51.

Bernard, C. (2022) *Intersectionality for Social Workers: An Introduction to Theory and Practice*. Abingdon: Routledge.

Betteridge, H. (2024) 'Introduction', in Louis, S. and Betteridge, H. (eds) *Let's Talk about Race in the Early Years*. Abingdon: Routledge, pp. 1–28.

Bialystok, E., Craik, F.I. and Luk, G. (2012) 'Bilingualism: Consequences for mind and brain', *Trends in Cognitive Sciences*, 16(4), 240–50.

Bokova, I. and Figueres, C. (2015) 'Why education is the key to sustainable development', *World Economic Forum*. Available at: https://www.weforum.org/stories/2015/05/why-education-is-the-key-to-sustainable-development/ (Accessed 27 March 2025).

Bonetti, S. (2019) *The Early Years Workforce in England: A Comparative Analysis Using the Labour Force Survey*. Available at: https://epi.org.uk/publications-and-research/the-early-years-workforce-in-england (Accessed 27 March 2025).

Bowlby, J. (1969). *Attachment. Attachment and Loss*, Vol. 1. New York: Basic Books.

Bromley, N. (2014) *Open Very Carefully – A Book With a Bite!* London: Nosy Crow Ltd.

Bronfenbrenner, U. (1977) 'Toward an experimental ecology of human development', *American Psychologist*, 32(7), 513–31.

Brundtland, G. (1987) *Report of the World Commission on Environment and Development: Our Common Future*. United Nations General Assembly document A/42/427

Burke, N. (2018) *Musical Development Matters*. Available at: https://early-education.org.uk/wp-content/uploads/2021/12/Musical-Development-Matters-ONLINE.pdf (Accessed 27 March 2025).

Cain, K. (2010) *Reading Development and Difficulties*. Chichester: BPS Blackwell.

Campbell, R. (2010) *Dear Zoo*. London: Macmillan Children's Books.

Carle, E. (1997) *Brown Bear, Brown Bear, What Do You See?* London: Puffin.

Carneiro, P., Cattan, S. and Ridpath, N. (2024) 'The short-and medium-term impacts of Sure Start on educational outcomes', Institute for Fiscal Studies. Available at: https://ifs.org.uk/publications/short-and-medium-term-impacts-sure-start-educational-outcomes (Accessed 27 March 2025).

Carr, M. (2001) *Assessment in Early Childhood Settings: Learning Stories*. London: Sage.

Carrazza, C. and Levine, S.C. (2025) 'Less is not always more: Rich and meaningful counting books lead to greater gains in number understanding than sparse counting books', *Developmental Psychology*, 61(3), 446–60.

Center on the Developing Child (2011) 'Building the brain's "air traffic control" system: How early experiences shape the development of executive function'. Available at: https://developingchild.harvard.edu/wp-content/uploads/2024/10/How-Early-Experiences-Shape-the-Development-of-Executive-Function.pdf (Accessed 27 March 2025).

Chalmers, H. and Murphy, V. (2021) 'Multilingual learners, linguistic pluralism and implications for education and research', in Ernesto, M. and Woore, R. (eds) *Debates in Second Language Education*. Abingdon: Routledge, pp. 66–88.

Chief Medical Officers (2019) *Physical Activity Guidelines*. Available at: https://assets.publishing.service.gov.uk/media/5d839543ed915d52428dc134/uk-chief-medical-officers-physical-activity-guidelines.pdf (Accessed 27 March 2025).

Child Poverty Action Group (CPAG) (2025) 'Child poverty facts and figures'. Available at: https://cpag.org.uk/child-poverty/child-poverty-facts-and-figures (Accessed 27 March 2025).

Children Act (1989) Available at: www.legislation.gov.uk/ukpga/1989/41/contents (Accessed 27 March 2025).

Choudhury, T. and Hodgkiss, A. (2021) 'How do young Bangladeshi and Sylheti-speaking children talk and play at home? An update on an ongoing research project'. Available at: https://researchschool.org.uk/eastlondon/news/how-do-young-bangladeshi-and-sylheti-speaking-children-talk-and-play-at-home-an-update-on-an-ongoing-research-project (Accessed 27 March 2025).

Christ, T. and Wang, X. (2011) 'Closing the vocabulary gap?: A review of research on early childhood vocabulary practices', *Reading Psychology*, 32(5), 426–458.

Christ, T. and Chiu, M.M. (2018) 'Hearing words, learning words: How different presentations of novel vocabulary words affect children's incidental learning', *Early Education and Development*, 29(6), 831–851.

Clements, D.H. and Sarama, J. (2014) *Learning and Teaching Early Math: The Learning Trajectories Approach*. Abingdon: Routledge.

Clements, D.H. and Sarama, J. (2017) Play, mathematics, and false dichotomies. Available at: https://dreme.stanford.edu/news/play-mathematics-and-false-dichotomies (Accessed 27 March 2025).

Clements, D.H. and Sarama, J. (2018) Myths of early math. Available at: https://eric.ed.gov/?id=EJ1199517 (Accessed 27 March 2025).

Clements, D.H. and Sarama, J. (2021) *Learning and Teaching Early Math: The Learning Trajectories Approach* (3rd edn). Abingdon: Routledge.

Cooke, G. and Lawton, K. (2008) *For Love or Money: Pay, Progression and Professionalisation of the 'Early Years' Workforce*. London: Institute for Public Policy Research.

Cooper, H. (1999) *Pumpkin Soup*. London: Corgi Children's.

Coram (2024) Childcare survey 2024. Available at: www.coram.org.uk/resource/childcare-survey-2024 (Accessed 27 March 2025).

Counsell, C. (2018) 'Senior curriculum leadership 1: The indirect manifestation of knowledge – (A) curriculum as narrative'. Available at: https://thedignityofthething blog.wordpress.com/2018/04/07/senior-curriculum-leadership-1-the-indirect-manifestation-of-knowledge-a-curriculum-as-narrative (Accessed 27 March 2025).

Dahl, R. (2016) *The Enormous Crocodile*. London: Puffin.

Dale, P. (1990) *Ten in the Bed*. London: Walker Books.

Davies, M. (2003) *Movement and Dance in Early Childhood* (2nd edn). London: Paul Chapman.

Department for Education (DfE) (2009) *Building Futures: Believing in Children. A Focus on Provision for Black Children in the Early Years Foundation Stage*. Available at: https://dera.ioe.ac.uk/8958/7/ey_bca_bldfuture0000809_Redacted.pdf (Accessed 27 March 2025).

Department for Education (DfE) (2018) *Improving the Home Learning Environment*. Available at: https://assets.publishing.service.gov.uk/government/uploads/system/uploads/attachment_data/file/919363/Improving_the_home_learning_environment.pdf (Accessed 27 March 2025).

Department for Education (DfE) (2022a) 'Early years foundation stage: Exemplification materials'. Available at: www.gov.uk/guidance/early-years-foundation-stage-exemplification-materials (Accessed 27 March 2025).

Department for Education (DfE) (2022b) Progress check at age 2. Available at: www.gov.uk/government/publications/progress-check-at-age-2 (Accessed 27 March 2025).

Department for Education (DfE) (2023) *Development Matters: Non-Statutory Curriculum Guidance for the Early Years Foundation Stage*. Available at: https://assets.publishing. service.gov.uk/media/64e6002a20ae890014f26cbc/DfE_Development_Matters_Report_ Sep2023.pdf (Accessed 27 March 2025).

Department for Education (DfE) (2024a) 'Schools, pupils and their characteristics'. Available at: https://explore-education-statistics.service.gov.uk/find-statistics/school-pupils-and-their-characteristics (Accessed 27 March 2025).

Department for Education (DfE) (2024b) 'SEND code of practice: 0 to 25 years'. Available at: www.gov.uk/government/publications/send-code-of-practice-0-to-25 (Accessed 27 March 2025).

Department for Education (DfE) (2025) *Early Years Foundation Stage Statutory Framework for group and school-based providers*. Available at: https://www.gov.uk/ government/publications/early-years-foundation-stage-framework--2 (Accessed 3 September 2025).

Dickinson, D.K., McCabe, A. and Sprague, K. (2003) 'Teacher Rating of Oral Language and Literacy (TROLL)', *The Reading Teacher*, 56(6), 554–64.

Dingley's Promise (2024) 'Early years SEND assessment guidance'. Available at: https:// help-for-early-years-providers.education.gov.uk/support-for-practitioners/send-assessment/ (Accessed 27 March 2025).

Dockrell, J., Law, J., Mathers, S., Forrest, C., Charlton, J., Dobinson, K. and Hewitt, L. (2023) 'Empowering staff to enhance oral language in the early years: Cluster randomised trial', UCL Discovery. Available at: https://discovery.ucl.ac.uk/id/ eprint/10170459/ (Accessed 27 March 2025).

Dweck, C.S. (2007) 'The perils and promises of praise', *ASCD*, 65(2), 34–9.

Early Intervention Foundation (2022) 'Less than one in five under 6s getting the physical activity they should following the pandemic'. Available at: www.eif.org.uk/ press-release/less-than-one-in-five-under-6s-getting-the-physical-activity-they-should-following-the-pandemic (Accessed 27 March 2025).

Early Years Alliance (2022) *Too Little, Too Late*. Available at: www.eyalliance.org.uk/ sites/default/files/send_funding_eya_report_final_march_2022_2.pdf (Accessed 27 March 2025).

Early Years Coalition (2021) *Birth to 5 Matters: Guidance by the Sector, for the Sector*. Available at: https://birthto5matters.org.uk (Accessed 27 March 2025).

Education Endowment Foundation (EEF) (2018) *Preparing for Literacy: Improving Communication, Language and Literacy in the Early Years. Guidance Report*. Available at: https://educationendowmentfoundation.org.uk/education-evidence/guidance-reports/literacy-early-years (Accessed 27 March 2025).

Education Endowment Foundation (EEF) (2020a) *Improving Mathematics in the Early Years and Key Stage 1: Guidance Report*. Available at: https://educationendowment foundation.org.uk/education-evidence/guidance-reports/early-maths (Accessed 27 March 2025).

Education Endowment Foundation (EEF) (2020b) *Special Educational Needs in Mainstream School: Guidance Report*. Available at: https://educationendowmentfoundation.org.uk/education-evidence/guidance-reports/send (Accessed 27 March 2025).

Education Endowment Foundation (EEF) (2021) *Effective Professional Development: Guidance Report*. Available at: https://educationendowmentfoundation.org.uk/education-evidence/guidance-reports/effective-professional-development (Accessed 27 March 2025).

Education Endowment Foundation (EEF) (2023a) 'Interactive reading'. Available at: https://educationendowmentfoundation.org.uk/early-years/evidence-store/early-literacy?approach=interactive-reading-in-early-literacy (Accessed 27 March 2025).

Education Endowment Foundation (EEF) (2023b) *Guide to Effective Professional Development in the Early Years*. Available at: https://educationendowmentfoundation.org.uk/early-years/professional-development-guide (Accessed 27 March 2025).

Education Endowment Foundation (EEF) (2023c) 'Contexts for teaching and learning: the early years pedagogical continuum'. Available at: https://d2tic4wvo1iusb.cloudfront.net/production/documents/pages/EY_Pedagogical_Continuum_0.3.pdf?v=1674479416 (Accessed 27 March 2025).

Education Endowment Foundation (EEF) (2024a) 'Personal, social and emotional development'. Available at: https://educationendowmentfoundation.org.uk/early-years/evidence-store/personal-social-and-emotional-development (Accessed 27 March 2025).

Education Endowment Foundation (EEF) (2024b) 'Promoting physical activity'. Available at: https://educationendowmentfoundation.org.uk/early-years/evidence-store/physical-development?approach=promoting-physical-activity-in-physical-development (Accessed 27 March, 2025).

Education Endowment Foundation (EEF) (2024c) 'Improving early education through high-quality interactions'. Available at: https://educationendowmentfoundation.org.uk/early-years/high-quality-interactions (Accessed 27 March, 2025).

Education Endowment Foundation (EEF) (2025) 'Early Years Toolkit'. Available at: https://educationendowmentfoundation.org.uk/early-years/toolkit (Accessed 27 March 2025).

Education Policy Institute (2024) *Annual Report 2024*. London: EPI.

Edwards, C., Gandini, L. and Forman, G. (eds) (2011) *The Hundred Languages of Children: The Reggio Emilia Experience in Transformation*. Westport, CT: Praeger Publishers.

Eglinton, K.A. (2003) *Art in the Early Years*. London: Routledge.

Elfer, P. (2015) 'Positive relationships: Emotion – mixed feelings'. Available at: www.nurseryworld.co.uk/features/article/positive-relationships-emotion-mixed-feelings (Accessed 27 March 2025).

Elfer, P. (2018) *Developing Close, Thoughtful Attention to Children and Families in the Early Years Pedagogy*. Available at: https://eyhub.co.uk/wp-content/uploads/2021/04/Work-Discussion-Evaluation-Final-Report-to-Froebel-Trust-30-April-2018-2.pdf (Accessed 27 March 2025).

Ehlert, L. (2014) *Leaf Man*. London: Clarion Books.

Epstein, A. (2007) *The Intentional Teacher: Choosing the Best Strategies for Young Children's Learning*. Washington, DC: National Association for the Education of Young Children.

Epstein, D. (1993) 'Too small to notice? Constructions of childhood and discourses of "race" in predominantly white contexts', *Curriculum Studies*, 1(3), 317–34.

Equality Act (2010) Available at: www.legislation.gov.uk/ukpga/2010/15/contents (Accessed 27 March 2025).

Erikson Early Math Collaborative (2014) *Big Ideas of Early Mathematics: What Teachers of Young Children Need to Know*. Hoboken, NJ: Pearson.

Evangelou, M., Sylva, K., Kyriacou, M., Wild, M. and Glenny, G. (2009) *Early Years Learning and Development Literature Review*. London: DCSF.

Farran, E.K., Gilmore, C. and Gilligan-Lee, K.A (2023) 'What is spatial reasoning?' Available at: www.surrey.ac.uk/sites/default/files/2023-12/spatial-reasoning-for-policy-makers.pdf (Accessed 27 March 2025).

Farran, E.K., Gripton, C., Gilligan-Lee, K.A., Lancaster, A., Williams, H., Borthwick, A., Bates, K.E., Williams, A.Y. and Gifford, S. (2022). 'Spatial reasoning in early childhood: Practitioner explainer videos'. Available at: https://osf.io/jqupn/ (Accessed 27 March 2025).

Fawcett Society (2020) *Unlimited Potential: The Final Report of the Commission on Gender Stereotypes in Early Childhood*. Available at: www.fawcettsociety.org.uk/unlimited-potential-the-final-report-of-the-commission-on-gender-stereotypes-in-early-childhood (Accessed 27 March 2025).

Fisher, J. (2020) *Moving on to Key Stage 1: Improving Transition into Primary School*. Maidenhead: Open University Press.

Foorman, B., Beyler, N., Borradaile, K., Coyne, M., Denton, C.A., Dimino, J., Furgeson, J., Hayes, L., Henke, J., Justice, L. and Keating, B. (2016) *Foundational Skills to Support Reading for Understanding in Kindergarten through 3rd Grade: Educator's Practice Guide* (NCEE 2016-4008). Washington, DC: National Center for Education Evaluation and Regional Assistance (NCEE), Institute of Education Sciences, US Department of Education.

Francis, B. (2020) 'Why superficial compliance with research is dangerous'. Available at: www.tes.com/magazine/archive/why-superficial-compliance-research-dangerous (Accessed 27 March 2025).

Froebel, F. (1912) *Froebel's Chief Writings on Education*. London: Edward Arnold.

Froebel Trust (2024) 'Family time in nature'. Available at: www.froebel.org.uk/case-studies/family-time-in-nature (Accessed 27 March 2025).

Gelman, R. and Gallistel, C.R. (1986) *The Child's Understanding of Number*. Cambridge, MA: Harvard University Press.

Gifford, S., Gripton, C., Williams, H.J., Lancaster, A., Bates, K.E., Williams, A.Y., Gilligan-Lee, K., Borthwick, A. and Farran, E.K. (2022) 'Spatial reasoning in early childhood'. Available at: https://psyarxiv.com/jnwpu (Accessed 27 March 2025).

Gilmore, C., Gobel, S. and Inglis, M. (2018) *An Introduction to Mathematical Cognition*. Abingdon: Routledge.

Goldschmied, E. and Jackson, S. (1993) *People Under Three: Young Children in Day Care*. London: Routledge.

Gopnik, A. (2009) 'Amazing babies'. Available at: www.edge.org/conversation/alison_gopnik-amazing-babies (Accessed 27 March 2025).

Gopnik, A., Meltzoff, A.N. and Kuhl, P.K. (1999) *The Scientist in the Crib: Minds, Brains, and How Children Learn*. New York: William Morrow.

Goswami, U. (2015) 'Children's cognitive development and learning', *Cambridge Primary Review Trust*. Available at: https://cprtrust.org.uk/wp-content/uploads/2015/02/COMPLETE-REPORT-Goswami-Childrens-Cognitive-Development-and-Learning.pdf (Accessed 27 March 2025).

Grenier, J. (2025) 'Taking the early years seriously: Rethinking workforce professionalism', *Impact*, 23, 14–17.

Grimmer, T. (2021) *Developing a Loving Pedagogy in the Early Years: How Love Fits with Professional Practice*. Abingdon: Routledge.

Grøver, V., Snow, C.E., Evans, L. and Strømme, H. (2023) 'Overlooked advantages of interactive book reading in early childhood? A systematic review and research agenda', *Acta Psychologica*, 239, 103997.

Harmey, S., James, F., Chung, J. and Castillo-Rabanal, I. (2024) *Write from the Beginning*. London: UCL Institute of Education.

Hill, E. (2013) *Where's Spot?* London: Puffin.

Hirsh-Pasek, K., Adamson, L.B., Bakeman, R., Owen, M.T., Golinkoff, R.M., Pace, A., Yust, P.K. and Suma, K. (2015) 'The contribution of early communication quality to low-income children's language success', *Psychological Science*, 26(7), 1071–83.

Hodgkiss, A. (2021) 'Home language learning: What factors matter, and how do we support families?', *EAL Journal E-Issue*, 14, 78–82.

House of Lords Library (2024) 'Child poverty: Statistics, causes and the UK's policy response'. Available at: https://lordslibrary.parliament.uk/child-poverty-statistics-causes-and-the-uks-policy-response/ (Accessed 27 March 2025).

Huang, R., Siraj, I. and Melhuish, E. (2024) 'Promoting effective teaching and learning through a professional development program: A randomized controlled trial', *Journal of Educational Psychology*, 116(8), 1352–67.

Jabadao (2009) 'More of me'. Available at: www.jabadao.org/post/more-of-me (Accessed 27 March 2025).

James, F (2022) 'The ShREC approach – Four evidence informed strategies to promote high quality interactions with young children'. Available at: https://educationendowmentfoundation.org.uk/news/the-shrec-approach-four-evidence-informed-strategies-to-promote-high-quality-interactions-with-young-children (Accessed 27 March 2025).

Jenkins J, Watts T, Magnuson K, Gershoff, E., Clements, D., Sarama, J. and Duncan, G.J. (2018) 'Do high-quality kindergarten and first-grade classrooms mitigate preschool fadeout?', *Journal of Research on Educational Effectiveness*, 11(3), 339–74.

John, K. (2012) 'Supervision, part 2: Achieving effectiveness'. Available at: www.nurseryworld.co.uk/features/article/supervision-part-2-achieving-effectiveness (Accessed 27 March 2025).

Jones Bartoli, A. (2018) *Using Storytelling to Promote Literacy, Communication and Socio-Emotional Development in the Early Years*. Available at: https://research.gold.ac.uk/id/eprint/24937/1/Tales%20Toolkit%20Final%20Report_24pp.pdf (Accessed 27 March 2025).

Justice, L. (2002) 'Word exposure conditions and preschoolers' novel word learning during shared storybook reading', *Reading Psychology*, 23(2), 87–106.

Justice, L. and Ezell, H. (2004) 'Print referencing: An emergent literacy enhancement strategy and its clinical applications', *Language, Speech, and Hearing Services in Schools*, 35(2), 185–93.

Kelly, D.J., Quinn, P.C., Slater, A.M., Lee, K., Gibson, A., Smith, M., Ge, L. and Pascalis, O. (2005) 'Three-month-olds, but not newborns, prefer own-race faces', *Developmental Science*, 8(6), F31–6.

Kingston, D. and Siraj, I. (2017) 'Supporting the implementation of the foundation phase through effective professional development', *Wales Journal of Education*, 19, 39–68.

Kraft, M.A. and Papay, J.P. (2014) 'Can professional environments in schools promote teacher development? Explaining heterogeneity in returns to teaching experience', *Educational Evaluation and Policy Analysis*, 36(4), 476–500.

Kress, G. (1997) *Before Writing: Rethinking the Paths to Literacy*. London: Routledge.

Kuypers, L.M. (2011) *The Zones of Regulation: A Curriculum Designed to Foster Self-Regulation and Emotional Control*. San Jose, CA: Think Social Publishing, Inc.

Lacome, J. (2012) *Walking Through the Jungle*. Leighton Buzzard: Access2Books.

Lane, J. (2008) *Young Children and Racial Justice: Taking Action for Racial Equality in the Early Years – Understanding the Past, Thinking about the Present, Planning for the Future*. London: National Children's Bureau.

Law, J., Theakston, A., Gascoigne, M., Dockrell, J., McKean, C. and Charlton, J. (2017) *Early Language Development: Needs, Provision and Intervention for Preschool Children from Socioeconomically Disadvantaged Backgrounds*. Available at: https://educationendowmentfoundation.org.uk/education-evidence/evidence-reviews/early-language (Accessed 27 March 2025).

Llenas, A. (2015) *The Colour Monster*. Dorking: Templar Publishing.

Lucas, M., Hope, C and Sharp, C. (2021) *IELS Thematic Report: Young Children's Physical Development in England*. Available at: https://assets.publishing.service.gov.uk/media/60ed85a78fa8f50c75b6ad77/IELS_Physical_Development_Report.pdf (Accessed 27 March 2025).

Lumsden, E. (2021) 'Rethinking early childhood services – change from within'. Available at: www.nurseryworld.co.uk/news/article/rethinking-early-childhood-services-change-from-within (Accessed 27 March 2025).

Lumsden, E. (2024) 'The MANDELA Model'. Available at: https://tapestry.info/the-mandela-model-workbook-2/ (Accessed 27 March 2025).

Mackenzie, N.M. and Scull, J. (eds) (2018) *Understanding and Supporting Young Writers from Birth to 8*. Abingdon: Taylor & Francis.

Manners, L. (2018) 'Physical development training – Time for action'. Available at: www.nurseryworld.co.uk/content/features/physical-development-training-time-for-action/ (Accessed 27 March 2025).

Marmot, M. (2020) 'Health equity in England: The Marmot review 10 years on', *BMJ*, 368.

Marmot, M. (2022) 'The health impacts of inequality'. Available at: www.ucl.ac.uk/news/headlines/2022/oct/health-impacts-inequality (Accessed 27 March 2025)

Mathers, S. (2020) 'Observing Language Pedagogy (OLP): Developing and piloting a contexualised video-based measure of early childhood teachers' pedagogical language knowledge', Doctoral dissertation, University College London.

Mathers, S. (2021) 'Using video to assess preschool teachers' pedagogical knowledge: Explicit and higher-order knowledge predicts quality', *Early Childhood Research Quarterly*, 55, 64–78.

Mathers, S. and Siraj, I. (2021) 'Researching pre-school teachers' knowledge of oral language pedagogy using video', *Frontiers in Education*, 6, 748347.

McArdle, F. and Wright, S. (2014) 'First literacies: Art, creativity, play, constructive meaning-making', in Barton G.M. (ed). *Literacy in the Arts: Retheorising Learning and Teaching*. Cham: Springer International Publishing, pp. 21–38.

McMillan, M. (1930) *The Nursery School*. London: J.M. Dent & Sons Ltd.

Melhuish, E. and Gardiner, J. (2021) *Study of Early Education and Development (SEED): Impact Study on Early Education Use and Child Outcomes up to Age Seven Years*. Available at: https://assets.publishing.service.gov.uk/media/617a9b79e90e0719751282e4/SEED_Age_7_Impact_Report.pdf (Accessed 27 March 2025).

Miller, E. and Almon, J. (2009) 'Crisis in the kindergarten: Why children need to play in school', Alliance for Childhood (NJ3a).

Ministry of Education and Culture, Finland (2016) 'Joy, play and doing together; Recommendations for physical activity in early childhood'. Available at: https://julkaisut.valtioneuvosto.fi/handle/10024/78924 (Accessed 27 March 2025).

Murphy, J. (1990) *Peace at Last*. Horsham: Ingham Yates.

Murphy, K. (2023) A Beginner's Guide to Self-Directed Neurodivergent Play. Available at: https://tapestry.info/wp-content/uploads/2023/12/A-Beginners-Guide-to-Self-Directed-Neurodivergent-Play-Dec-2023.pdf (Accessed 27 March 2025).

Murphy, K. (2025) 'Neuro affirming practice – Early Years advice from Kerry Murphy'. Available at: www.teachearlyyears.com/a-unique-child/view/neurodiversity-affirming-practice-in-early-years (Accessed 27 March 2025).

National Audit Office (2024) *Improving Educational Outcomes for Disadvantaged Children*. Available at: www.nao.org.uk/reports/improving-educational-outcomes-for-disadvantaged-children/?nab=0#publication-details (Accessed 27 March 2025).

National Scientific Council on the Developing Child (2004) 'Young children develop in an environment of relationships: Working Paper No. 1'. Available at: https://pediatrics.developingchild.harvard.edu/wp-content/uploads/2021/12/Young-Children-Develop-in-an-Environment-of-Relationships.pdf (Accessed 27 March 2025).

National Society for Education in Art and Design (NSEAD) (2021) 'Anti-racist Art Education (ARAE) curriculum checklist'. Available at: www.nsead.org/resources/curriculum/arae-curriculum-checklist (Accessed 27 March 2025).

Nelinger, A., Album, J., Haynes, A. and Rosan, C. (2021) Their Challenges are Our Challenges: A Summary Report of the Experiences Facing Nursery Workers in the UK in 2020. London: Anna Freud National Centre for Children and Families.

O'Sullivan, J. and Sakr, M (2022) *Social Leadership in Early Childhood Education and Care: An Introduction*. London: Bloomsbury.

Ofcom (2023) *Children and Parents: Media Use and Attitudes*. Available at: www.ofcom.org.uk/siteassets/resources/documents/research-and-data/media-literacy-research/children/childrens-media-use-and-attitudes-2023/childrens-media-use-and-attitudes-report-2023.pdf?v=329412 (Accessed 27 March 2025).

Office for National Statistics (2024) 'Gender pay gap in the UK: 2024'. Available at: www.
ons.gov.uk/employmentandlabourmarket/peopleinwork/earningsandworkinghours/
bulletins/genderpaygapintheuk/2024/previous/v1 (Accessed 27 March 2025).

Office for Standards in Education (Ofsted) (2024) 'Best start in life part 3'. Available at:
www.gov.uk/government/publications/best-start-in-life-a-research-review-for-early-
years/best-start-in-life-part-3-the-4-specific-areas-of-learning (Accessed 27 March
2025).

Osgood, J. (2011) 'Contested constructions of professionalism within the nursery', in
Miller, L. and Cable, C. (eds) *Professionalization, Leadership and Management in the
Early Years*. London: Sage.

Ouellette, G. and Sénéchal, M. (2017) 'Invented spelling in kindergarten as a predictor
of reading and spelling in Grade 1: A new pathway to literacy, or just the same road,
less known?', *Developmental Psychology*, 53(1), 77–88.

Paley, V.G. (1990) *The Boy Who Would be a Helicopter*. Cambridge, MA: Harvard
University Press.

Philip, S. and Gaggiotti, L. (2020) *I Really Want to Shout!* London: Templar.

Piaget, J. (1952) *The Origins of Intelligence in Children*. New York: Norton.

Price, D. and Tayler, K. (2015) *LGBT Diversity and Inclusion in Early Years Education*.
Abingdon: Routledge.

Raver, C.C., Blair, C. and Willoughby, M. (2013) 'Poverty as a predictor of 4-year-olds'
executive function: New perspectives on models of differential susceptibility',
Developmental Psychology, 49(2), 292–304.

Rice, M.L., Taylor, C.L. and Zubrick, S.R. (2008) 'Language outcomes of 7-year-old
children with or without a history of late language emergence at 24 months', *Journal
of Speech, Language and Hearing Research*, 51(2), 394–407.

Ridgway, C., Ong, K. and Tammelin, T. (2009) 'Infant motor development predicts
sports participation at age 14 years: Northern Finland birth cohort of 1966', *PLoS
One*, 4, e6837.

Rogoff, B. (2003) *The Cultural Nature of Human Development*. Oxford: Oxford University
Press.

Rosen, M. (2000) *We're Going on a Bear Hunt*. London: Walker Books.

Rowe, D.W. and Wilson, S.J. (2015) 'The development of a descriptive measure of early
childhood writing: Results from the Write Start! writing assessment', *Journal of
Literacy Research*, 47(2), 245–92.

Rustin, M. (2008) *Work Discussion: Implications for Research and Policy*. London: Karnac
Books.

Sammons, P., Toth, K., Sylva, K., Melhuish, E., Siraj, I. and Taggart, B. (2015) 'The long-
term role of the home learning environment in shaping students' academic
attainment in secondary school', *Journal of Children's Services*, 10(3), 189–201.

Sarama, J. and Clements, D. (2009) 'Building blocks and cognitive building blocks:
Playing to know the world mathematically', *American Journal of Play*, 1(3), 313–337.

Schoon, I., Nasim, B., Sehmi, R. and Cook, R. (2015) *The Impact of Early Life Skills on
Later Outcomes*. Available at: https://discovery.ucl.ac.uk/id/eprint/10051902/1/
Schoon_2015%20The%20Impact%20of%20Early%20Life%20Skills%20on%20
Later%20Outcomes_%20Sept%20fin2015.pdf (Accessed 27 March 2025).

Seltzer, M.C. and O'Brien, L.M. (2024) 'Fostering racial literacy in early childhood contexts', *Early Childhood Educational Journal*, 52, 181–9.

Sen, A. (2013) 'The ends and means of sustainability', *Journal of Human Development and Capabilities: A Multi-disciplinary Journal for People-Centered Development*, 14(1), 6–20.

Service, O., Hallsworth, M., Halpern, D., Algate, F., Gallagher, R., Nguyen, S., Ruda, S. and Sanders, M. (2015) *EAST: Four Simple Ways to Apply Behavioural Insights*. Available at: www.bi.team/publications/east-four-simple-ways-to-apply-behavioural-insights (Accessed 27 March 2025).

Shuey, E. and M. Kankaraš (2018) 'The power and promise of early learning', OECD Education Working Papers, No. 186, OECD Publishing, Paris.

Simpson, D., Loughran, S., Lumsden, E., Mazzocco, P., McDowall Clark, R. and Winterbottom, C. (2018) 'Talking heresy about "quality" early childhood education and care for children in poverty', *Journal of Poverty and Social Justice*, 26(1), 3–18.

Simpson, D., Loughran, S., Lumsden, E., McDowall Clark, R. and Winterbottom, C. (2017) '"Seen but not heard": Practitioners work with poverty and the organising out of disadvantaged children's voices and participation in the early years', *European Early Childhood Education Research Journal*, 25(2), 177–88.

Simpson, D., Lumsden, E. and McDowall Clark, R. (2015) 'Pre-school practitioners, child poverty and social justice', *International Journal of Sociology and Social Policy*, 35(5/6), 325–39.

Siraj, I., Kingston, D., Neilsen-Hewett, C., Howard, S., Melhuish, E., de Rosnay, M., Duursma, E. and Luu, B. (2016) 'Fostering effective early learning: A review of the current international evidence considering quality in early childhood education and care programmes in delivery, pedagogy and child outcomes'. Available at: https://ro.uow.edu.au/sspapers/4287 (Accessed 27 March 2025).

Siraj, I., Mathews, S., Gross, J. and Buchanan, C. (2024) 'The role of early language development & social mobility', Working Paper. Available at: www.bera.ac.uk/wp-content/uploads/2021/05/Presidential-roundtable-working-paper_Siraj-et-al_final.pdf (Accessed 27 March 2025).

Siraj, I., Melhuish, E., Howard, S., Neilsen-Hewett, C., Kingston, D., de Rosnay, M., Duursma, E., Feng, X. and Luu, B. (2018) 'Fostering effective early learning (FEEL) study'. Available at: https://ora.ox.ac.uk/objects/uuid:8230da2d-4d14-4b5e-bd86-a4ff045533ab/files/m06b45eae1f09c3bb5eb226b81ca9b86c (Accessed 27 March 2025).

Siraj, I., Melhuish, E., Howard, S.J., Neilsen-Hewett, C., Kingston, D., de Rosnay, M., Huang, R., Gardiner, J. and Luu, B. (2023) 'Improving quality of teaching and child development: A randomised controlled trial of the leadership for learning intervention in preschools', *Frontiers in Psychology*, 13, 1092284.

Siraj-Blatchford, I., Muttock, S., Sylva, K., Gilden, R. and Bell, D. (2002) *Researching Effective Pedagogy in the Early Years*. Available at: https://dera.ioe.ac.uk/4650/1/RR356.pdf (Accessed 27 March 2025).

Skene, K., O'Farrelly, C.M., Byrne, E.M., Kirby, N., Stevens, E.C. and Ramchandani, P.G. (2022) 'Can guidance during play enhance children's learning and development in educational contexts? A systematic review and meta-analysis'. Available at: https://srcd.onlinelibrary.wiley.com/doi/full/10.1111/cdev.13730 (Accessed 27 March 2025).

Smith, A., Staunton, R., Sahasranaman, A. and Worth, J. (2023) 'Impact evaluation of Nuffield Early Language Intervention (NELI) Wave Two'. Available at: https://d2tic4wvo1iusb.cloudfront.net/production/documents/projects/NELI-wave-2-scale-up-impact-evaluation-report-FINAL.pdf?v=1742732160 (Accessed 27 March 2025).

Soukakou, E.P. (2012) *Inclusive Classroom Profile (ICP)*. Baltimore, MD: Brookes Publishing.

Sylva, K. and Eisenstadt, N. (2024) *Transforming Early Childhood: Narrowing the Gap between Children from Lower- and Higher-Income Families*. Available at: www.nesta.org.uk/report/transforming-early-childhood-narrowing-the-gap-between-children-from-lower-and-higher-income-families/ (Accessed 27 March 2025).

Sylva, K., Siraj, I., Taggart, B. and Kingston, D. (2025) *Early Childhood Quality Rating Scale – Emergent Curriculum (ECQRS–EC)*. London: David Fulton Publishers.

Tabors, P. (1997) *One Child, Two Languages*. Baltimore, MD: Brookes Publishing.

Te Ihuwaka/New Zealand Education Evaluation Centre (2021) *Science in the Early Years*. Available at: https://ero.govt.nz/sites/default/files/2021-04/Science%20in%20the%20Early%20Years%20Early%20Childhood%20and%20Years%201%20to%204.pdf (Accessed 27 March 2025).

Te Tari Arotake Mātauranga/New Zealand Education Review Office (2016) *Early Mathematics: A Guide for Improving Teaching and Learning*. Available at: https://ero.govt.nz/our-research/early-mathematics-a-guide-for-improving-teaching-and-learning (Accessed 27 March 2025).

Teacher Development Trust (2016) 'DfE CPD Standard'. Available at: https://tdtrust.org/research/dfe-cpd-standard/ (Accessed 27 March 2025).

Tedam, P. (2011) 'The MANDELA model of practice learning: An old present in new wrapping?', *The Journal of Practice Teaching and Learning*, 11(2), 60–76.

Tedam, P. (2015) 'Understanding diversity', in Waller, T. and Davies, G. (eds) *An Introduction to Early Childhood* (3rd edn). London: Sage, pp. 90–109.

Tedam, P. (2020) *Anti-oppressive Social Work Practice*. London: Sage.

Thomas, E. (2025) 'Anti-racism in early childhood spaces', in Tarry, E. (ed.) *Principles and Practice to Help Young Children Belong*. Abingdon: Routledge.

Thompson, N. (2021) *Anti-Discriminatory Practice* (7th edn). London: Red Globe Press.

Tickell, C. (2011) *The Early Years: Foundations for Life, Health and Learning – An Independent Report on the Early Years Foundation Stage to Her Majesty's Government*. Available at: https://assets.publishing.service.gov.uk/government/uploads/system/uploads/attachment_data/file/180919/DfE-00177-2011.pdf (Accessed 27 March 2025).

Tovey, H. (2016) *Bringing the Froebel Approach to Your Early Years Practice*. London: Taylor & Francis.

Tremblay, R. (2002) 'Prevention of injury by early socialization of aggressive behavior', *Injury Prevention*, 8(suppl. 4), iv17–iv21.

United Nations (2016) 'The 17 goals'. Available at: https://sdgs.un.org/goals (Accessed 27 March 2025).

United Nations Children's Fund (UNICEF) (2019) 'A summary of the UN Convention on the Rights of the Child'. Available at: www.unicef.org.uk/rights-respecting-schools/wp-content/uploads/sites/4/2017/01/Summary-of-the-UNCRC.pdf (Accessed 27 March 2025).

van den Heuvel-Panhuizen, M. and Elia, I. (2012) 'Developing a framework for the evaluation of picturebooks that support kindergartners' learning of mathematics', *Research in Mathematics Education*, 14(1), 17–47.

Venkadasalam, V.P. and Ganea, P.A. (2018) 'Do objects of different weight fall at the same time? Updating naive beliefs about free-falling objects from fictional and informational books in young children', *Journal of Cognition and Development*, 19(2), 165–81.

Vygotsky, L.S. (1978) *Mind in Society: The Development of Higher Psychological Processes* (Vol. 86). Cambridge, MA: Harvard University Press.

Weale, S. (2018) 'Ofsted warns teachers against "gimmicks" such as Brain Gym'. Available at: www.theguardian.com/education/2018/dec/04/ofsted-teachers-gimmicks-brain-gym-schools (Accessed 27 March 2025).

White, J. (2013) *Playing and Learning Outdoors: Making Provision for High Quality Experiences in the Outdoor Environment with Children 3–7*. Abingdon: Routledge.

Whitebread, D., Anderson, H., Coltman, P., Page, C., Pasternak, D.P. and Mehta, S. (2005) 'Developing independent learning in the early years', *Education 3–13*, 33(1), 40–50.

Wigfield, J. and Guthrie, A. (2000) 'Engagement and motivation in reading', in Kamil, M., Mosenthal, P., Pearson, D. and Barr, R. (eds) *Handbook of Reading Research* (3rd edn). New York: Longman.

Wiliam, D. (2013) *Principled Curriculum Design*. Available at: https://webcontent.ssatuk.co.uk/wp-content/uploads/2013/09/Dylan-Wiliam-Principled-curriculum-design-chapter-1.pdf (Accessed 27 March 2025).

Williams, J. (2023) 'Prioritising play to protect against the harms of homelessness in pre-school children', in *PEDAL Play and Mental Health Conference 2023*, University of Cambridge.

Wilson, S., Jacob, C.J. and Powell, D. (2011) 'Behavior-change interventions to improve hand-hygiene practice: A review of alternatives to education', *Critical Public Health*, 21(1), 119–27.

World Health Organization (WHO) (2018) *Nurturing Care for Early Childhood Development: A Framework for Helping Children Survive and Thrive to Transform Health and Human Potential*. Available at: https://apps.who.int/iris/bitstream/handle/10665/272603/9789241514064-eng.pdf (Accessed 27 March 2025).

Youth Futures Foundation (2024) 'Discrimination and work: Breaking down the barriers faced by ethnically minoritised young people'. Available at: https://youthfuturesfoundation.org/wp-content/uploads/2024/03/Discrimination-and-work-report.pdf (Accessed 27 March 2025).

Zauche, L.H., Thul, T.A., Mahoney, A.E.D. and Stapel-Wax, J.L. (2016) 'Influence of language nutrition on children's language and cognitive development: An integrated review', *Early Childhood Research Quarterly*, 36, 318–33.

Index